LiveCode Mobile Development HOTSHOT

Create your own exciting applications with
10 fantastic projects

Edward D Lavieri Jr.

BIRMINGHAM - MUMBAI

LiveCode Mobile Development HOTSHOT

First published: October 2013

Production Reference: 1171013

Published by Packt Publishing Ltd.
Livery Place
35 Livery Street
Birmingham B3 2PB, UK.

ISBN 978-1-84969-748-4

www.packtpub.com

Cover Image by Jarek Blaminsky (milak6@wp.pl)

Credits

Author

Edward D Lavieri Jr.

Reviewers

Randy Hengst

Geoff Canyon

Mark Rauterkus

Acquisition Editors

Pramila Balan

Mary Nadar

Lead Technical Editor

Susmita Panda

Technical Editors

Amit Ramadas

Harshad Vairat

Project Coordinator

Rahul Dixit

Proofreaders

Stephen Copestake

Lauren Harkins

Indexer

Rekha Nair

Production Coordinator

Shantanu Zagade

Cover Work

Shantanu Zagade

About the Author

Edward D Lavieri Jr. has a strong academic background with multiple graduate degrees. He has 12 years of experience as a college instructor teaching computer programming and other computer science and information systems courses. He retired from the U.S. Navy after 25 years as an Intelligence Specialist and Command Master Chief. He started his own software design and development studio in 2008. His passion is developing educational games.

As founder and creative director of his own software design and development studio, he is constantly developing software. He uses LiveCode as one of his primary development tools.

He authored a book on software consulting entitled *Software Consulting: A Revolutionary Approach* and was the technical editor of the *Excel Formulas and Functions for Dummies* book. He has also authored numerous computer science and information systems college courses.

I would like to thank my wife and life partner Brenda, above all else. She creates the balance in life that makes anything possible. Thank you for the eternal smile on my heart and for being so supportive. Also, thank you Lona, my favorite author on the planet, for being an inspiration. Lastly, I am thankful for the amazing work that the following people have pioneered: Grace Hopper, Tim Berners-Lee, Jack Kilby, Douglas Engelbart, and Kevin Miller. Without their efforts, this book would not have been a reality.

About the Reviewer

Randy Hengst is a professor and co-chair in the Education Department of Augustana College in Rock Island, IL, USA. He teaches Educational Psychology, methods classes for elementary education majors, and supervises student teaching experiences in elementary schools.

He is also the lead developer of Classroom Focused Software. Within that work he has developed numerous iOS apps for use in the Number Sense Project that is part of the preparation program for elementary education majors at Augustana. Refer to www.augustana.edu/numbersense.

www.PacktPub.com

Support files, eBooks, discount offers and more

You might want to visit www.PacktPub.com for support files and downloads related to your book.

Did you know that Packt offers eBook versions of every book published, with PDF and ePub files available? You can upgrade to the eBook version at www.PacktPub.com and as a print book customer, you are entitled to a discount on the eBook copy. Get in touch with us at service@packtpub.com for more details.

At www.PacktPub.com, you can also read a collection of free technical articles, sign up for a range of free newsletters and receive exclusive discounts and offers on Packt books and eBooks.

http://PacktLib.PacktPub.com

Do you need instant solutions to your IT questions? PacktLib is Packt's online digital book library. Here, you can access, read and search across Packt's entire library of books.

Why Subscribe?

- ▸ Fully searchable across every book published by Packt
- ▸ Copy and paste, print and bookmark content
- ▸ On demand and accessible via web browser

Free Access for Packt account holders

If you have an account with Packt at www.PacktPub.com, you can use this to access PacktLib today and view nine entirely free books. Simply use your login credentials for immediate access.

Table of Contents

Preface

There are over 2,000 programming languages and several that can be used to program mobile applications. LiveCode has proven itself a strong competitor in the mobile application development market. The power of this easy-to-learn programming environment will get you to start developing mobile apps with the very first project.

LiveCode Mobile Development Hotshot is a hands-on guide to developing games and other apps for mobile devices using LiveCode. You will learn tricks and techniques for tackling even the most difficult mobile application topics. Best of all, you will be provided with 100 percent of the source code with each line of code explained.

The approach taken in this book is to present a hands-on mission in each project. This approach will help you learn faster and more efficiently. You can enter the code listed in the book, or download it from the Packt Publishing website.

You'll be exposed to introductory mobile applications such as **Hello Planet** and **Interface Fun**. Each project is successively more complex. Additional projects include games, a calculator, and much, much more.

By the time you complete all the projects in this book, you'll have the confidence and skills necessary to develop your own mobile applications using LiveCode.

What this book covers

Project 1, *Developing Hello Planet!*, introduces LiveCode for mobile devices. In this project, you'll build your first mobile application.

Project 2, *Developing User Interfaces*, explains how to develop user interfaces including orientations and navigation.

Project 3, Using Math – Mobile Calculator, demonstrates how to create a mobile app calculator that supports addition, subtraction, multiplication, and division. This project also introduces the concept of random numbers.

Project 4, Building Menus – Menu of Menus, introduces LiveCode menus to include swipe, pulldown, option, combobox, pop up, tab, picker, and dropdown.

Project 5, Creating How Smart Am I? – A Quiz Game, explains how to create a mobile app quiz. Question types of true/false, multiple choice, sequencing, short answer, and picture-based are demonstrated.

Project 6, Creating the Find the Bananas Game, explains how to create a game based on the classic three-shell game. This project introduces how to use reference images and why it is so important.

Project 7, Creating the Jungle Dance Party Mobile App, introduces the concept of basic animation.

Project 8, Creating the My Database Mobile App, introduces you to creating and using databases in LiveCode.

Project 9, Advanced Fun with the Advanced Fun Mobile App, introduces you to several advanced features of LiveCode.

Project 10, In-app Purchases and Advertising for iOS and Android, explains how to implement in-app purchases and advertising for both iOS and Android mobile devices.

Appendix, Mobile App Development Primer, explains how to prepare your LiveCode mobile apps for submission to app stores.

What you need for this book

In order to follow the examples provided in this book, you'll need a copy of LiveCode Community 6.1.1. or greater. This software is available for free at `http://livecode.com/download/`.

Who this book is for

This book is written for people that are already familiar with the LiveCode development environment, but have not yet explored how to use their knowledge of LiveCode to create mobile apps.

Conventions

In this book, you will find several headings appearing frequently.

To give clear instructions of how to complete a procedure or task, we use:

Mission Briefing

This section explains what you will build, with a screenshot of the completed project.

Why Is It Awesome?

This section explains why the project is cool, unique, exciting, and interesting. It describes what advantage the project will give you.

Your Hotshot Objectives

This section explains the major tasks required to complete your project.

▶ Task 1

▶ Task 2

▶ Task 3

▶ Task 4, and so on

Mission Checklist

This section explains any pre-requisites for the project, such as resources or libraries that need to be downloaded, and so on.

Task 1

This section explains the task that you will perform.

Prepare for Lift Off

This section explains any preliminary work that you may need to do before beginning work on the task.

Engage Thrusters

This section lists the steps required in order to complete the task.

Objective Complete - Mini Debriefing

This section explains how the steps performed in the previous section allow us to complete the task.

Classified Intel

The extra information in this section is relevant to the task.

You will also find a number of styles of text that distinguish between different kinds of information. Here are some examples of these styles, and an explanation of their meaning.

Code words in text, database table names, folder names, filenames, file extensions, pathnames, dummy URLs, user input, and Twitter handles are shown as follows: "We also added a call to that command at the end of the `timeup` command."

A block of code is set as follows:

```
on openStack
    answer "Greetings!" titled "Hello Planet!"
end openStack
```

New terms and **important words** are shown in bold. Words that you see on the screen, in menus or dialog boxes for example, appear in the text like this: "So, navigate to **File | Standalone Application Settings**."

[Warnings or important notes appear in a box like this.]

[Tips and tricks appear like this.]

Reader feedback

Feedback from our readers is always welcome. Let us know what you think about this book—what you liked or may have disliked. Reader feedback is important for us to develop titles that you really get the most out of.

To send us general feedback, simply send an e-mail to feedback@packtpub.com, and mention the book title via the subject of your message.

If there is a topic that you have expertise in and you are interested in either writing or contributing to a book, see our author guide on www.packtpub.com/authors.

Customer support

Now that you are the proud owner of a Packt book, we have a number of things to help you to get the most from your purchase.

Downloading the example code

You can download the example code files for all Packt books you have purchased from your account at `http://www.packtpub.com`. If you purchased this book elsewhere, you can visit `http://www.packtpub.com/support` and register to have the files e-mailed directly to you.

Errata

Although we have taken every care to ensure the accuracy of our content, mistakes do happen. If you find a mistake in one of our books—maybe a mistake in the text or the code—we would be grateful if you would report this to us. By doing so, you can save other readers from frustration and help us improve subsequent versions of this book. If you find any errata, please report them by visiting `http://www.packtpub.com/submit-errata`, selecting your book, clicking on the **errata submission form** link, and entering the details of your errata. Once your errata are verified, your submission will be accepted and the errata will be uploaded on our website, or added to any list of existing errata, under the Errata section of that title. Any existing errata can be viewed by selecting your title from `http://www.packtpub.com/support`.

Piracy

Piracy of copyright material on the Internet is an ongoing problem across all media. At Packt, we take the protection of our copyright and licenses very seriously. If you come across any illegal copies of our works, in any form, on the Internet, please provide us with the location address or website name immediately so that we can pursue a remedy.

Please contact us at `copyright@packtpub.com` with a link to the suspected pirated material.

We appreciate your help in protecting our authors, and our ability to bring you valuable content.

Questions

You can contact us at `questions@packtpub.com` if you are having a problem with any aspect of the book, and we will do our best to address it.

Project 1
Developing Hello Planet!

There are several ways of learning how to program. The most proven method is to program by actually programming. I know that sounds intuitive, but so many programming books just show you code and have you retype it. The approach taken in this book is to show you programming techniques, demonstrate how to apply them in code, and to have you apply what you have learned by using the new knowledge in your own programming projects. Each project consists of a specific project that we'll code together. Projects have been specifically designed to demonstrate key functions and features of LiveCode.

Mission Briefing

For our first project, we'll start with a small derivation of the popular **Hello World!** application. We'll develop a mobile application that greets the user with a custom message. Our application will target the iOS 6.0 development platform and run on iPads, iPhones, and iTouches with at least iOS 6.0 installed.

Why Is It Awesome?

It is important to start with a relatively simple mobile application. This will allow you to quickly grasp key functions and features of developing mobile applications with LiveCode. Don't worry, we'll start developing more complex mobile applications in subsequent projects.

Your Hotshot Objectives

To develop our **Hello Planet!** mobile application, we'll use several capabilities and features to include the following:

- ▸ Answer dialog
- ▸ System time
- ▸ Evaluate user input
- ▸ Custom pop ups
- ▸ Locational services

Mission Checklist

You do not need plugins or additional software for LiveCode in order to accomplish this mission. You're all set, so let's get started.

Using pop-up dialogs

Let's get started by creating a new main stack with basic properties. You can set these properties in the properties inspector.

Prepare for Lift Off

First, we will create a new stack and name it `HelloPlanet`.

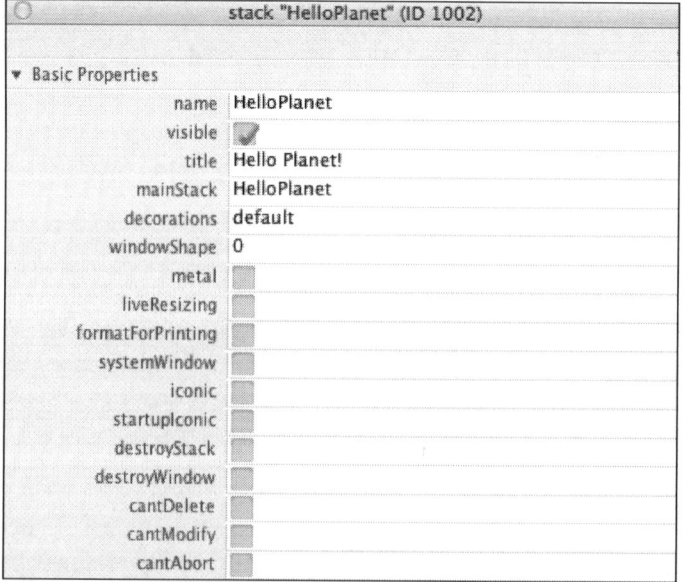

 Make sure to create your App ID and Provisioning Profile via your Apple developer account before you move past this point.

Now, we need to tell LiveCode that this will be a mobile app. So, navigate to **File |
Standalone Application Settings**. You'll want to deselect **Mac**, **Windows**, and **Linux** as
standalone options. Those are the default settings, and because you'll be developing a
mobile app, you do not need to create desktop versions. After you adjust your settings, your
Standalone Application Settings for HelloPlanet – iOS dialog should look something like the
following screenshot:

Standalone Application Settings for HelloPlanet – iOS									
General	Stacks	Copy Files	Mac	Windows	Linux	Web	iOS	Android	Bug Reports

Build for: ☑ iOS   [iPod, iPhone and iPad ▼]   [6.0 or later ▼]   [Universal ▼]

Basic Application Settings

Display Name [HelloPlanet] Version [1.0.0]

Internal App ID [com.three19.helloplanet]

Profile [Project01 ▼]

Externals ☐ revZip ☐ revXML ☐ SQLite
          ☐ MySQL ☐ PDF Printing

Icons   ☐ Prerendered Icon

iPhone [⊗] [...]
Hi-Res iPhone [⊗] [...]
iPad [⊗] [...]
Hi-Res iPad [⊗] [...]

Splash Screens

iPhone [⊗] [...]
Hi-Res iPhone [⊗] [...]
4 Inch iPhone [⊗] [...]
iPad Portrait [⊗] [...]
iPad Lscape [⊗] [...]
Hi Res iPad Portrait [⊗] [...]
Hi-Res iPad Lscape [⊗] [...]

Orientation Options

iPhone Initial Orientation [Portrait ▼]

iPad Supported Initial Orientations:
☑ Portrait   ☐ Portrait Upside-Down
☐ Landscape Left   ☐ Landscape Right

Custom URL Scheme

URL Name [   ]

Requirements and Restrictions

☐ Persistent WiFi ☐ File Sharing ☐ Push Notifications

	Required	Prohibited	n/a
Telephony	○	○	◉
Peer–Peer	○	○	◉
SMS	○	○	◉
Still Camera	○	○	◉
Auto-Focus Camera	○	○	◉
Front-Facing Camera	○	○	◉
Camera Flash	○	○	◉
Video Camera	○	○	◉
Accelerometer	○	○	◉
Gyroscope	○	○	◉
Location Services	○	○	◉
GPS	○	○	◉
Magnetometer	○	○	◉
Microphone	○	○	◉
Game–Kit	○	○	◉
WiFi	○	○	◉
OpenGL ES 1.1	○	○	◉
OpenGL ES 2.0	○	○	◉

Status Bar

Status Bar ◉ Visible ○ Hidden

Status Bar Style [Default ▼]

Engage Thrusters

Okay, you're ready to start coding the mobile app. Let's write a script that results in a pop-up dialog appearing when the mobile app is first loaded. We'll do this with the following code on the main stack:

```
on openStack
    answer "Greetings!" titled "Hello Planet!"
end openStack
```

This code is executed when the app first loads. Because it is at the main stack level and is initiated with the `openStack` keyword, the `answer` command will result in a pop-up dialog before any other code is executed. Also, you'll see we've used two strings: one for the title and one for the message.

Objective Complete - Mini Debriefing

When we do not tell the `answer` command what buttons to display on the pop-up dialog, it defaults to an **OK** button.

Okay, that was not very exciting, but we had to start somewhere.

Detecting the time of day

Let's start adding features to our mobile app, first by displaying the time of day.

Engage Thrusters

Let's modify the code in the main stack to include code to get and display the current time.

```
on openStack
    local theTime

    put the time into theTime

    answer "Greetings!" & return & theTime titled "Hello Planet!"
end openStack
```

As you can see from this code, we created a local variable to temporarily hold the mobile device's current time. Next, we pulled the local time with the `put the time` command and stored it using into the `local` variable with the same line of code. Then, we simply modified the `answer` command to add a carriage return and the time. Take a look at our results.

Objective Complete - Mini Debriefing

So far, we have a mobile app that opens a dialog, displays a message that includes the current time, and presents the user with the single **OK** button. In the next task, we'll take steps to make this app a bit more interactive.

Evaluating user input

Our Hello Planet! app does take user input. The **OK** button must be tapped and that tap is something we can capture and potentially assign code to. What do we know about this button? We know that the user taps it (when they do). We also know at what date and time they tap it.

Engage Thrusters

So, let's count how many seconds it takes the user to tap that button. Here is the code:

```
on openStack
   global theStart
   local theTime

   put the seconds into theStart
   put the time into theTime

   answer "Greetings!" & return & theTime titled "Hello Planet!"
   timeup
end openStack
```

```
command timeup
   global theStart
   local theEnd

   put the seconds into theEnd

   answer "It took you " & (theEnd - theStart) & " seconds to tap that
button!" titled "I was Counting"
end timeup
```

We made a few adjustments to our app's code.

For the openStack code, we made the following changes:

- ▸ Added a global variable called theStart
- ▸ Captured the current time in seconds
- ▸ Stored the current time in the global theStart variable
- ▸ Added a command call to the new timeup command that executes immediately after the user releases the **OK** button

For the timeup code, we made the following changes:

- ▸ Added a reference to the global theStart variable
- ▸ Added a local variable called theEnd
- ▸ Captured the current time in seconds
- ▸ Stored the current time in the local theEnd variable
- ▸ Calculated how many seconds elapsed between displaying the pop-up dialog and when the user released the **OK** button; we accomplished this by subtracting theStart from theEnd

After the user releases the **OK** button, he/she will be greeted with a new pop-up dialog as shown in the following screenshot:

So far, we've only allowed the user to provide inputs by way of tapping a button. Let's get some additional information from them by asking a direct question. Here's the code:

```
command timeup
    global theStart
    local theEnd

    put the seconds into theEnd

    answer "It took you " & (theEnd - theStart) & " seconds to tap that
button!" titled "I was Counting"

    namefun
end timeup

command namefun
    ask "What is your name?"
end namefun
```

As you can see in the preceding code, we have added a new command, namefun. We also added a call to that command at the end of the timeup command. When we execute the code, we see that a new pop-up dialog appears that asks the user to enter their name. LiveCode helps us out here by automatically activating the mobile device's keyboard.

The user can now enter their name via their mobile device's keyboard. Let's do something with the text they enter.

What we'll do next is take the name the user inputs, count the number of letters, and determine how many of them are vowels. Then, we'll provide the results to the user in yet another pop-up dialog.

Here is the modified code for the namefun command:

```
command namefun
    local userName, theLen, theVowels, tLoop

    ask "What is your name?"
    put it into userName
    put the length of userName into theLen
    --
    put 0 into theVowels
    repeat with tLoop = 1 to theLen
        if character tLoop of userName is among the characters of
"aeiou" then
            add 1 to theVowels
        end if
    end repeat

    answer "You have " & theLen & " letters in your name; " & theVowels
& " of them are vowels."
end namefun
```

Okay, let's take a closer look at our new code:

```
local userName, theLen, theVowels, tLoop
```

We are using four local variables:

▸ userName: We use this to hold the input from the user

▸ theLen: We put the number of characters in the user's input into this variable

▸ theVowels: We store the number of vowels contained in the user's name

▸ tLoop: We use this variable for our repeat loop

Now, the next line of code is:

```
ask "What is your name?"
```

The ask command initiates the prompt with **What is your name?** as the prompt and the **OK** and **Cancel** buttons.

```
put it into userName
```

We use the preceding line of code to take the username and put it into the variable userName.

```
    put the length of userName into theLen
```

We use the preceding line of code to take the length of the username and put it into the variable userName. In this context, the length is defined by the number of characters in the username.

```
    put 0 into theVowels
    repeat with tLoop = 1 to theLen
        if character tLoop of userName is among the characters of
    "aeiou" then
            add 1 to theVowels
        end if
    end repeat
```

In the preceding code block, we cycle through the entire username, one character at a time. For each character, we check to see if it is a vowel by comparing it to the provided string (aeiou). Before entering the repeat loop, we give our counter variable, theVowels, a value of zero.

```
    answer "You have " & theLen & " letters in your name; " & theVowels
    & " of them are vowels."
```

Objective Complete - Mini Debriefing

Finally, we provide our user with an informative pop-up dialog using the answer command as shown in the following screenshot:

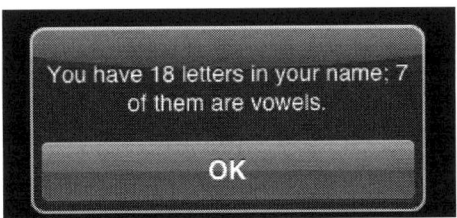

Custom pop ups

The ability to create custom pop-up dialogs provides the programmer with incredible flexibility in both displaying information to the user and obtaining information from them.

Prepare for Lift Off

In the last three tasks, we relied on the operating system to build our pop-up dialogs. What if you want to use pop ups with more customizations such as the layout and appearance? LiveCode gives us the flexibility to create our own pop-up dialogs. In fact, there are a couple of different ways of doing this. First, we can create a group of objects and then display the group when warranted. The second method is to create one or more cards in a new stack to be used for pop-up dialogs. We'll use the second method in this task because it exercises better programming style.

Programming style refers to how a programmer codes his/her applications. It is considered good style to use clear programming techniques that can easily be discerned if other programmers were to review the source code.

Engage Thrusters

In this task, we'll copy our Hello Planet! source code and name it `HelloPlanet_v2.livecode`. This will result in two different versions of our Hello Planet! mobile application. Both the versions will perform the same functions. The difference will be that the second version will use custom dialog boxes as pop ups instead of relying on the pop ups automatically generated by the `answer` and `ask` commands.

Here are the six steps we will take:

1. Customize the main stack.
2. Create and customize a card called `Greeting1`.
3. Create and customize a card called `Greeting2`.
4. Create and customize a card called `Counting`.
5. Create and customize a card called `GetName`.
6. Create and customize a card called `Final`.

We have a lot to do, so let's get started.

Customizing the main stack

You'll remember that our mobile application's title was simply Hello Planet!. For clarity, let's change that to `Hello Planet! v2` via the main stack's properties inspector.

Now, let's customize the main stack by giving it a background color of black. This will become the default color of the new cards we create.

Now, we are ready to create and customize the five cards that will correspond to the five pop-up dialogs in our Hello Planet! v2 mobile application.

Creating and customizing a new card called Greeting1

As our main application window is just a blank blue screen, we can easily mimic pop-up dialogs by creating objects on additional cards with the same background color as the stack.

When we created the main stack, our first card was automatically created. So, let's rename that card to `Greeting1`.

You'll recall that this first dialog in the initial version of this app simply displayed a pop-up dialog that had a title, message, and an OK button. We'll build that pop-up dialog on the **Greeting1** card by following these steps:

1. Go to the **Greeting1** card.
2. Draw a rounded rectangle on the card so that it is located just below the top of the card. Change the following settings:
   1. Set **Opaque** of the rectangle to true.
   2. Change the fill color to blue so that there is a contrast with the background of the card.
   3. Set the border to `0`.
   4. Set the text to bold and the font size to **18**.
   5. Set the drop shadow to true.
   6. Change the drop shadow color to a light color such as white.
   7. Lock the size and position.
3. Drag a Label field on top of the rectangle and also change the following settings:
   1. Change the label's text color to white.
   2. Center the label's text.
   3. Change the label's text size to **24**.
   4. Set the label's text to bold.
   5. Change the label's contents to `Hello Planet! v2`.
   6. Resize the label's physical size to `292` wide and `42` high. This will ensure the text is properly displayed on the card.

4. Drag a second Label field onto the middle of the rounded rectangle and update the following settings:

    1. Change the label's text color to white.
    2. Center the label's text.
    3. Change the label's text size to **24**.
    4. Change the label's text to `Greetings!`.
    5. Resize the label's physical size to `292` wide and `42` high. This will ensure the text is properly displayed on the card.

5. Draw a second rounded rectangle on the bottom-center of the first rounded rectangle and update the following settings:

    1. Set **Opaque** of the rectangle to true.
    2. Change the fill color to a lighter color to contrast with the background of the card.
    3. Change the name to `OK`.
    4. Set the border to `0`.
    5. Set the text to bold and the font size to **18**.
    6. Set the drop shadow to true.
    7. Change the drop shadow color to a light color such as white.

Your custom pop-up dialog should look similar to the following screenshot:

Next, we need to code the **OK** rectangle so that the app continues processing the dialog interfaces we've previously programmed. Here is the code for that rectangle:

```
on mouseUp
   timeup
end mouseUp
```

Now, we will need to modify the code in the `openStack` command to remove the call to the `answer` command. As you can see in the following code block, you can simply comment out the last two lines of code:

```
on openStack
    global theStart
    local theTime

    put the seconds into theStart
    put the time into theTime

    // v1 code no longer required
    //answer "Greetings!" & return & theTime titled "Hello Planet!"
    //timeup
end openStack
```

You can see that we eliminated the `answer` command and moved the call to the `timeup` command to the new **OK** button we created. Now we are ready to create our second pop-up dialog.

Creating and customizing a new card called Greeting2

Our **Greeting2** card will simply add the current time to the message provided by the **Greeting1** card. Let's use a shortcut to create our second pop-up dialog card. The quickest route to success is to copy the elements from the first card and paste them on the new card.

Once you have all four objects (two rounded rectangles and two labels) copied to the **Greeting2** card, make the following modifications:

1. Unlock the size and position of the large rounded rectangle.
2. Change the height of the large rounded rectangle to `160`.
3. Lock the size and position of the large rounded rectangle.
4. Move the smaller rounded rectangle with the **OK** label to the bottom of the larger rounded rectangle.
5. Copy the label that currently has `Greetings!` as the content.
6. Paste the new label and position it above the **OK** rounded rectangle.
7. Change the name of the new label to `timeDisplay`.
8. Empty the contents of the new `timeDisplay` label.

Now we need to modify the `openStack` code as follows:

```
on openStack
   global theStart
   //local theTime

   put the seconds into theStart
   put the time into fld "timeDisplay" on card "Greeting2"
   go to card "Greeting2"
   // v1 code no longer required
   //answer "Greetings!" & return & theTime titled "Hello Planet!"
   //timeup
end openStack
```

We commented out the local variable `theTime` because we no longer need it. Instead, we can pass the system time direction into the `timeDisplay` field. Once the time is put into the `timeDisplay` field, we open the **Greeting2** card with the `go to card "Greeting2"` statement.

When we run the application in the mobile simulator, the screen displays the greeting message and time in the simulated pop-up dialog as shown in the following screenshot:

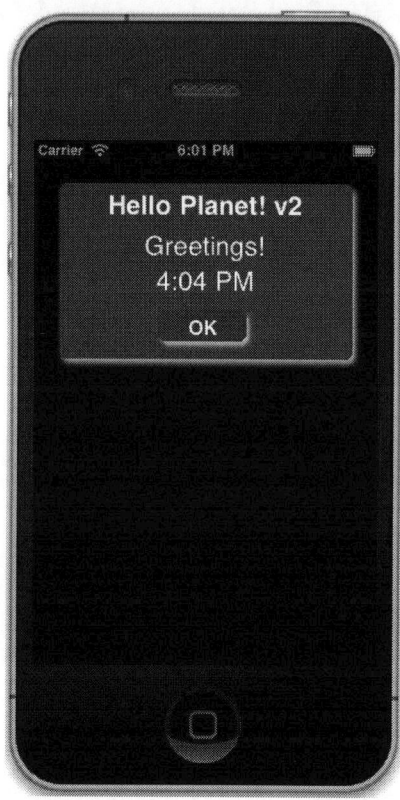

Creating and customizing a new card called Counting

Our next step is to create a pop up that will display the **I was Counting** message from the first version of our Hello Planet! mobile application. To do this, we will copy the objects on the **Greeting2** card and paste them onto a new card named **Counting**.

Here are the steps to customize the Counting card:

1. Rename the label `timeDisplay` to `countDisplay`.
2. Delete the label with the current contents of `Greetings!`.
3. Change the height of the label `countDisplay` from **42** to `72`.
4. Change the contents of the top label (currently contains **Hello Planet! v2**) to `I was Counting`.

Now, we just need to modify the command `timeup` source code to calculate the seconds and display the feedback message on the **Counting** card. Here is the modified source code:

```
command timeup
   global theStart
   local theEnd

   put the seconds into theEnd
   put "It took you " & (theEnd - theStart) & " seconds" & return &
"to tap that button!" into fld "countDisplay" on card "Counting"
   go to card "Counting"
   //v1 code no longer required
   //answer "It took you " & (theEnd - theStart) & " seconds to tap
that button!" titled "I was Counting"
   // namefun
end timeup
```

As you can see, we commented out the `answer` command and the call to `namefun`. We replaced the `answer` command with the `put` command. Because we commented out the call to `namefun`, we'll need to call that command once the user clicks on the **OK** button. Instead of keeping the `namefun` command at the stack level, we will, in the next task, move that code to the **GetName** card. So, we'll just need to go from the **Counting** card to the **GetName** card. Here is that source code:

```
on mouseUp
   go to card "GetName"
end mouseUp
```

Once the new code is run in an emulator, you should receive the following output, with the amount of seconds being the actual time you took to tap the **OK** button:

Creating and customizing a new card called GetName

Our next step is to create and customize a card named **GetName** that prompts the user for their name. So, we'll need a message, the ability to input text, and two buttons labeled **Cancel** and **OK**.

Here are the required steps:

1. Copy the objects from the **Greeting1** card.

2. Create a new card and name it `GetName`.

3. Paste the copied objects from the **Greeting1** card onto the **GetName** card.

4. Delete the Label field containing `Hello Planet! v2`.

5. Move the Label field containing `Greetings!` to the top of the blue rounded rectangle.

6. Change the contents of the remaining Label field to `What is your name?`.

7. Add a text entry field under the label and above the **OK** button.

8. Name the text entry field `theName`.

9. Change the text size of the field `theName` to **24**.

10. Change the background color of the field `theName` to white.

11. Move the **OK** button to the right of the blue rounded rectangle.

12. Duplicate the **OK** rectangle and place it to the left of the **OK** rectangle.

13. Change the name of the new rectangle to `Cancel`.

14. Resize the **Cancel** and **OK** rectangles so they span the width of the `theName` field.

Once you complete these steps, your card should look similar to the following screenshot:

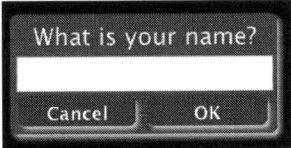

LiveCode will automatically display the keyboard when the user taps the text entry field (`theName`), so we do not need to add any code to make it happen. We do need to code both the **Cancel** and **OK** rectangles. Let's start with the **Cancel** rectangle.

When the user taps the **Cancel** button, we just want to go back to the previous card—the Counting card. Here is the code for the **Cancel** button:

```
on mouseUp
    go to card "Counting"
end mouseUp
```

The code for the **OK** rectangle is a bit more complex and can be slightly modified from the `namefun` command that we coded in the first version of our application. So, your first action is to copy the entire `namefun` command from the stack level and paste the code into the **OK** graphic's on `mouseUp` command.

Next, we'll modify the source code to use the input from our text entry field to calculate the number of characters and vowels in the name entered by the user. Here is the source code:

```
on mouseUp
    local userName, theLen, theVowels, tLoop
    local theResults

    put the text of fld "theName" into userName
    put the length of userName into theLen
    --
    put 0 into theVowels
    repeat with tLoop = 1 to theLen
        if character tLoop of userName is among the characters of
"aeiou" then
            add 1 to theVowels
        end if
    end repeat

    put "You have " & theLen & " letters in your name; " & theVowels &
" of them are vowels." into theResults
end mouseUp
```

You'll notice that much of the original source code from the `namefun` command remains unchanged. We added a new local variable, `theResults`, to hold the entire final result's string. We'll use this to populate our final card. The `put the text of fld "theName" into username` code captures any text entered by the user. From there, the rest of the source code is unchanged until the final `put` command, which replaced the `answer` command.

We should also code in some basic housekeeping. When the GetName card is displayed, we want to ensure the text entry field (`theName`) is blank. Here is the code we will use to accomplish that:

```
on preOpenCard
    put empty into fld "theName"
end preOpenCard
```

Because this code is placed at the card level using the `preOpenCard` command, any text in the text entry field will be removed before it is displayed to the user.

When you are finished with this fifth step, your simulator test should resemble the following output:

Our final step is to create and customize a new card called **Final**.

Creating and customizing a new card called Final

For this final step, we'll start by creating a new card and naming it `Final`. Next, copy the objects from the Counting card and paste them in the new Final card. Then, complete the following customizations:

1. Delete the Label field with the contents `I was Counting`.

2. Rename the `countDisplay` Label field as `finalResults`.

3. Move the `finalResults` Label field to the top of the large blue rectangle.

4. Change the text size from **24** to `18`.

5. Deselect **Don't Wrap Text** on the `finalResults` field.

6. Expand the **OK** rectangle to the width of the large blue rectangle leaving a small space on both sides.

7. Move the **OK** rectangle up so that is just below the `finalResults` Label field.

8. Resize the large blue triangle so that there is not a large gap between the bottoms of the two rectangles.

Now we are ready to perform our final coding. First, we'll need to edit the on `mouseUp` command of the **OK** rectangle on the GetName card. Instead of putting the final results into a local variable, we'll modify the code to put the results directly into the `finalResults` Label field on the Final card. Here is the modified source code:

```
on mouseUp
    local userName, theLen, theVowels, tLoop

    put the text of fld "theName" into userName
    put the length of userName into theLen
    --
    put 0 into theVowels
    repeat with tLoop = 1 to theLen
        if character tLoop of userName is among the characters of
"aeiou" then
            add 1 to theVowels
        end if
    end repeat

    put "You have " & theLen & " letters in your name; " & theVowels &
" of them are vowels." into fld "finalResults" on card "Final"
    go to card "Final"
end mouseUp
```

As you can see, we have only made two changes to this source code. First, we deleted the `local theResults` line of code, as we no longer need that local variable. We also changed the final put command to put the compiled results into the field `finalResults` on the Final card instead of a local variable. Lastly, we make a call to the card Final.

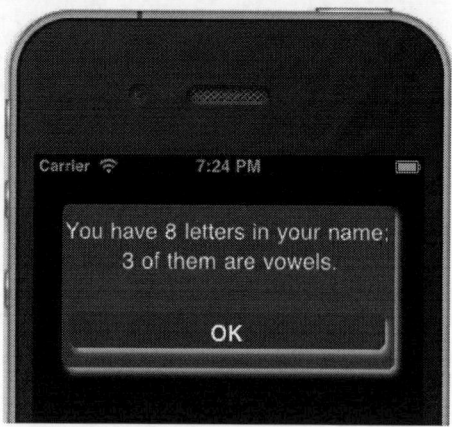

Our final action is to assign an action to the **OK** rectangle on the Final card. There are a couple of options. We can quit the application or we can loop back to the very beginning. As the user can exit the application by using their mobile device buttons (such as the Home button on an iPhone), we do not always need to offer that functionality. Therefore, let's simply code the **OK** button to reopen the Greeting2 card. Here is the code we'll use:

```
on mouseUp
    go to card "Greeting2"
end mouseUp
```

That's it for our look at custom pop ups.

Objective Complete - Mini Debriefing

Working with custom pop ups is something that you'll likely do a lot if you develop mobile applications with LiveCode. Using standard pop ups is usually acceptable for business or finance types of applications. While you are developing educational and entertainment applications, the use of custom pop ups is more desirable.

Using locational services

Locational services allow applications to use information gathered from networks (Wi-Fi, cellular, and GPS) to determine the device's location. This information can be used in a variety of ways to include mapping and providing the user with locality-relevant information.

Prepare for Lift Off

Let's use an advanced feature with another pop up. We'll determine the location of the mobile device and display the results in a standard pop-up dialog.

Engage Thrusters

The first thing we need to do is to make a copy of the original Hello Planet! LiveCode file. You can name the copied file `HelloPlanet_v3.livecode`.

With the LiveCode source file open, add the following code at the stack level:

```
on preOpenStack
   local theLocation

   if mobileSensorAvailable("location") is true then
      mobileStartTrackingSensor "location", true
      get mobileSensorReading("location", true)
      if it is an array then
         combine it using return and ":"
      end if
      put it into theLocation
      answer theLocation titled "Current Location"
      mobileStopTrackingSensor "location"
   else
      answer "Your mobile location sensor is not available" titled
"Sorry"
   end if
end preOpenStack
```

On the second line of code, we declare a local variable to hold the location results. Next is an if-then-else block with the `if mobileSensorAvailable` statement. This statement tests to see if the mobile device's location sensor is available. If it is not available, the `answer "Your mobile location sensor is not available" titled "Sorry"` statement displays an informative message to the user.

If the location sensor is available, the following block of code is executed:

```
mobileStartTrackingSensor "location", true
get mobileSensorReading("location", true)
if it is an array then
   combine it using return and ":"
end if
put it into theLocation
answer theLocation titled "Current Location"
mobileStopTrackingSensor "location"
```

Let's look at the description for each of the eight lines of code in detail.

- ▸ **Line 1**: With this statement, we are initiating the tracking sensor.

- ▸ **Line 2**: This statement obtains the reading from the location sensor. The `true` parameter provides detailed results. We could have replaced the `true` parameter with `false`, which would have only provided basic results.

- ▸ **Line 3**: This conditional `if` statement tests to see if results from line 2 are in the form of an array. If the mobile device is working properly, the results will always be in the form of an array.

- ▸ **Line 4**: Here we use the `combine` command to convert the array into an easily readable list.

- ▸ **Line 5**: This closes the conditional block of code.

- ▸ **Line 6**: This statement places the newly formatted results into the variable `theLocation`.

- ▸ **Line 7**: This is the output statement that calls the pop up and displays the contents of the variable `theLocation`.

- ▸ **Line 8**: With this statement, we stop the tracking sensor.

While using a mobile device's sensors, you'll want to be mindful of how much additional processing is required by the device. Excessive processing can cause the device to heat up and the battery to drain faster.

Once you enter the new code, you're ready to test it. Because this code interacts with the mobile device's hardware, you will not be able to test it in an emulator. If you attempt to do so, you will receive an error such as the one shown in the following screenshot:

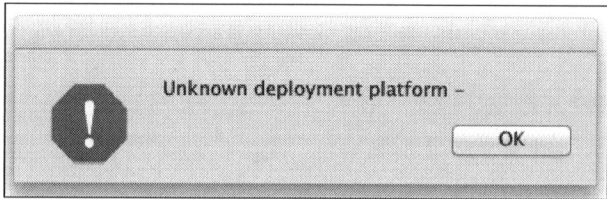

You'll need to install the mobile app on an actual device to test your newly revised app. The first time you run the app on your device, the mobile operating system should display a system dialog indicating that the app wants to use the device's current location. Refer to the following screenshot for an example:

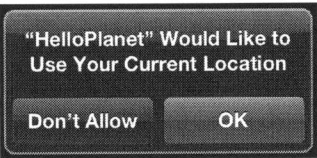

Objective Complete - Mini Debriefing

Once you click on the **OK** button, the Hello Planet! app will determine and display your device's current location. The output will be similar to the following screenshot:

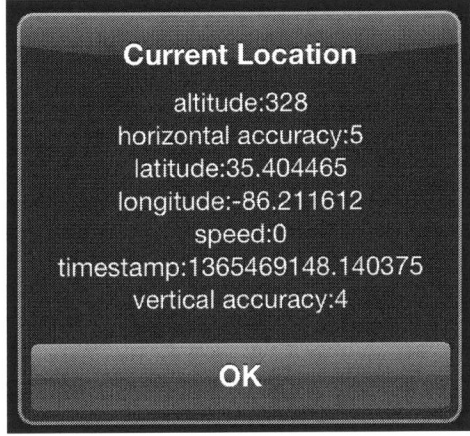

Let's wrap up this project with a project debrief in the next section.

Mission Accomplished

You completed your first project. I encourage you to explore and experiment with the source code. This strategy will help you fully understand the code as well as learn how making changes in the code impacts the application's output.

With this project, we explored how to use pop-up dialogs on mobile devices. In addition to using system-generated pop ups, we created some of our own. We also detected the time of day, evaluated user input, and captured data from the mobile device's location sensor.

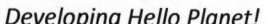

For system-generated pop ups, we made use of the `answer` and `ask` commands. While we explored several ways of creating custom pop ups, we simulated pop ups with custom-designed cards.

A Hotshot Challenge

This developer's challenge is designed to take what you learned about pop ups, and through self discovery, extend your knowledge. For this challenge, modify the source code that captures and displays the locational information to accomplish the following:

- ▸ Inform the user if the location sensor is available or not
- ▸ Ask the user if they prefer detailed or basic location information
- ▸ Instead of displaying all the location information, provide a button for each data piece and allow the user to select individual buttons to see the specific data

That's it. Good luck.

Project 2

Developing User Interfaces

A key concept to keep in mind when developing mobile applications is that there are layers. At the bottom layer is the mobile device's operating system, such as iOS or Android. At the top layer is your user. And, of course, the middle layer is where your mobile application is. The users never see your source code, but they do see the graphics, buttons, and text that your application displays. These components are collectively known as user interfaces. Users interact with your application's user interface.

Mission Briefing

In this project, we'll build an application that allows users to cycle through various screens to learn information about colors. We will also deal with mobile device orientations (portrait and landscape) in this project.

Why Is It Awesome?

We conquer two main **User Interface Components** (**UICs**): multiple ways to transition between cards and orientations. Spending time learning how to handle different mobile device orientations is important because different users use their devices differently. Learning how to compensate for this varied use will be time well spent.

Your Hotshot Objectives

To develop our Interface Fun mobile application, we'll use several capabilities and features to include:

- ▸ Portrait orientation
- ▸ Landscape orientation
- ▸ Card navigation
- ▸ Buttons
- ▸ Graphics
- ▸ Label fields

Mission Checklist

You do not need anything special to accomplish this mission. You're all set, so let's get started.

Orientation

Orientation refers to how a mobile device is held or viewed. When the device is held vertically, the display screen's height is more than its width. This is known as the **portrait** orientation. When the mobile device is held horizontally, the display screen's width is more than its height. This is known as the **landscape** orientation.

Engage Thrusters

Let's try an experiment. Grab your mobile device and notice how you pick it up and how you hold it. This is known as user behavior. Knowing how users use their mobile devices is important when you design and develop mobile applications.

Next, experiment with several different applications that you already have on your mobile device. Determine what happens when you switch your device's orientation between portrait and landscape.

Objective Complete - Mini Debriefing

You should now have a good understanding of the concept of orientation. This understanding will help you determine what orientation to use when you are developing your own mobile applications.

Classified Intel

The terms portrait and landscape come from the ideal canvas orientation for viewing a painting of a person (portrait) and viewing a painting of an outdoor scene (landscape).

Working with cards

Cards can be an important part of designing user interfaces. Each card represents a screen in your application. Depending upon the type of application that you are building, you might only need one card, or you could use many of them.

Engage Thrusters

Cards can be used in LiveCode to provide different interfaces and screens; they can also be used to organize your mobile app's content. Let's take a closer look at how to use cards for your mobile application.

Examining card properties

Let's begin by creating a new main stack named InteractiveFun_v2. The size of the stack should be 320 x 480 pixels. Once you create the new stack, review the **Application Browser** (shown in the following screenshot) to gain access to the default card:

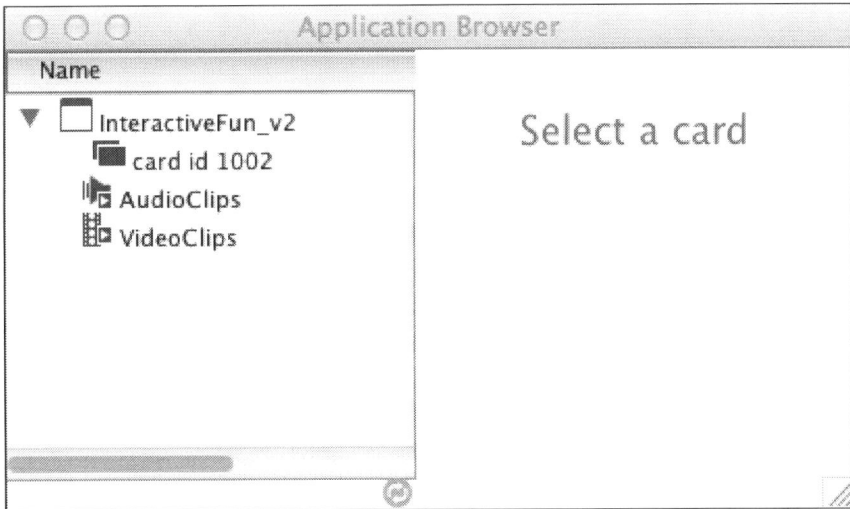

When new main stacks are created, those stacks will contain one card. You can access the card directly by double-clicking on it. When you right-click on the card in the **Application Browser**, you can access the card's scripts and properties. The properties inspector is another way to access cards. This inspector provides us access to the following areas:

- ▸ **Basic Properties**
- ▸ **Colors and Patterns**
- ▸ **Custom Properties**
- ▸ **Geometry**
- ▸ **Blending**
- ▸ **Property Profiles**
- ▸ **Size and Position**
- ▸ **Text formatting**

Cards in action

Let's create Version 2 of our Interactive Fun application by performing the following steps:

1. Rename the current card to Red.
2. Create a second card and name it Green.
3. Create a third card and name it Blue.
4. Change the background color of each card to the color matching the name of the card.
5. On the **Red** card, create two buttons. Label one Go to Green and the other Go to Blue. Place both buttons towards the bottom of the card; exact placement is not important.
6. Edit the code of each button to so that when the onMouseUp handler is called, that navigation changes to the appropriate colored card. For example, the "Go to Green" button's code should be:

```
on mouseUp
    go to card "Green"
end mouseUp
```

7. On the **Green** card, create two buttons. Label one Go to Red and the other Go to Blue. Place both the buttons in the same location as you did for the **Red** card.
8. Edit the code of each button to so that when the onMouseUp handler is called, that navigation changes to the appropriate colored card as you did in step 6.
9. On the **Blue** card, create two buttons. Label one Go to Red and the other Go to Green. Place both buttons in the same location as you did for the **Red** and **Green** cards.

10. Edit the code of each button to so that when the `onMouseUp` handler is called, that navigation changes to the appropriate colored card as you did in step 6.

It is time to test your app using the simulator. Your app should allow easy navigation between the cards. Using the red, green, and blue color scheme provides you with visual proof that your application is working properly.

Card transitions

We have several options regarding transitioning between cards. In the previous section, we saw that the new card simply appeared without any fanfare. We can enhance our user interface by using visual effects when navigating from one card to another. We accomplish this by using the `visual effect` command.

To use the `visual effect` command, we simply make a call to that command, right before the command to go to another card. Here is an example of the code you would use:

```
visual effect dissolve
go to card "Red"
```

Not all of LiveCode's visual effects will work for mobile devices. The following effects are the ones that do work:

- plain
- dissolve
- push up
- push down
- push right
- push left
- reveal up
- reveal down
- reveal right
- reveal left
- scroll up
- scroll left
- scroll down
- scroll right
- curl up (iOS only, not Android)
- curl down (iOS only, not Android)
- flip left (iOS only, not Android)
- flip right (iOS only, not Android)

We can also include a speed parameter to the `visual effect` command. If no speed parameter is provided, then the `visual effect` command occurs at normal speed. Here are the speed options:

- very slow
- slow
- normal
- fast
- very fast

The following code is an example of how you would add speed to your `visual effect` command:

```
visual effect dissolve very slowly
go to card "Red"
```

We can even add audio clips that play during the visual effect. This is accomplished by using the following sample code:

```
visual effect dissolve very slowly with sound "chesse.wav"
go to card "Red"
```

Let's modify our Red card to demonstrate some of these visual effects.

1. Create a button called `Go to Green dissolve fast`. Add the following code to the button:

    ```
    on mouseUp
        visual effect dissolve fast
        go to card "Green"
    end mouseUp
    ```

2. Create a button called `Go to Green reveal up slowly`. Add the following code to the button:

    ```
    on mouseUp
        visual effect reveal up slowly
        go to card "Green"
    end mouseUp
    ```

3. Create a button called `Go to Green reveal down very slowly`. Add the following code to the button:

    ```
    on mouseUp
        visual effect reveal down very slowly
        go to card "Green"
    end mouseUp
    ```

4. Create a button called `Go to Green scroll left`. Add the following code to the button:

    ```
    on mouseUp
        visual effect scroll left
        go to card "Green"
    end mouseUp
    ```

5. Create a button called `Go to Green scroll right`. Add the following code to the button:

    ```
    on mouseUp
        visual effect scroll right
        go to card "Green"
    end mouseUp
    ```

6. Create a button called `Go to Green curl up`. Add the following code to the button:

    ```
    on mouseUp
        visual effect curl up
        go to card "Green"
    end mouseUp
    ```

7. Create a button called `Go to Green curl down`. Add the following code to the button:

    ```
    on mouseUp
        visual effect curl down
        go to card "Green"
    end mouseUp
    ```

8. Create a button called `Go to Green flip left`. Add the following code to the button:

    ```
    on mouseUp
        visual effect flip left
        go to card "Green"
    end mouseUp
    ```

9. Create a button called `Go to Green flip right`. Add the following code to the button:

    ```
    on mouseUp
        visual effect flip right
        go to card "Green"
    end mouseUp
    ```

10. Organize your buttons (you should have 11 of them) on the Red card. How you organize them is up to you.

Objective Complete - Mini Debriefing

The following screenshot is an example of one such solution:

Classified Intel

So far, we've referenced cards by their name (that is, **Red**). We can also refer to them by their index number. Each card is given an index number starting with 1. Numbers are assigned sequentially. As you can see from the following screenshot of the Application Browser, our three cards (**Red, Green**, and **Blue**) are also cards **1, 2**, and **3**.

Name	Num
▼ ☐ InteractiveFun_v2	
🖼 Red	1
🖼 Green	2
🖼 Blue	3

So, we can say `go to card Blue` and `go to card 3`. Both commands will have the same effect. We can also say `go to next card` or `go to previous card`. Both of those commands will cycle through the card index. So, if you are on card 3 and there is no card 4, the `go to next card` will navigate from card 3 to card 1. The same is true if you are on card 1 and use the `go to previous card` command. In this case, navigation will go from card 1 to card 3 (the last card of the current stack).

Buttons

LiveCode provides us with easy access to push buttons, default buttons, and rectangle buttons on the tool palette. Once we drag any of these interface objects onto a card, we can change its style via the properties inspector. This gives us the ability to change a button to any of the following styles: push, square, rounded, transparent, opaque, shadow, checkbox, or radio.

Engage Thrusters

There are several messages related to buttons that are very useful when developing mobile applications. The most frequently used are `mouseDown` and `mouseUp`. Typically, only the `mouseUp` message is used; however, there are cases when you might want to use the `mouseDown` message. Let's experiment with both.

1. Let's begin by creating a new main stack named `InteractiveFun_v3`. The size of the stack should be `320 x 480` pixels.

2. Using the **Colors and Patterns** inspector, change the background color of the card to any color.

3. Drag a Label field from the **Tools** palette onto the card. Name the field `header`. Change the contents to `Mouse Messages`. Align it to the center and bold the text. Set the width to `264` and height to `21`. Set the location of the field to `157, 16`.

4. Drag a Scrolling Field from the **Tools** palette onto the card. Name the field messages. Set the width to 264 and height to 286. Set the location of the field to 157, 175. Using the **Basic Properties**, inspector, make sure you remove the checkmark next to **Focusable** which will set the tranverseOn to off and ensure the keyboard is not automatically activated when the mobile app is run.

5. Drag a Rectangle Button from the **Tools** palette onto the card. Name the button Button 1. Set the location of button Button 1 to 93,363.

6. Drag a Rectangle Button from the **Tools** palette onto the card. Name the button Button 2. Set the location of button Button 2 to 227,363.

7. Drag a Rectangle Button from the **Tools** palette onto the card. Name the button Quit. Set the location of button Quit to 157,425.

Objective Complete - Mini Debriefing

When you've completed the preceding seven steps, run your app in the simulator. It should resemble the following screenshot:

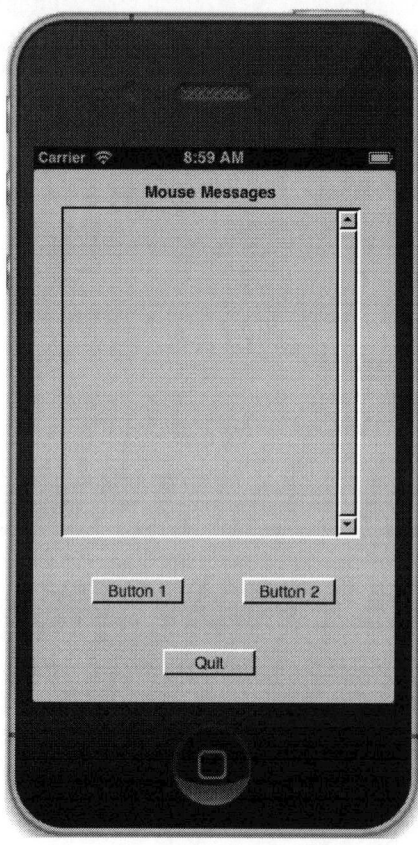

Now we can program our three buttons. What we will do is capture the messages from the three buttons and display them on sequential lines in the Scrolling Field.

Enter the following code for button `Button 1`:

```
on mouseDown
   local nextLine

   put the number of lines of fld "messages" into nextLine
   put the name of me & " mouseDown" into line (nextLine +1) of fld
"messages"
end mouseDown

on mouseUp
   local nextLine

   put the number of lines of fld "messages" into nextLine
   put the name of me & " mouseUP" into line (nextLine +1) of fld
"messages"
end mouseUp
```

As you can see, we created two listeners, one each for the `mouseDown` and `mouseUp` messages. We start by declaring a local variable called `nextLine` to temporarily hold the number of lines currently in the field `messages`. To obtain that number, we use `put the number of lines of fld "messages" into the nextLine` line of code. Next, we build a string and display it on the next blank line of the field.

We use the `put the name of me` code snippet to display the name of the button along with the message the button sent. This allows us to simply copy the code from button `Button 1` and paste it into `Button 2`.

Let's copy the code from button Button 1 and paste it into the code of button Button 2. Now, test the app in the simulator again. As you can see from the following screenshot, mouseDown and mouseUp messages are being captured and displayed for both buttons:

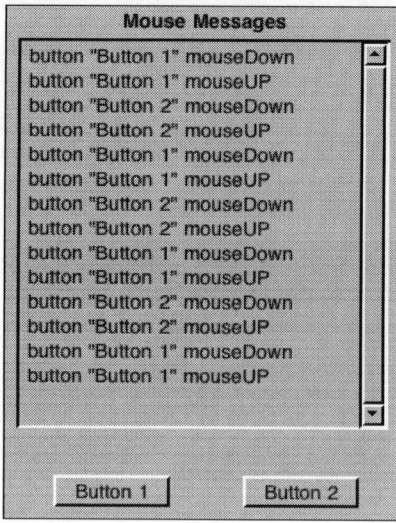

All that is left is to add code to our Quit button. Enter the following code for that button:

```
on mouseDown
    local nextLine

    put the number of lines of fld "messages" into nextLine
    put the name of me & " mouseDown" into line (nextLine +1) of fld
"messages"
end mouseDown

on mouseUp
    quit
end mouseUp
```

As you can see, we simply copy and pasted the on mouseDown listener from either of the other buttons. No code change was required. We also added code to quit the app when the user takes their finger off of the mouse, triggering the mouseUp message to be sent.

Classified Intel

The concept of LiveCode messages should not be new to you. If you are unfamiliar with messages, you can open the Message Watcher window, which is available from the **Development** drop-down menu in LiveCode. You can monitor the messages your stacks and cards are receiving using this tool.

Graphics

LiveCode graphics are objects that are drawn, customized, and programmed within the LiveCode development environment. As illustrated in the following diagram, the graphic types are **Rectangle**, **Rounded Rectangle**, **Oval**, **Line**, **Freehand**, **Polygon**, and **Freehand Polygon**. Regardless of the type of graphic, you refer to them as `grc` or `graphic` in code.

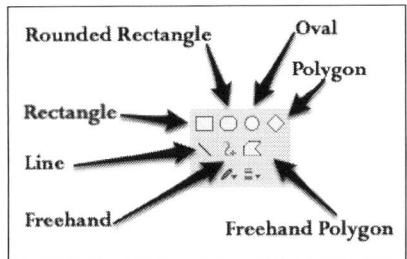

Engage Thrusters

Let's create Version 4 of our Interactive Fun mobile application.

1. Begin by creating a new main stack named `InteractiveFun_v4`. The size of the stack should be 320 x 480 pixels.

2. Set the background color to white.

3. Using the **Standalone Application Settings** dialog, hide the **Status Bar**. We are disabling the **Status Bar** so that we can have additional screen real estate. The **Status Bar**'s height is 20 pixels and, for `Interactive Fun v4`, we'll need as much screen real estate as possible. See the following screenshot for details:

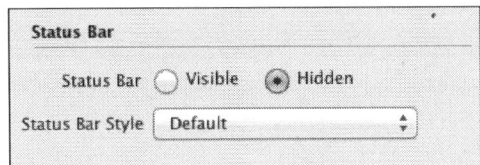

4. Select the Rectangle tool from the **Tools** palette and draw a rectangle on the card. Set the width to 138 and height to 50. Set the location to 221,41. Set the **Opaque** to True. Select a background color of your choosing.

5. Select the Rounded Rectangle tool from the **Tools** palette and draw a rounded rectangle on the card. Set the width to 134 and height to 48. Set the location to 221,105. Set the **Opaque** to True. Select a background color of your choosing.

6. Select the Oval tool from the **Tools** palette and draw an oval on the card. Set the width to 74 and height to 60. Set the location to 221,75. Set the **Opaque** to True. Select a background color of your choosing.

7. Select the Polygon tool from the **Tools** palette and draw a polygon on the card. Set the width to 72 and height to 72. Set the location to 221,257. Set the **Opaque** to True. Select a background color of your choosing.

8. Select the Line tool from the **Tools** palette and draw a line on the card. Set the width to 128 and height to 4. Set the location to 221,310. Set the **Opaque** to True. Set the line size to 3 by editing the border size field of the **Basic Properties** inspector.

9. Select the Freehand tool from the **Tools** palette and draw any shape on the card. Set the approximate width and height to 73 and 71. Set the location to 221,363. Set the **Opaque** to True. Select a background color of your choosing.

10. Select the Freehand Polygon tool from the **Tools** palette and draw a freehand polygon on the card. Set the approximate width and height to 110 and 50. Set the location to 221,439. Set the **Opaque** to True. Select a background color of your choosing.

11. Drag a Label field onto the left of the rectangle on the card. Change the contents of the label to Rectangle. Apply the bold and center formatting to the text.

12. Drag a Label field onto the left of the rounded rectangle on the card. Change the contents of the label to Rounded Rectangle. Apply the bold and center formatting to the text.

13. Drag a Label field onto the left of the oval on the card. Change the contents of the label to Oval. Apply the bold and center formatting to the text.

14. Drag a Label field onto the left of the polygon on the card. Change the contents of the label to Polygon. Apply the bold and center formatting to the text.

15. Drag a Label field onto the left of the line on the card. Change the contents of the label to Line. Apply the bold and center formatting to the text.

16. Drag a Label field onto the left of the freehand object on the card. Change the contents of the label to Freehand. Apply the bold and center formatting to the text.

17. Drag a Label field onto the left of the freehand polygon on the card. Change the contents of the label to Freehand Polygon. Apply the bold and center formatting to the text.

18. Center-align each Label field to the corresponding graphic.

19. Center-align all seven labels to one another.

Objective Complete - Mini Debriefing

Once you have completed the preceding steps, your app should look similar to the following screenshot:

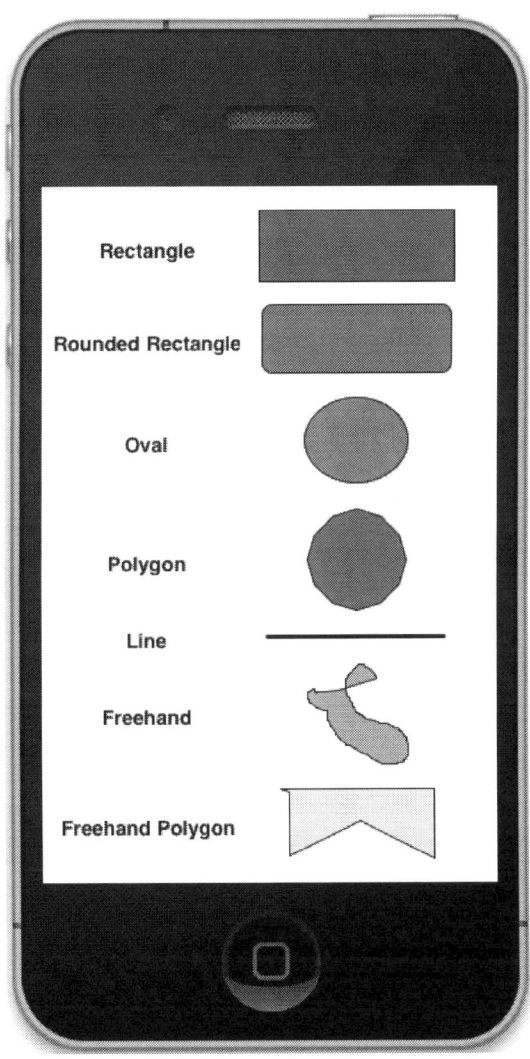

Classified Intel

Graphics can be powerful interface objects. We can apply customizations to their appearance, animate them, apply code to them, and even create them programmatically. You can use graphics to replace standard buttons to give your mobile app a look that is unique.

Mission Accomplished

You completed your second project with four different versions. You can use what you've learned about orientation, cards, buttons, and graphics, to create your own unique interactive interfaces.

We created four versions of our Interactive Fun mobile application. The first version helped us understand how to handle portrait and landscape orientations. The second version focused on navigating between cards with and without visual effects. In our third version, we experimented with buttons. Our final and fourth version was used to create the seven types of graphics.

As you have become accustomed to the projects in this book, we tackled this project's core learning topics of orientation, cards, buttons, and graphics, through hands-on programming and experimentation. I encourage you to continue to experiment with each of the four versions of this project.

A Hotshot Challenge

Let's take what you've learned in this project to a new level. For this challenge, try to accomplish the following with a fifth version of the Interactive Fun application:

- ▶ On card 1, provide the user with the ability to indicate one selection from each of the three categories: visual effect, visual effect speed, and card to navigate to
- ▶ Create seven additional cards, each with a unique graphic
- ▶ Cards 2 through 8 should permit the user to navigate back to card 1

That's it. Have fun with this challenge. Good luck!

Project 3

Using Math – Mobile Calculator

Mobile devices do a great job with mathematical equations, from adding and subtracting to performing more complex calculations. Most people take calculators for granted stating that, "they just work." We'll take a project-based approach to create our own mobile calculator. This look behind the curtains should give you an appreciation for the complexities of even the simplest of calculators.

Mission Briefing

In this project, we will build a mobile calculator that supports addition, subtraction, multiplication, and division. We will also include the ability to generate random numbers as part of our calculations.

Our mobile calculator will carefully process user input to help prevent mistakes. So, our mission is to create a user-friendly mobile calculator that performs accurate calculations and supports random number processing.

Here is a preview of what the mobile app that we will build in this project looks like:

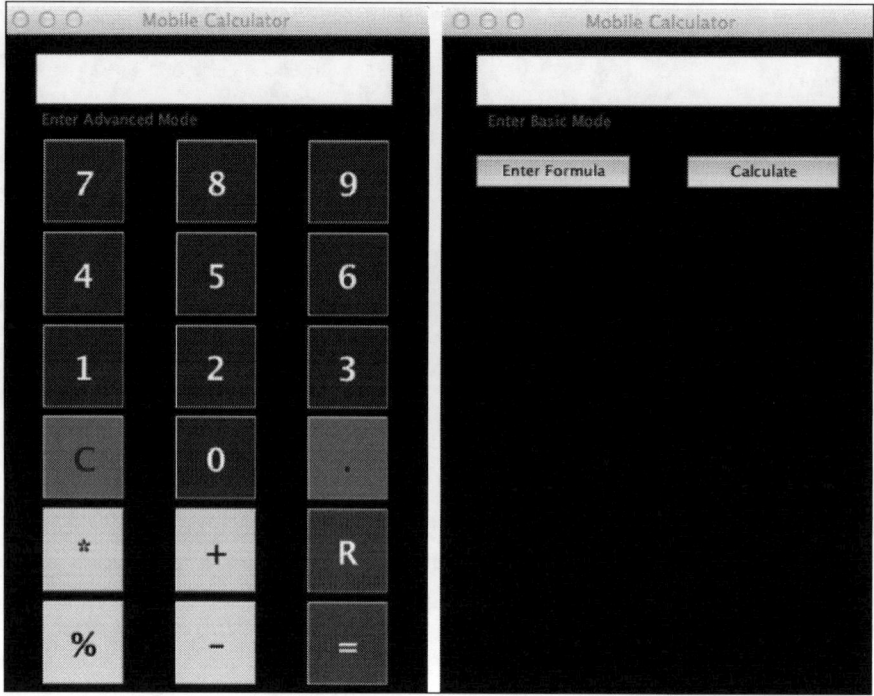

Why Is It Awesome?

When you have completed the Mobile Calculator project, you will have a good understanding of how to perform mathematical calculations using LiveCode for mobile applications. You'll also learn the importance of planning for user input issues and potential user errors. These learning points will be important to you as you work on subsequent projects in this book and develop your own mobile applications using LiveCode.

Your Hotshot Objectives

To complete the Mobile Calculator project, we'll accomplish the following tasks:

▶ Creating the user interface

▶ Accepting user input

▶ Validating user input

▶ Performing calculations

▶ Using the order of precedence

▶ Using random numbers

Mission Checklist

Whenever you develop mobile applications that use math, you should have an external source for validating the calculations. You can use a physical calculator, a calculator on your computer, or a spreadsheet software such as Microsoft Excel. Once you have a means of performing mathematical calculations, you'll be ready to get started.

Creating the user interface

Our first task is to build the user interface for our Mobile Calculator application. There will be a total of 20 interface objects for our project. We'll handle adding LiveCode scripts to each button in the next section.

Prepare for Lift Off

Here is the list of interface objects we'll need for our application:

- Number buttons (0, 1, 2, 3, 4, 5, 6, 7, 8, and 9)
- Calculation buttons
    - Addition (+)
    - Subtraction (-)
    - Multiplication (*)
    - Division (%)
- The decimal button
- The clear (C) button
- The equals (=) button
- The random (R) button
- Two label fields

Engage Thrusters

1. Let's begin by creating a new main stack named `MobileCalculator`. Using the properties inspector, make the following customizations to the main stack:
    1. Change the size of the stack to `320 x 480` pixels.
    2. Set the title of the stack to `Mobile Calculator`.
    3. Set the background color to black.

2. Next, we will create a button to use as a template.

    1. Drag a Rectangle Button onto the card.

    2. Change the size of the button to 60 x 60 pixels. This will result in a standard square button.

    3. Set the location to 62, 106. This will be the future spot of the 7 button.

    4. Change the name of the button to 7.

    5. Put 7 into the button's label.

    6. Set the text size to **24**.

    7. Set the style to bold.

    8. Set the background color to dark brown.

    9. Set the foreground color to white.

    10. Change the border width to 1.

    11. Set **Lock size and position** of the button to true. Do this by checking the **Lock size and position** checkbox in the **Size & Position** section of the properties inspector. Since this is our button template, we'll want to be sure we do not accidentally change the button's location.

So far, your interface should look like the following screenshot:

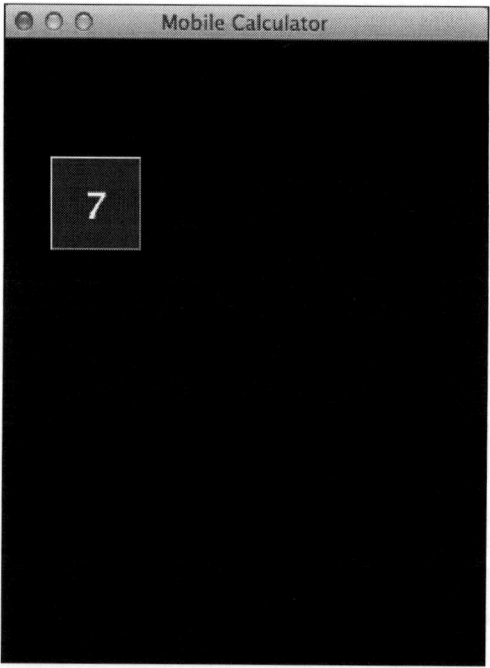

3. With our template created, we can use it to quickly create the rest of the number buttons. Make nine copies of the **7** button and customize each button using the following table:

Button	Location
0	161, 306
1	62, 240
2	161, 240
3	260, 240
4	62, 173
5	161, 173
6	260, 173
7	62, 106
8	161, 106
9	260, 106

Set **Lock size and position** of each for the new buttons to true as explained earlier.

Upon completion of step 3, your interface should look like the following screenshot:

As you can see, we've left enough room above the numbers for the calculation display, and below the number buttons for the remaining interface buttons.

4. Next, we'll create our clear and decimal point buttons.

□ Copy the **0** button and make the following modifications to the new button:

1. Name the button `Clear`.
2. Set the label to `C`.
3. Set the location of the button to `62, 306`.
4. Change the background color to a dark orange color.
5. Change the foreground color to the same dark brown color you used in step 2.
6. Set **Lock size and position** to true.

□ Copy the **C** button and make the following modifications to the new button:

1. Name the button `Decimal`.
2. Set the label to `..`
3. Set the location of the button to `260, 306`.
4. Set **Lock size and position** to true.

Upon completion of step 4, your interface should look like the following screenshot:

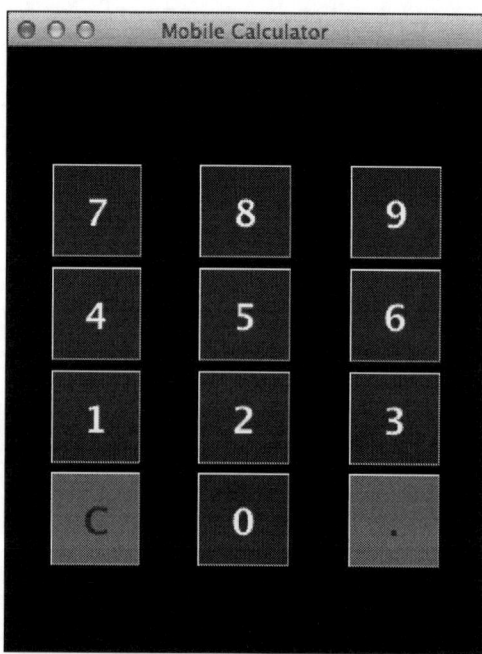

5. We are ready to create our calculation buttons.

    ❑   Copy the **C** button and make the following modifications to the new button:

        1. Name the button `Multiply`.

        2. Set the label to `*`.

        3. Set the location of the button to `62, 373`.

        4. Change the background color to a light tan color.

        5. Change the foreground color to black.

        6. Set **Lock size and position** to true.

    ❑   Copy the * button and make the following modifications to the new button:

        1. Name the button `Divide`.

        2. Set the label to `%`.

        3. Set the location of the button to `62, 440`.

        4. Set **Lock size and position** to true.

    ❑   Copy the * button and make the following modifications to the new button:

        1. Name the button `Plus`.

        2. Set the label to `+`.

        3. Set the location of the button to `161, 373`.

        4. Set **Lock size and position** to true.

    ❑   Copy the * button and make the following modifications to the new button:

        1. Name the button `Minus`.

        2. Set the label to `-`.

        3. Set the location of the button to `161, 440`.

        4. Set **Lock size and position** to true.

Upon completion of step 5, your interface should look like the following screenshot:

As you can see, we are indicating button organization by color and placement.

6. Let's create a button that will allow the user to use random numbers.

  ❑ Copy the **+** button and make the following modifications to the new button:

     1. Name the button Random.
     2. Set the label to R.
     3. Set the location of the button to 260, 373.
     4. Change the background color to dark red.
     5. Set **Lock size and position** to true.

7. We only have one button left to create for our interface – the equals button.

  ❑ Copy the **+** button and make the following modifications to the new button:

     1. Name the button Equals.
     2. Set the label to =.
     3. Set the location of the button to 260, 440.

4. Change the background color to dark green.

5. Set **Lock size and position** to true.

Upon completion of this step, your interface should look like the following screenshot:

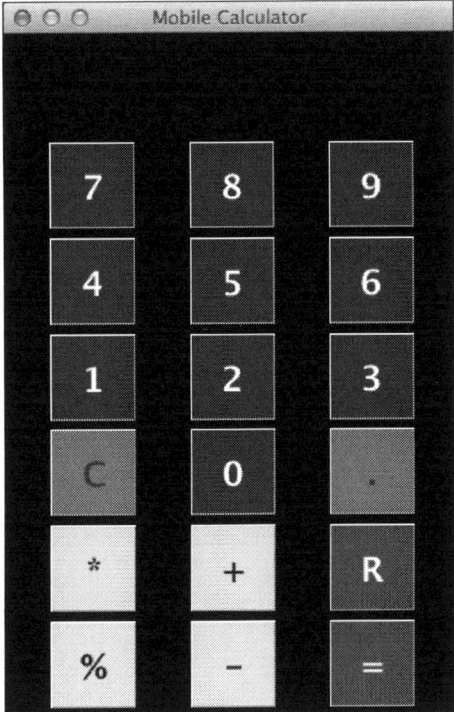

8. Now, we are ready to create the first of our two labels. Our first label will display output to the user.

1. Drag a Label field onto the card.

2. Name the field `Results`.

3. Change the width to `266` and height to `36`.

4. Set the location to `159`, `32`.

5. Change the contents to `0`.

6. Set **Opaque** to true.

7. Set the background color to white.

8. Set the text size to **24**.

9. Set **Lock size and position** to true.

9. Our last label will be an interface element that allows the user to switch between basic and advanced modes.

   1. Drag a Label field onto the card.
   2. Name the field `Mode`.
   3. Set the contents to `Enter Advanced Mode`.
   4. Change the width to `128` and height to `21`.
   5. Set the location to `90, 60`.
   6. Set the foreground color to red.
   7. Set **Lock size and position** to true.

Objective Complete - Mini Debriefing

We used nine steps to create 20 interface objects for our mobile application. One of the techniques we used to be more efficient was to create button templates. This saved us time by only having to make minor changes to buttons created with templates.

Your completed interface should look like the following screenshot:

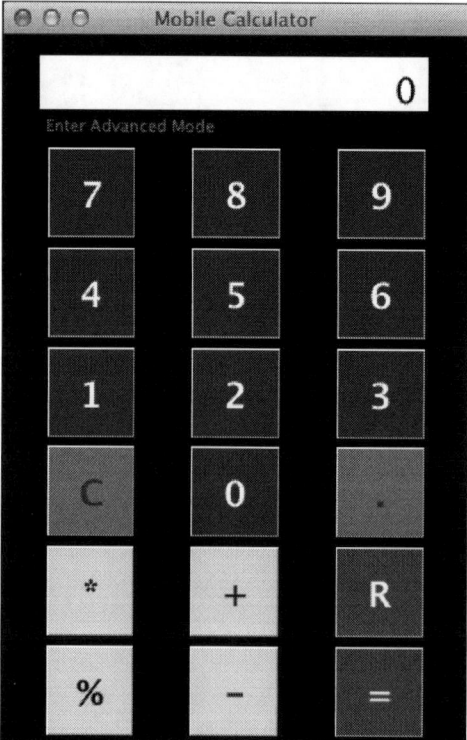

Classified Intel

When you have multiple interactive interface objects in a mobile application, you'll want to ensure you have enough spacing between them to prevent user input mistakes. If, for example, your buttons are too close to one another, it will be easier for users to tap the wrong buttons. So, keep that in mind while designing your interfaces, and run lots of tests afterwards.

Accepting user input

In this section, we will add LiveCode scripts to our mobile application's interface objects. We will first create a set of global variables at the stack level so that user input can be captured and used. We will use the "first number operator second number" schema for our calculations.

Engage Thrusters

Accepting user input can be a very important component of mobile applications. The key to successfully handling user input is to ensure the proper variables are set up. We'll begin with global variables next.

Creating and initializing global variables

Our first step is to create a set of global variables in the stack. Enter the following code:

```
on preOpenStack
    global firstNumber, secondNumber, theOperator, theMode

    clearAll
end preOpenStack
```

Each time the app is loaded, the `preOpenStack` message is received by the stack and our associated code does two things. First, it initializes the following four global variables:

- `firstNumber`: This is the number before the operator in our "first number operator second number" schema

- `secondNumber`: This is the number after the operator in our "first number operator second number" schema

- `theOperator`: This variable will hold the mathematical operation selected by the user (multiplication, division, addition, or subtraction)

- `theMode`: This variable will track which mode the calculator is in, basic or advanced

The second thing our `preOpenStack` code does is call the `clearAll` command. Here is the code for that command. Be sure to enter it at the stack level.

```
command clearAll
    global firstNumber, secondNumber, theOperator, theMode

    put empty into firstNumber
    put empty into secondNumber
    put empty into theOperator
    --
    put "Basic" into theMode
    put "Enter Advanced Mode" into fld "Mode"

end clearAll
```

The purpose of the `clearAll` command is to reset all our global variables, clear the output displayed in the Results field, and put the calculator back in Basic mode. We accomplish this by declaring the global variables, putting empty into `firstNumber`, `secondNumber`, and `theOperator`. We also populate Basic into `theMode`. Lastly, we put `Enter Advanced Mode` into the field **Mode**.

Programming the number buttons

Our next step is to program each of the number buttons (0-9). We do not want to duplicate a bunch of code for each number button. So, let's create a command to accept a number when the user enters it. Then, we can have each number button call the same command and pass its number as a parameter.

Before programming this command, let's look at some of the logic required. When a user taps a number button, we need a method of knowing if that number is the first digit in the first number, second, or a subsequent digit in the first number, or the first digit in the second number, second, or a subsequent digit in the second number. This can get complicated, so let's look at the four possible conditions that can exist when a user taps a number button.

Case	firstNumber	theOperator	secondNumber
1	is empty	is empty	is empty
2	is a number	is empty	is empty
3	is a number	is not empty	is empty
4	is a number	is not empty	is a number

After review of the preceding table, we see that there are only four conditions that will exist when a user enters numbers. So, let's create a command that processes the numbers based on these four cases.

```
command processNumber theNumber
    global firstNumber, secondNumber, theOperator

    // Case 1
    if (firstNumber is empty) then
        put theNumber into firstNumber
        // Case 2
    else if (firstNumber is a number) AND (theOperator is empty) then
        put theNumber after firstNumber
        // Case 3
    else if (theOperator is not empty) AND (secondNumber is empty) then
        put theNumber into secondNumber
        // Case 4
    else if (secondNumber is a number) then
        put theNumber after secondNumber
    end if
end processNumber
```

As you can see with the command declaration statement, we are identifying `theNumber` to receive the value passed to us by the 0-9 buttons. With the `processNumber` command, we use an if-then-else set of statements to determine which of the four cases exist and then take the appropriate action. Compare the code to the following table to see which conditions we are testing for and what action is taken:

Case	Conditions	Action
1	(firstNumber is empty)	put theNumber into firstNumber
2	(firstNumber is a number) AND (theOperator is empty)	put theNumber after firstNumber
3	(theOperator is not empty) AND (secondNumber is empty)	put theNumber into secondNumber
4	(secondNumber is a number)	put theNumber after secondNumber

Now that we have a command that can accept any number, we just need to program each of the 10 number buttons (0-9) so that the `processNumber` command knows which number is being passed to it. Here is the code:

```
on mouseUp
    processNumber(the short name of me)
end mouseUp
```

We only needed one identical line of code for each of the number buttons. Each button passes its short name to the `processNumber` command.

 Be sure that you enter the code `processNumber(the short name of me)` in each of the number buttons' (0, 1, 2, 3, 4, 5, 6, 7, 8, and 9) on `mouseUp` scripts.

We also need to update the display so the user knows that whatever they are entering is being displayed. So, let's slightly modify our `processNumber` command. Here is the code:

```
command processNumber theNumber
    global firstNumber, secondNumber, theOperator

    // Case 1
    if (firstNumber is empty) then
        put theNumber into firstNumber
        set the text of fld "Results" to firstNumber
        // Case 2
    else if (firstNumber is a number) AND (theOperator is empty) then
        put theNumber after firstNumber
        set the text of fld "Results" to firstNumber
        // Case 3
    else if (theOperator is not empty) AND (secondNumber is empty) then
        put theNumber into secondNumber
        set the text of fld "Results" to secondNumber
        // Case 4
    else if (secondNumber is a number) then
        put theNumber after secondNumber
        set the text of fld "Results" to secondNumber
    end if
end processNumber
```

We only added four lines of code, one for each of the four cases. We simply set the text of the field **Results** to the first or second number, depending upon which number was being entered by the user.

Programming the operator buttons

Our next task is to program the operator (*, %, +, -) buttons. We'll use the same technique we did with our number buttons and create one command that accepts the input from the four operator buttons.

First, let's create the LiveCode script for the four operator buttons:

```
on mouseUp
    processOperator(the short name of me)
end mouseUp
```

This script passes the short name of the operator button to the command `processOperator`. Next, we'll program the `processOperator` command. But first, we should again review what the possible conditions might be when one of the operators is pressed.

Case	firstNumber	theOperator	secondNumber
1	is empty	is empty	is empty
2	is a number	is empty	is empty
3	is a number	is not empty	is empty
4	is a number	is not empty	is a number

Based on this table, here is the script for the `processOperator` command. Be sure to enter this code at the stack level.

```
command processOperator passedOperator
    global firstNumber, secondNumber, theOperator

    // Case 1
    if (firstNumber is empty) then
        beep
        // Case 2
    else if (firstNumber is a number) AND (theOperator is empty) then
        put passedOperator into theOperator
        // Case 3
    else if (theOperator is not empty) AND (secondNumber is empty) then
        put passedOperator into theOperator
        // Case 4
    else if (secondNumber is a number) then
        put calculate() into firstNumber
        put passedOperator into theOperator
        put empty into secondNumber
    end if
end processOperator
```

In case 1, no number has been entered yet, so pressing an operator key is considered invalid.

In case 2, the first number has already been entered, and the operator is now being defined.

In case 3, the first number and the operator have already been entered, but the second number has not been entered yet. In this case, we simply update the operator based on the latest user input.

In case 4, the first number, operator, and the second number have already been entered. When the user enters an operator after having entered the second number, that indicates a calculation is ready to be entered. So, we'll take the calculation results and make it the new first number, and the newest operator is recorded.

Our `processOperator` script calls a `calculate()` function. Let's write that next.

Programming the calculation function

Here is the code:

```
function calculate
    global firstNumber, secondNumber, theOperator
    local tempResults

    switch theOperator
      case "Multiply"
          put firstNumber * secondNumber into tempResults
          break
      case "Divide"
          put firstNumber / secondNumber into tempResults
          break
      case "Plus"
          put firstNumber + secondNumber into tempResults
          break
      case "Minus"
          put firstNumber - secondNumber into tempResults
          break
    end switch

    set the text of field "Results" to tempResults
    return tempResults
end calculate
```

Our `calculate` function does not have to be too sophisticated because we know that when this function is called, the user has already entered the first number, the mathematical operator, and the second number. This allows us to create a switch statement based on the operator.

After we complete the calculation, we update the **Results** field and return the value, so processing can continue with the `processOperator` script.

Programming the clear command

When the user clicks on the **C** button, they will want their latest input to be cleared from memory and the display. There are only four possible cases in which the **C** button will need to perform any operations. These cases are presented in the following table:

Case	firstNumber	theOperator	secondNumber
1	is empty	is empty	is empty
2	is a number	is empty	is empty
3	is a number	is not empty	is empty
4	is a number	is not empty	is a number

We can re-use most of the code we've already written for the `processOperator` command. Here is the modified code:

```
command processClear
    global firstNumber, secondNumber, theOperator

    // Case 1
    if (firstNumber is empty) then
        set the text of field "Results" to empty
        // Case 2
    else if (firstNumber is a number) AND (theOperator is empty) then
        if the len of firstNumber > 1 then
            delete the last char of firstNumber
            set the text of field "Results" to firstNumber
        else
            put empty into firstNumber
            set the text of field "Results" to empty
        end if
        // Case 3
    else if (theOperator is not empty) AND (secondNumber is empty) then
        put empty into theOperator
        // Case 4
    else if (secondNumber is a number) then
        if the len of secondNumber > 1 then
            delete the last char of secondNumber
            set the text of field "Results" to secondNumber
        else
```

```
        put empty into secondNumber
        set the text of field "Results" to empty
      end if
    end if
end processClear
```

In case 1, no values have been entered for the first number, so our code simply empties any displayed results in the **Results** field.

In case 2, the first number has been entered, but an operator has not been identified. This tells us that the user wants to clear out the last digit of the first number. We need to check to see if the first number has more than one digit. If it is only one digit, we simply empty the `firstNumber` variable; otherwise, we remove the last digit of the number.

In case 3, the first number has been entered and an operator has been identified, but the second number has not been entered yet. In this case, we want to empty the previously entered operator from the `theOperator` variable.

In case 4, the user has entered the second number. Similar to what we did for case 2, we need to determine if the second number has more than one digit and then edit the second number accordingly.

The next thing for us to do is to enter code for the **C** button that calls the `processClear` command. Here is the code for the **C** button:

```
on mouseUp
   processClear
end mouseUp
```

This code simply calls the `processClear` command each time it is clicked.

Programming the equals button

The last thing we need to do is program the equals button. We previously programmed the `calculate()` function, so we'll use it again for the equals functionality. Here is the code for the equals button:

```
on mouseUp
   global firstNumber, secondNumber, theOperator

   if (firstNumber is a number) AND (theOperator is not empty) AND
(secondNumber is a number) then
      put calculate() into firstNumber
      put empty into theOperator
      put empty into secondNumber
   else
      beep
   end if
end mouseUp
```

Before calling the `calculate()` function, we check to ensure that we have both the first and second numbers as well as an operator. If we do not have these three components, we send a system beep to the user.

In the case that we do have all three data components, we call the `calculate()` function, put the results in the `firstNumber` variable, and empty the variables `theOperator` and `secondNumber`.

Objective Complete - Mini Debriefing

Now we have a fully functioning mobile calculator. We created 20 individual interface objects and programmed the number buttons (0-9), the operator buttons (+, -, *, %), the **C** (clear) button, and the equals button. We used calls to functions and commands to make our source code efficient.

With this phase of our project behind us, you should take time to thoroughly test the application.

Validating user input

So far, we have done a great job in preventing user error. Each interface object has specific input associated with it. When a user clicks on the **7** button, for example, only a 7 can be entered into our equation. What if you gave the user access to the keyboard? That would introduce a wide range of possible data input errors. In this section, we'll delve into the area of validating user input.

Engage Thrusters

Our Mobile Calculator application only has one card. Let's get started by naming that card `Basic`. Next, we'll create a new card and name it `Advanced`. Next, follow these steps to set up the user interface on the **Advanced** card.

1. Copy the **Results** field from the **Basic** card and paste it onto the **Advanced** card.
2. Copy the **Mode** field from the Basic card and paste it onto the Advanced card.
3. Change the contents of the field **Mode** to `Enter Basic Mode`.
4. Change the text alignment of field **Mode** to left.
5. Drag a Rectangle Button onto the Advanced card and make the following customizations:
    1. Set the width to `112` and height to `23`.
    2. Set the location to `82, 97`.
    3. Set the name to `Formula`.

4. Set the label to `Enter Formula`.

5. Set **Lock size and position** to true.

6. Drag a square button onto the Advanced card and make the following customizations:

   1. Set the width to `112` and height to `23`.

   2. Set the location to `236`, `97`.

   3. Set the name to `Calculate`.

   4. Set the label to `Calculate`.

   5. Set **Lock size and position** to true.

Your user interface on the Advanced card should look like the following screenshot:

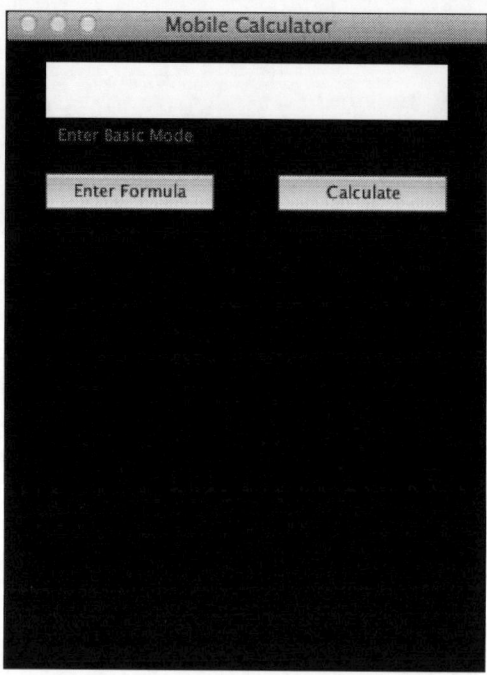

7. Now, let's code the button with the **Enter Formula** label. Enter the following code for that button:

```
on mouseUp
    global tOne, tTwo, tOperator

    put empty into fld "Results"

    ask "Enter the first number" titled "First Number"
```

```
   put it into tOne
   set the text of field "Results" to tOne
   --
   ask "Enter an Operator (+, -, *, %)" titled "Operator
Selection"
   put it into tOperator
   set the text of field "Results" to tOne & space & tOperator
   --
   ask "Enter the second number" titled "Second Number"
   put it into tTwo
   set the text of field "Results" to tOne & space & tOperator &
space & tTwo
end mouseUp
```

We created three global variables to hold our first number (tOne), second number (tTwo), and the operator (tOperator). Next, we cleared the Results field. The rest of our code is broken into three sections, one for each global variable. Each of these sections gets input from the user, stores the results into the appropriate variable, and updates the Results field.

As you can see from the following screenshot, our code works as it was designed to:

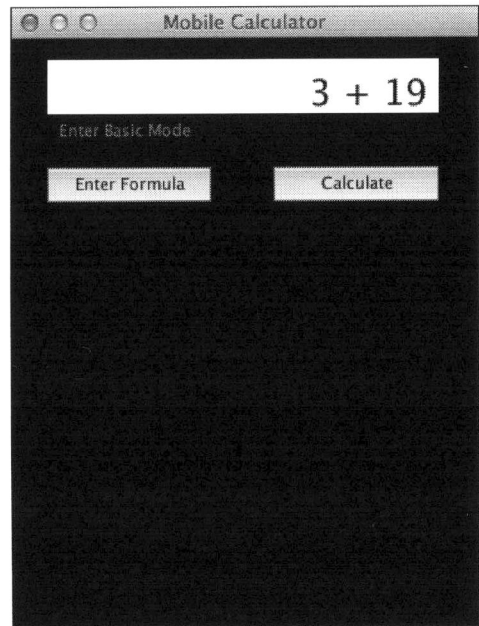

What if the user enters invalid data? Some users will do it on purpose and others will do it by mistake. We want to do our best to prevent users from entering incorrect data. One method of preventing erroneous data is to simply use buttons as we did on the Basic card. Let's demonstrate this by changing the `ask` dialog that gets the mathematical operator from the user to an `answer` dialog with four buttons, one for each operator. Here is the new code for that section of code:

```
answer "Select an Operator" with "+" or "-" or "*" or "%" titled
"Operator Selection"
  put it into tOperator
  set the text of field "Results" to tOne & space & tOperator
```

Our new dialog only permits the user to select one of the authorized operators. Refer to the following screenshot for details:

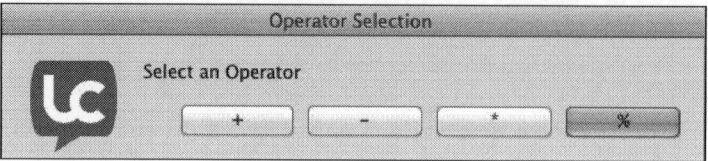

8. We still need to ensure that users are only entering numbers for the first and second numbers. There are a couple of ways of accomplishing this. One method is to check that both variables are actually numbers. We can do that with the following code:

```
on mouseUp
    global tOne, tTwo, tOperator

    put empty into fld "Results"

    ask "Enter the first number" titled "First Number"
    put it into tOne
    if tOne is a number then
        set the text of field "Results" to tOne
        --
        answer "Select an Operator" with "+" or "-" or "*" or "%"
titled "Operator Selection"
        put it into tOperator
        set the text of field "Results" to tOne & space & tOperator
        --
        ask "Enter the second number" titled "Second Number"
        put it into tTwo
        if tTwo is a number then
            set the text of field "Results" to tOne & space &
tOperator & space & tTwo
        else
```

```
        answer "Invalid " & quote  & "Second Number" & quote & "
input."
        put empty into fld "Results"
      end if
   else
      answer "Invalid " & quote  & "First Number" & quote & "
input."
   end if
end mouseUp
```

We added two if-then statements, one for each number (first and second). If the data input was not a number, processing ends.

Another method of accomplishing this would be to ensure only numbers can be entered.

9. We will program the **Calculate** button in the next section. So, the last thing we need to be able to do is to switch between Basic and Advanced modes. On the Advanced card, enter the following script into the **Mode** field:

```
on mouseUp
   global theMode

   put "Basic" into theMode
   go to card "Basic"
end mouseUp
```

As you can see, we are simply changing the contents of the variable theMode and going back to the Basic card. Now, let's add code to the **Mode** field on the Basic card.

```
on mouseUp
   global theMode

   put "Advanced" into theMode
   go to card "Advanced"
end mouseUp
```

This code changes the contents of the variable theMode to Advanced and switches to the Advanced card.

Objective Complete - Mini Debriefing

Validating user input is very important for most mobile applications. While testing your applications, you should have as many people test them as possible. Ask them to try to crash your app, even offer them a reward if they succeed. The more potential problems you can fix before release, the better.

Classified Intel

Another method of controlling what characters users are allowed to input would be to display the keyboard that best fits the current functionality. For example, if you want a user to only enter numbers, you might make a call to the `mobileSetKeyboardType "numeric"` command.

Performing calculations

Let's navigate to the Advanced card in our mobile application. We will focus on the **Calculate** button to demonstrate how to code math into your mobile applications.

Engage Thrusters

Enter the following LiveCode script for the **Calculate** button:

```
on mouseUp
   global tOne, tTwo, tOperator
      local tempResults

   switch tOperator
      case "*"
         put tOne * tTwo into tempResults
         break
      case "%"
         put tOne / tTwo into tempResults
         break
      case "+"
         put tOne + tTwo into tempResults
         break
      case "-"
         put tOne - tTwo into tempResults
         break
   end switch

   set the text of field "Results" to tOne & space & tOperator & space
& tTwo & " = " & tempResults
end mouseUp
```

We used a `switch` statement with four possible cases, one for each mathematical operator. We then performed the basic mathematical function and display the results. An example output is shown in the following screenshot:

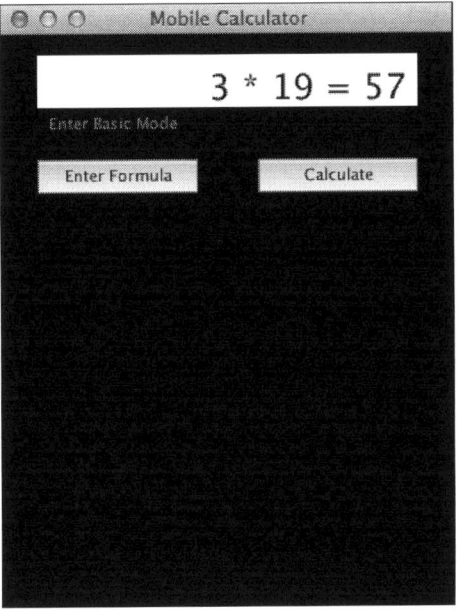

What about more complex calculations? LiveCode has a great capability to process advanced mathematical functions and operations. Here is a list of some mathematical functions that you can use in your mobile applications:

▶ cos()
▶ asin()
▶ max()
▶ abs()
▶ exp10()
▶ trunc()
▶ sin(x)
▶ min()
▶ round()
▶ exp2()
▶ sqrt()
▶ pi

Objective Complete - Mini Debriefing

While LiveCode is not a statistical tool, it has very strong built-in calculation capabilities.

Using the order of precedence

You may be familiar with the order of operators or operator precedence from your early school years. Now is the time to brush up on that area of mathematics. Let's examine the mathematical equation of 10 + 6 / 3. If we process the equation left to right, we get 10 + 6 = 16 divided by 3, which results in 5.333333. This is the incorrect solution.

If we remember that we should divide before we add, we would divide 6 by 3 with a result of 2, then add it to 10 with a result of 12. This is the correct solution.

It becomes very clear that we cannot simply perform calculations programmatically without specific knowledge of the order of precedence.

Engage Thrusters

The following table shows the proper operator order of precedence:

Precedence	Name	Symbol	Explanation
1	Grouping	( )	Expressions in parenthesis are evaluated first. When nested, the innermost dataset is evaluated first.
2	Unary	`not` `bitNot` `there is a` `there is no`	Unary operations act on a single operand only.
3	Exponent	^	This is also referred to as the power of a number.
4	Multiplication/ Division	`*` `%` `div` `mod`	Each of these has the same order of precedence. If more than one is used in an equation, they are computed left to right.
5	Addition / Subtraction	+ _	Both of these have the same order of precedence. If more than one is used in an equation, they are computed left to right.
6	Concatenation	& && ,	These are string operators (join strings).

Precedence	Name	Symbol	Explanation
7	Comparison	`<`	These operators compare two values.
		`>`	
		`<=`	
		`>=`	
		`contains`	
		`is/is not among`	
		`is/is not in`	
		`is/is not within`	
		`is/is not a`	
8	Equality	`=`	These operators compare two values for equality.
		`is`	
		`<>`	
		`!=`	
		`is not`	
9	bitAnd	`bitAnd`	
10	bitXOr	`bitXOr`	
11	bitOr	`bitOr`	
12	and	`and`	
13	or	`or`	
14	function calls		This is the lowest priority operator.

Objective Complete - Mini Debriefing

As you've seen, there is more to operator precedence than most people realize. Fortunately, we have everything we need to know in the preceding table.

Using random numbers

Let's navigate to the Basic card in our mobile application. We will focus on the **R** button to demonstrate how to use random numbers in our mobile applications. Random numbers are commonly used in mobile games and games of chance.

Engage Thrusters

Add the following code to the **R** button on the Basic card:

```
on mouseUp
    set the randomSeed to the long seconds

    ask "Enter any number" titled "Upper Limit"
    answer random(it) & " is a random number between 1 and " & it
titled "Results"
end mouseUp
```

This code accomplishes three things. First, it sets a random seed. Using a random seed helps improve the randomness of results. Next, the code prompts the user for input. The user is being asked for an upper limit number.

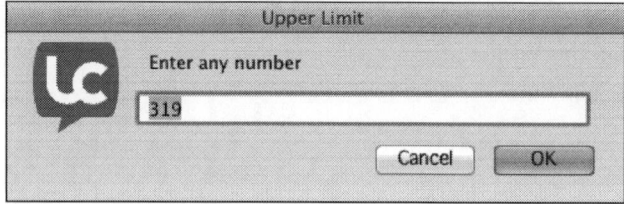

Lastly, our code calculates a random number between 1 and the number entered by the user and displays the results. Refer to the following screenshots for details:

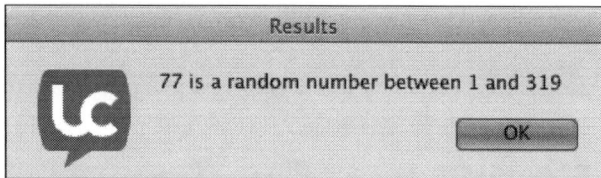

Objective Complete - Mini Debriefing

We aptly demonstrated how to use random numbers to include the necessity for using a random seed. We used both the `randomSeed` and `random()` functions.

Classified Intel

It is important to use a unique random seed each time you need to generate a random number. Using a function such as the long seconds is a good technique. The long seconds returns the number of seconds since midnight, January 1st, 1970 (GMT).

Mission Accomplished

This project had you delving into how LiveCode handles mathematical functions and operations. Along the way, we discovered how to program and use our own functions and commands, how to accept and validate user input, and how to use random numbers.

Here is a screenshot of the two modes (Basic and Advanced) that we created for our Mobile Calculator project:

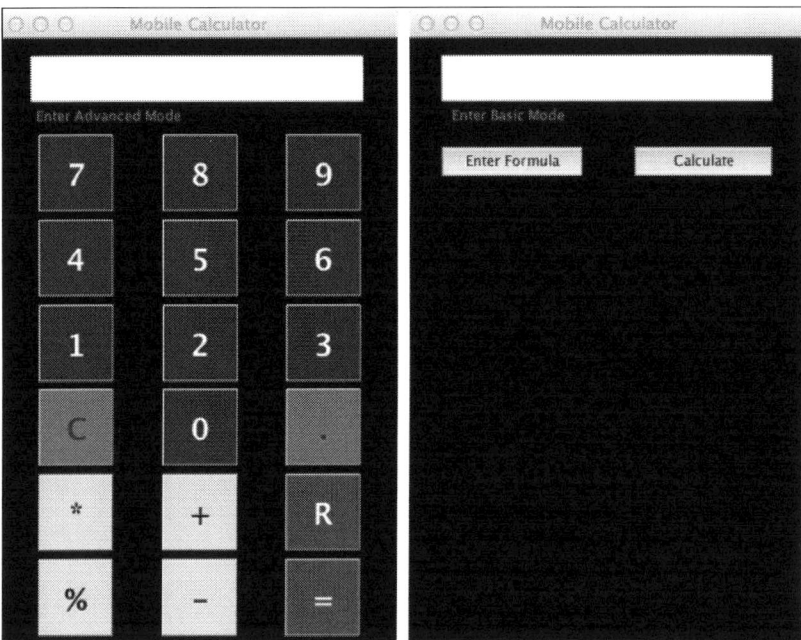

A Hotshot Challenge

You might have noticed that we created a decimal button on the Basic card. You might have also realized that we did not program it. Right now it is just sitting there taking up space. Your challenge, should you choose to accept it, is to program that button and make any other necessary changes to the mobile app so that users can use the calculator with a decimal point. Good luck!

Project 4

Building Menus – Menu of Menus

Mobile applications often present users with options. These options might include selecting a date and time for a meeting, a color, a number, or a host of other options. How to present the options to the user deserves careful consideration. Fortunately, LiveCode offers several different menu interface objects. In this project, we will look at how to use each of LiveCode's menu interface objects specifically for mobile devices.

Mission Briefing

In this project, we will build a mobile application called **Menu of Menus**. We will use a single stack with eight cards. Each card will feature a different type of menu interface object:

- swipe
- pulldown
- option
- combobox
- pop-up
- tab
- picker
- dropdown

Our app's main purpose is to demonstrate various menu objects working on a mobile device. We'll add some components to our project along the way to ensure developing this app is fun.

The following screenshot is a preview of what the mobile app that we will build in this project looks like:

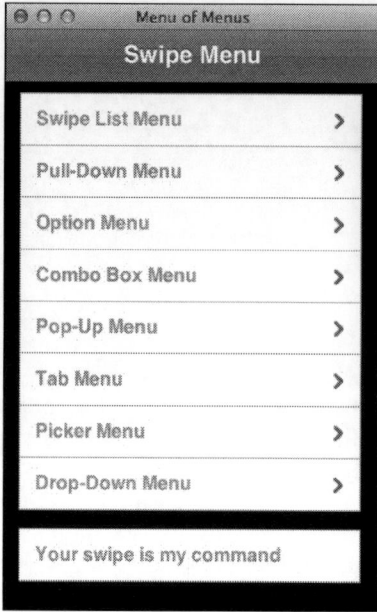

This project requires the use of a third-party commercial plugin called MobGUI. This plugin works with the commercial version of LiveCode and is available at a nominal fee. Even if you do not want to purchase the plugin, it is worth your time reading through this project's pages.

Why Is It Awesome?

It is very important to become familiar with menu interface objects for mobile devices. Your users will need to interact with the apps you develop. Menu interface objects are advanced user interface objects, in that they have embedded functionality in LiveCode that makes their use a powerful tool for you as a LiveCode developer.

You might think that menus are not important to you because you are only going to develop game apps for mobile devices. Even in this case, menu interface objects are typically used. One common example is to select a difficulty setting from a drop-down menu list.

Even if your immediate mobile application project does not call for the use of menus, this project will provide you with the ability to easily use menu interface objects in future LiveCode mobile application projects.

Your Hotshot Objectives

To complete the Menu of Menus project, we'll accomplish the following tasks:

- ▶ Creating the main stack
- ▶ Creating the project shell
- ▶ Creating a swiping menu interface
- ▶ Creating a pull-down menu interface
- ▶ Creating an option menu interface
- ▶ Creating a combobox menu interface
- ▶ Creating a pop-up menu interface
- ▶ Creating a tab menu interface
- ▶ Creating a picker menu interface
- ▶ Creating a drop-down menu interface

Mission Checklist

Throughout this project, we will make use of the `MobGUI LiveCode` plugin. You can obtain this plugin at the LiveCode store. It is very reasonably priced. Once you have purchased the `MobGUI` plugin, you will be provided with a download link. With the plugin downloaded to your computer, you will need to ensure it is placed in the appropriate folder. As shown in the following screenshot, the `revMobGUI.livecode` file should be placed in the `Plugins` folder of your LiveCode installation:

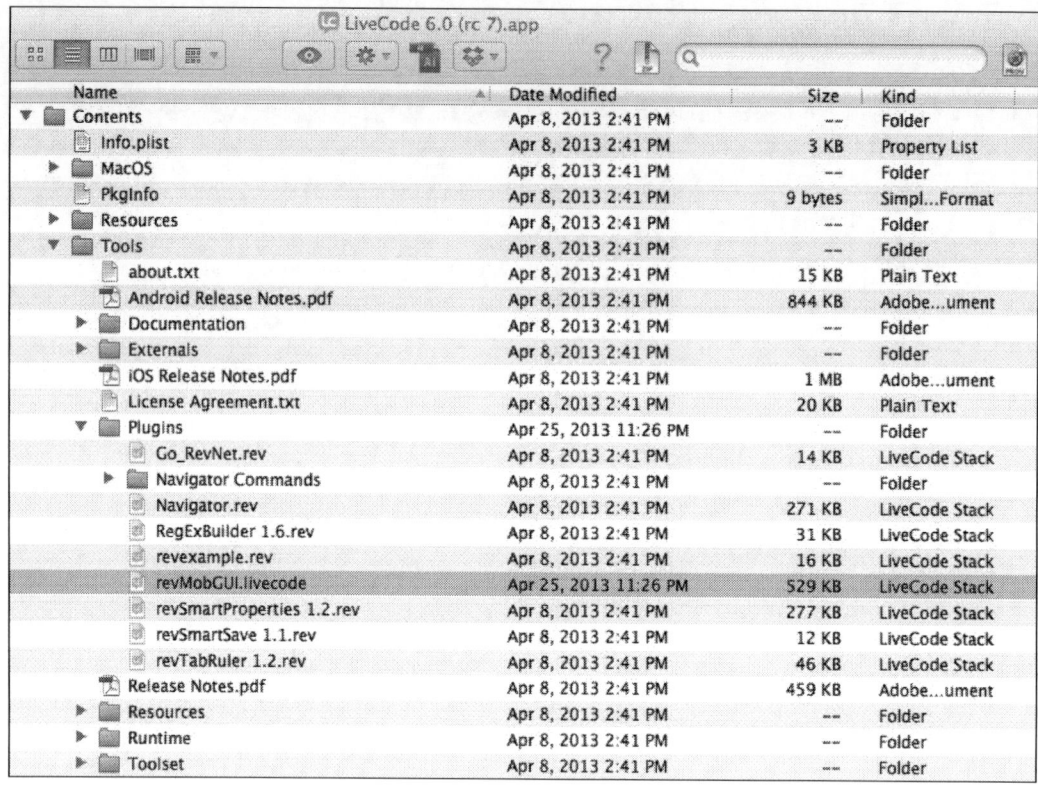

Creating the main stack

Our first task is to create the main stack for our Menu of Menus application. There will be eight cards in our stack; we'll create those in the next section and then, in subsequent sections, add appropriate LiveCode scripts to them.

Prepare for Lift Off

Open LiveCode and double-check to ensure you have the MobGUI plugin installed. Simply select **Plugins** from the **Development** drop-down menu and ensure that revMobGUI is listed.

Engage Thrusters

1. Let's begin by creating a new main stack named Menus. Using the properties inspector, make the following customizations to the main stack:

    1. Change the size of the stack to 320 x 480 pixels.

    2. Set the name of the stack to Menus.

    3. Set the title of the stack to Menu of Menus.

    4. Set the background color to black.

2. Open the MobGUI plugin by selecting the **Development** drop-down menu, then **Plugins**, and finally, revMobGUI.

3. With the MobGUI stack in focus, click on the **Menus** main stack.

4. In the MobGUI stack, make the following configuration changes:

    1. Under the **Design size & orientation** section, select **iPhone** and **Portrait**.

    2. Under the **Runtime allowed orientations** section, select **Portrait** and deselect **Portrait upside down**, **Landscape left**, and **Landscape right**.

When you complete the four steps, the MobGUI interface should resemble the following screenshot:

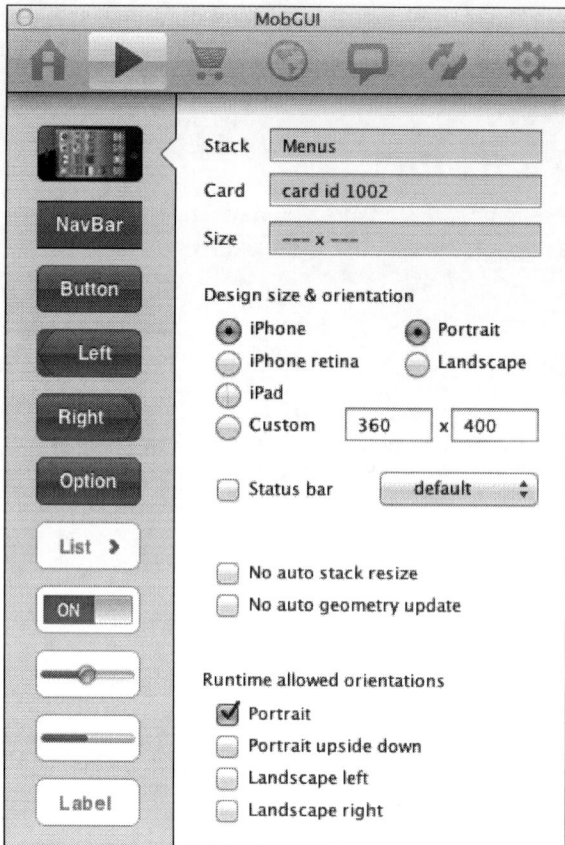

Objective Complete - Mini Debriefing

Now we have a main stack named Menus that uses the MobGUI plugin. This will be our canvas for the remaining tasks required of this project.

Classified Intel

You can accomplish everything in this project without using the MobGUI plugin. Using the plugin is therefore not required, but it is advisable. The benefits of using the MobGUI plugin are that you can save a tremendous amount of time when creating and scripting your interface. MobGUI is a third-party plugin and is only available when purchased along with a commercial license of LiveCode.

Creating the project shell

In this section, we will create a shell for the project that consists of eight cards. Cards 2 through 8 will have navigational controls that permit the user to go back to card 1.

Engage Thrusters

1. LiveCode automatically created the first card when we created the main stack. Make the following changes to card 1:

   1. Rename the card to `Swipe`.

   2. Drag a navigation bar from the `MobGUI` stack onto the Swipe card.

   3. Change the label of the Navigation Bar to `navBar`.

   4. Set the label of `navBar` to `Swipe Menu`.

2. Create a second card and make the following configuration changes:

   1. Rename the card to `Pull`.

   2. Drag a navigation bar from the `MobGUI` stack onto the card.

   3. Change the title of the Navigation Bar to `navBar`.

   4. Set the label of `navBar` to `Pull-Down Menu`.

   5. Drag a left navigational button from the `MobGUI` stack onto the card.

   6. Rename the left button to `Back`.

   7. Change the label text of the Back button to `Back`.

   8. Remove all of the Back button's code.

   9. Add the following code to the Back button:

   ```
   on mouseUp
       go to card 1
   end mouseUp
   ```

   This code will take the user to the first card, which is our main menu.

3. Create a third card with the following details:

   1. Rename the card to `Option`.

   2. Copy the `navBar` and `Back` objects from the first card and paste them onto the new card.

   3. Change the label of `navBar` to `Option Menu`.

4. Create a fourth card with the following details:

    1. Rename the card to `Combo`.

    2. Copy the `navBar` and `Back` objects from the first card and paste them onto the new card.

    3. Change the label of `navBar` to `Combo Box Menu`.

5. Create a fifth card with the following details:

    1. Rename the card to `Pop`.

    2. Copy the `navBar` and `Back` objects from the first card and paste them onto the new card.

    3. Change the label of `navBar` to `Pop-Up Menu`.

6. Create a sixth card with the following details:

    1. Rename the card to `Tab`.

    2. Copy the `navBar` and `Back` objects from the first card and paste them onto the new card.

    3. Change the label of `navBar` to `Tab Menu`.

7. Create a seventh card with the following details:

    1. Rename the card to `Picker`.

    2. Copy the `navBar` and `Back` objects from the first card and paste them onto the new card.

    3. Change the label of `navBar` to `Picker Menu`.

8. Create an eighth card with the following details:

    1. Rename the card to `Drop`.

    2. Copy the `navBar` and `Back` objects from the first card and paste them onto the new card.

    3. Change the label of `navBar` to `Drop-Down Menu`.

Objective Complete - Mini Debriefing

Now we have a main stack with eight cards. Cards 2 through 8 have navigational bars with an appropriate label. These cards also all have a Back button that takes the user back to card 1.

Classified Intel

We made quick work of creating cards 3 through 8 by copying objects from card 2 and making minor edits. This type of approach is intended to save you time. Programming in LiveCode need not be tedious.

Creating a swiping menu interface

In this section, we will edit the first card of your mobile application. The card will hold swiping menu interface objects, one for each type of menu used in this project.

Engage Thrusters

1. Drag a Label field from the `MobGUI` stack onto the **Swipe** card. Make the following modifications to the label.

    1. Change the label to `Footer`.

    2. Set the text to `Your Swipe is my command`.

    3. Set the location to `158, 434`.

2. Next we will add eight list button groups from the `MobGUI` stack to our card. Here are the steps:

    1. Right-click on the list button group on the `MobGUI` stack and select the number `8`.

    2. Drag the list button group from the `MobGUI` stack onto the Swipe card.

3. Edit the first list button group and make the following configuration changes:

    1. Change the name of the list button group to `Swipe`.

    2. Change the label to `Swipe List Menu`.

    3. Set the location to `158, 74`.

4. Edit the second list button group and make the following configuration changes:

    1. Change the name of the list button group to `Pull`.

    2. Change the label to `Pull-Down Menu`.

    3. Set the location to `158, 117`.

    4. Edit the `on touchEnd` script to point to the Pull card. Here is the code:

    ```
    on touchEnd pId
       mobGUIUntouch the long id of me
       visual effect push left very fast
       go card "Pull"
    end touchEnd
    ```

5. Edit the third list button group and make the following configuration changes:

    1. Change the name of the list button group to `Option`.

    2. Change the label to `Option Menu`.

    3. Set the location to `158, 160`.

    4. Edit the `on touchEnd` script to point to the Option card. Here is the code:

        ```
        on touchEnd pId
            mobGUIUntouch the long id of me
            visual effect push left very fast
            go card "Option"
        end touchEnd
        ```

6. Edit the fourth list button group and make the following configuration changes:

    1. Change the name of the list button group to `Combo`.

    2. Change the label to `Combo Box Menu`.

    3. Set the location to `158, 203`.

    4. Edit the `on touchEnd` script to point to the Combo card. Here is the code:

        ```
        on touchEnd pId
            mobGUIUntouch the long id of me
            visual effect push left very fast
            go card "Combo"
        end touchEnd
        ```

7. Edit the fifth list button group and make the following configuration changes:

    1. Change the name of the list button group to `Pop`.

    2. Change the label to `Pop-Up Menu`.

    3. Set the location to `158, 246`.

    4. Edit the `on touchEnd` script to point to the Pop card. Here is the code:

        ```
        on touchEnd pId
            mobGUIUntouch the long id of me
            visual effect push left very fast
            go card "Pop"
        end touchEnd
        ```

8. Edit the sixth list button group and make the following configuration changes:

    1. Change the name of the list button group to `Tab`.

    2. Change the label to `Tab Menu`.

    3. Set the location to `158, 289`.

    4. Edit the `on touchEnd` script to point to the Tab card. Here is the code:

    ```
    on touchEnd pId
        mobGUIUntouch the long id of me
        visual effect push left very fast
        go card "Tab"
    end touchEnd
    ```

9. Edit the seventh list button group and make the following configuration changes:

    1. Change the name of the list button group to `Picker`.

    2. Change the label to `Picker Menu`.

    3. Set the location to `158, 332`.

    4. Edit the `on touchEnd` script to point to the Picker card. Here is the code:

    ```
    on touchEnd pId
        mobGUIUntouch the long id of me
        visual effect push left very fast
        go card "Picker"
    end touchEnd
    ```

10. Edit the eighth list button group and make the following configuration changes:

    1. Change the name of the list button group to `Drop`.

    2. Change the label to `Drop-Down Menu`.

    3. Set the location to `158, 375`.

    4. Edit the `on touchEnd` script to point to the Drop card. Here is the code:

    ```
    on touchEnd pId
        mobGUIUntouch the long id of me
        visual effect push left very fast
        go card "Drop"
    end touchEnd
    ```

Objective Complete - Mini Debriefing

Once you have completed the preceding 10 steps, you will have the main interface of the Menu of Menus mobile application completed. Your interface should look like the one in the following screenshot:

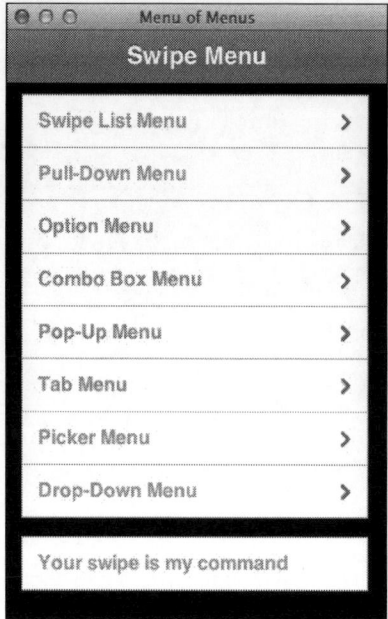

Creating a pull-down menu interface

In this section, we will create two pull-down menu interfaces on our Pull card. We will ask the user to first select a color, then an animal. We will include a Process button that provides results of the user's selections.

Engage Thrusters

1. Drag a Label field from the **Tools** palette onto the **Pull** card and make the following modifications to that label:

    1. Set the width to `134` and height to `21`.

    2. Set the location to `81, 64`.

    3. Change the foreground color to `white`.

    4. Align the text to left.

    5. Bold the text.

6. Change the text size to `14`.

7. Change the contents to select a color.

2. Drag a Pulldown Menu from the **Tools** palette onto the **Pull** card and make the following modifications to that object:

    1. Set the name to `color`.

    2. Set the width to `134` and height to `21`.

    3. Set the location to `219, 64`.

    4. Set the menu items text to `Red`, `Green`, `Blue`, and `Purple`.

    5. Set the `showName` to true by selecting the checkbox next to **Display Name** in the properties inspector.

    6. Edit the code so that it matches the following:

```
on menuPick pItemName
    global theColor
    put pItemName into theColor
end menuPick
```

3. Drag a Label field from the **Tools** palette onto the **Pull** card and make the following modifications to that label:

    1. Set the width to `134` and height to `21`.

    2. Set the location to `81, 198`.

    3. Change the foreground color to `white`.

    4. Align the text to left.

    5. Bold the text.

    6. Change the text size to `14`.

    7. Change the contents to `Select an animal`.

4. Drag a Pulldown Menu menu from the **Tools** palette onto the **Pull** card and make the following modifications to that object:

    1. Set the name to `animal`.

    2. Set the width to `134` and height to `21`.

    3. Set the location to `221, 198`.

    4. Set the menu items text to `Lion`, `Tiger`, `Bear`, and `Zebra`.

    5. Set the `showName` to `True`.

6. Edit the code so that it matches the following:

```
on menuPick pItemName
    global theAnimal
    put pItemName into theAnimal
end menuPick
```

5. Drag a Label field from the **Tools** palette onto the **Pull** card and make the following modifications to that label:

   1. Change the name to `Results`.

   2. Set the width to `276` and height to `68`.

   3. Set the location to `156, 406`.

   4. Change the foreground color to `yellow`.

   5. Align the text to center.

   6. Bold the text.

   7. Change the text size to `14`.

   8. Clear the default contents.

6. Drag a button from the `MobGUI` stack onto the **Pull** card and make the following modifications:

   1. Change the name to `Process`.

   2. Change the label to `Process`.

   3. Edit the `on touchEnd` script so that it matches the following code:

```
on touchEnd pId
    global theColor, theAnimal
    local part1, part2, newAnimal
    mobGUIUntouch the long id of me

    if theColor is empty OR theAnimal is empty then
        answer "Cannot compute. Check your selections."
    else
        switch theColor
            case "Red"
                put "R" into part1
                break
            case "Green"
                put "Gr" into part1
                break
            case "Blue"
                put "Bl" into part1
```

```
                  break
             case "Purple"
                 put "P" into part1
          end switch
          --
          switch theAnimal
             case "Lion"
                 put "ion" into part2
                 break
             case "Tiger"
                 put "iger" into part2
                 break
             case "Bear"
                 put "ear" into part2
                 break
             case "Zebra"
                 put "ebra" into part2
          end switch
          --
          put part1 & part2 into newAnimal
          put "You selected " & theColor & " and " & theAnimal &
  return & \\
             "Your new animal is:" & return & newAnimal into fld
  "Results"
           end if
        end touchEnd
```

As you review our Process button's code, you will see that we are accomplishing five things:

1. First, we check to make sure that the user has selected both a color and an animal. If they failed to make one selection in each category, we display a pop up and urge them to check their selections.

2. Next, we take the first part of the selected color and place it in the local variable part1. We use R for red, Gr for green, Bl for blue, and P for purple.

3. Our next step is to place part of the animal name into the local variable part2. We use ion for Lion, iger for Tiger, ear for Bear, and ebra for Zebra.

4. Next, we combine the variables part1 and part2 into a third variable named newAnimal.

5. Lastly, we output the results to the user.

The last thing we need to do is to add code to the card that clears the on-screen results and global variables each time the card is viewed. Here is that code:

```
on preOpenCard
   global theColor, theAnimal

   put empty into theColor
   put empty into theAnimal
   put empty into fld "Results"
end preOpenCard
```

As you can see by reviewing the preceding code, we start by declaring the two global variables (`theColor` and `theAnimal`). Next, we put `empty` into both of those variables. The last thing our code does is to clear the Results field.

Objective Complete - Mini Debriefing

Having followed the seven steps in this section, you should have the Pull card completely designed and programmed so that it serves as a good example of how to use pull-down menus for mobile applications developed using LiveCode. Your application should look similar to the following screenshot:

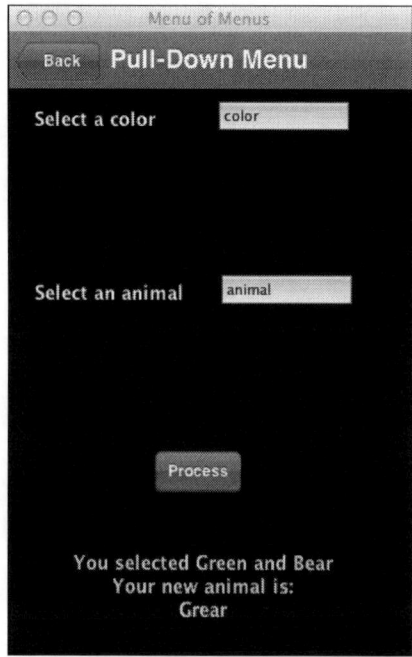

Creating an option menu interface

In this section, we will create three option menu interfaces on our Option card. We will prompt the user to select a country from the first option menu, a number from the second, and an animal, plant, or vegetable from the third menu. We will then present the user with a Process button to process the selections. Our final task will be to display the results to the user.

Engage Thrusters

As you progress through the steps in this task, you will use both the LiveCode **Tools** palette and the MobGUI interface. There are instances where you could accomplish steps using either interface. Let's stick to the steps as outlined to avoid confusion.

1. Navigate to the **Option** card.

2. Drag an Option Menu button from the LiveCode **Tools** palette onto the **Option** card and make the following modifications to that object:

    1. Set the name to Country.

    2. Set the width to 102 and height to 22.

    3. Set the location to 69, 91.

    4. Set the menu items text to at least five countries. I listed countries I have been to, but you can use anything, such as Australia, Canada, China, India, Russia, Singapore, South Korea, and the United States.

    5. Edit the code so that it matches the following:

    ```
    on menuPick pItemName
        global theCountry
        put pItemName into theCountry
    end menuPick
    ```

    This code simply takes the user's choice and puts the value into the global variable theCountry.

3. Drag an Option Menu from the **Tools** palette onto the **Option** card and make the following modifications to that object:

    1. Set the name to Number.

    2. Set the width to 50 and height to 22.

    3. Set the location to 160, 91.

    4. Set the menu items text to the following numbers: 2, 3, 4, 5, 10, and 20.

5. Edit the code so that it matches the following:

```
on menuPick pItemName
    global theNumber
    put pItemName into theNumber
end menuPick
```

This code simply takes the user's choice and puts the value into the global variable `theNumber`.

4. Drag an Option Menu from the **Tools** palette onto the **Option** card and make the following modifications to that object:

   1. Set the name to `Product`.

   2. Set the width to `102` and height to `22`.

   3. Set the location to `251, 91`.

   4. Set the menu items text to `Aardvark`, `Christmas tree`, `Lizard`, `Orchid`, and `Spinach`.

   5. Edit the code so that it matches the following:

```
on menuPick pItemName
    global theObject
    put pItemName into theObject
end menuPick
```

This code simply takes the user's choice and puts the value into the global variable `theObject`.

5. Drag a Label field from the **Tools** palette onto the **Option** card and make the following modifications to that label:

   1. Change the name to `Results`.

   2. Set the width to `276` and height to `92`.

   3. Set the location to `156, 418`.

   4. Change the foreground color to `yellow`.

   5. Align the text to center.

   6. Bold the text.

   7. Change the text size to **14**.

   8. Clear the default contents.

6. Drag a button from the `MobGUI` stack onto the **Option** card and make the following modifications:

   1. Change the name to `Process`.

   2. Change the label to `Process`.

   3. Edit the `on touchEnd` script so that it matches the following code:

```
on touchEnd pId
    global theCountry, theNumber, theObject
    local firstChar, aan
    mobGUIUntouch the long id of me

    if theCountry is empty OR theNumber is empty OR theObject
    is empty then
        answer "Cannot compute. Check your selections."
    else
        //put char 1 of theObject into firstChar
        if char 1 of theObject is among the characters of
        "aeiou" then
            put "an" into aan
        else
            put "a" into aan
        end if

        put "You will have a very happy life with your
        parents, spouse, and " \\
        & theNumber & " children living on " &  aan & space &
        theObject \\
        & " farm in " & theCountry & "." into fld "Results"
    end if
end touchEnd
```

As you review our **Process** button's code, you will see that we are accomplishing three things:

1. First, we check to make sure that the user has selected a country, a number, and an object. If they failed to make one selection in each category, we display a pop up and urge them to check their selections.

2. Next, we check to see if the first letter of value in the variable `theObject` is a vowel. If it is a vowel, we put "an" into the variable `aan`; otherwise we put "a" into that variable.

3. Lastly, we output the results to the user.

The last thing we need to do is to add code to the card that clears the on-screen results and global variables each time the card is viewed. Here is that code:

```
on preOpenCard
  global theCountry, theNumber, theObject

  put empty into theCountry
  put empty into theNumber
  put empty into theObject
  put empty into fld "Results"
end preOpenCard
```

As you can see by reviewing the preceding code, we start by declaring the three global variables (`theCountry`, `theNumber`, and `theObject`). Next, we put `empty` into all three of those variables. The last thing our code does is to clear the Results field.

Objective Complete - Misson Debriefing

Having followed the seven steps in this section, you should have the **Option** card completely designed and programmed so that it serves as a good example of how to use option menus for mobile applications developed using LiveCode. Your application should look similar to the following screenshot:

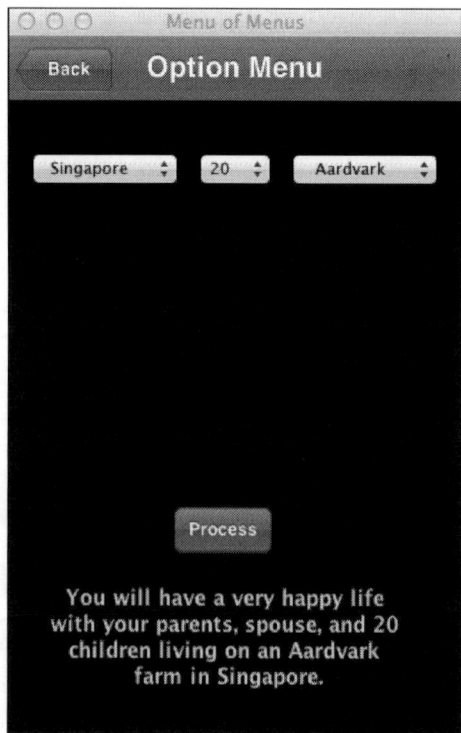

Creating a combobox menu interface

In this section, we will create a pop-up menu interface on our Combo card. Combo menus allow the user to select a menu choice already listed or enter their own selection via the keyboard.

Engage Thrusters

We'll work through four steps to accomplish our task.

1. Drag a Label field from the **Tools** palette onto the **Combo** card and make the following modifications to that field:
    1. Set the width to `202` and height to `21`.
    2. Set the location to `117, 88`.
    3. Change the foreground color to `white`.
    4. Align the text to left.
    5. Bold the text.
    6. Change the text size to `14`.
    7. Change the contents to `Select your favorite fruit`.

2. Drag a Label field from the **Tools** palette onto the **Combo** card and make the following modifications to that label:
    1. Change the name to `Results`.
    2. Set the width to `276` and height to `68`.
    3. Set the location to `156, 406`.
    4. Change the foreground color to `yellow`.
    5. Align the text to center.
    6. Bold the text.
    7. Change the text size to `14`.
    8. Clear the default contents.

3. Drag an Option Menu from the **Tools** palette onto the **Combo** card and make the following modifications to that object:
    1. Set the name to `Combo`.
    2. Set the width to `190` and height to `22`.
    3. Set the location to `155, 139`.

4. Set the menu items text to `Apples, Bananas, Coconut, Orange,` and `Watermelon`.

5. Edit the code so that it matches the following:

```
on menuPick pItemName
    set the text of fld "Results" to pItemName
end menuPick


on returnInField
    set the text of fld "Results" to the label of  me
end returnInField
```

With the `on menuPick` script, we capture any of the combobox menu options prepopulated and put the results in the Results field. With the second script, `on returnInField`, we capture anything the user types in when they hit the return key.

4. The last thing we need to do is to add code to the card that clears the on-screen results each time the card is viewed. Here is that code:

```
on preOpenCard
    put empty into fld "Results"
end preOpenCard
```

As you can see by reviewing the preceding code, we simply clear the Results field.

Objective Complete - Mission Debriefing

Having followed the four steps in this section, you should have the **Combo** card completely designed and programmed so that it serves as a good example of how to use combo menus for mobile applications developed using LiveCode. Your application should look similar to the following screenshot:

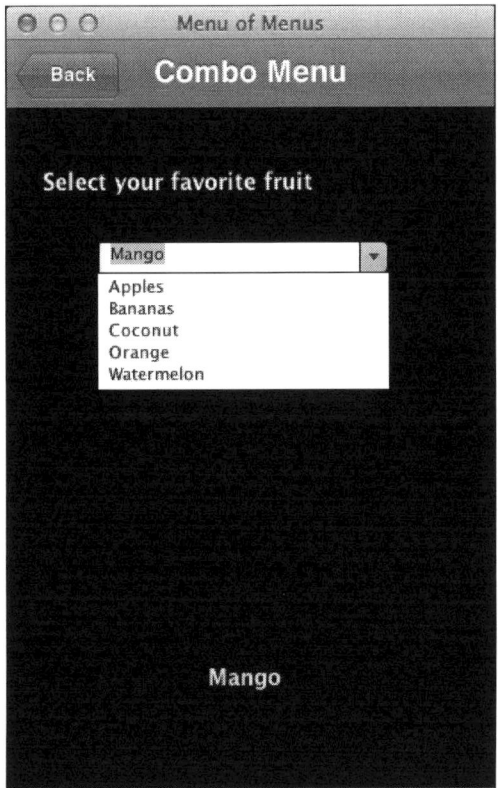

Creating a pop-up menu interface

In this section, we will create a pop-up menu interface on our Pop card. Pop-up menus are a nice menu interface that allows you to conserve precious screen real estate. When a user selects a pop-up menu, the menu choices appear in a popped-up interface.

Engage Thrusters

1. Drag a Label field from the **Tools** palette onto the **Pop** card and make the following modifications to that label:

    1. Change the name to `Results`.

    2. Set the width to `276` and height to `68`.

    3. Set the location to `156, 406`.

    4. Change the foreground color to `yellow`.

    5. Align the text to center.

6.   Bold the text.

7.   Change the text size to 14.

8.   Clear the default contents.

2.   Drag a Pop-Up Menu from the **Tools** palette onto the Pop card and make the following modifications to that object:

1.   Set the width to 222 and height to 22.

2.   Set the location to 155, 209.

3.   Set the menu items text to the 50 U.S States. You can find a file with the 50 states alphabetically listed in the Chapter 4 folder for this book, located on the www.packtpub.com site.

4.   Edit the code so that it matches the following:

```
on menuPick pItemName
    set the text of fld "Results" to pItemName
end menuPick
```

With the on menuPick script, we capture the selection made by the user and put the results in the Results field.

3.   The last thing we need to do is to add code to the card that clears the on-screen results each time the card is viewed. Here is that code:

```
on preOpenCard
    put empty into fld "Results"
end preOpenCard
```

As you can see by reviewing the preceding code, we simply clear the Results field.

Objective Complete - Mission Debriefing

Having followed the four steps in this section, you should have the **Pop** card completely designed and programmed so that it serves as a good example of how to use pop-up menus for mobile applications developed using LiveCode. Your application should look similar to the following screenshot:

Creating a tab menu interface

In this section, we will create a tab menu interface on our Tab card. Tab menus offer an excellent way of organizing information groups without having to switch between cards. In two steps, we will create a simple tab menu interface that has four tabs, one for each season.

Engage Thrusters

1. Drag a Tab Panel menu from the **Tools** palette and place it onto the **Tab** card. Make the following configuration changes to the object:

    1. Change the name to `Tabs`.

    2. Set the width to `280` and height to `144`.

    3. Set the location to `158, 150`.

    4. Set the background color to `white`.

    5. Change the tabs in the basic properties of the properties inspector to `Spring`, `Summer`, `Autumn`, and `Winter`.

    6. Set the `showName` to `True` by checking the **Display Name** checkbox in the properties inspector.

2. Add the following code to the **Tabs** panel menu object:

```
on menuPick pItemName
   switch pItemName
      case "Spring"
         set the label of me to "Longer Days" & return & \
               "Plant Growth" & return & "Unstable Weather" & \
               return & "Groundhog Day"
         break
      case "Summer"
         set the label of me to "Sunny" & return & "Picnics" & \
               return & "Vacation" & return & "Swimming" & \
               return & "Ice Tea"
         break
      case "Autumn"
         set the label of me to "Foliage Splendor" & return & \
               "Earlier Nights" & return & "September Equinox" & \
               return & "Thanksgiving"
         break
      case "Winter"
         set the label of me to "Coldest" & return & "Snow" & \
               return & "Ice" & "Freezing" & return & "Snowmen" &
\
               return & "Santa Claus"
         break
   end switch
end menuPick
```

Our source code uses a simple switch statement to change the text of the label based on which tab is selected.

Objective Complete - Mission Debriefing

Having followed the two steps in this section, you should have the **Tab** card completely designed and programmed so that it serves as a simple example of how to use tab panel menus for mobile applications developed using LiveCode. Your application should look similar to the following screenshot:

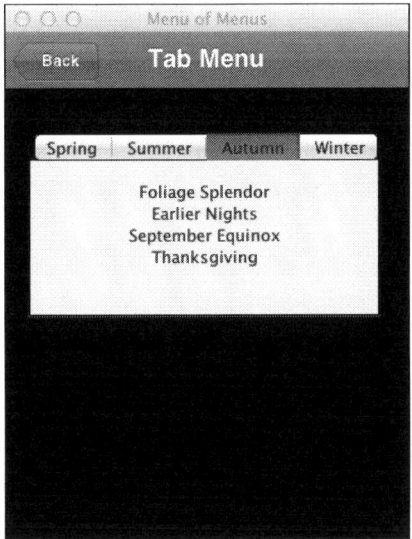

Creating a picker menu interface

In this section, we will create a picker menu interface on our Picker card. We will create a picker with three columns: the first and third for numbers, and the middle column for mathematical operators.

Engage Thrusters

There are no user interface objects required to instantiate a picker menu for mobile devices. We can accomplish this programmatically. Here is the source code required for the Picker card.

```
on openCard
   local t1, t2, t3

   put "1" & return & "2" & return & "3" & return & \
       "4" & return & "5" & return & "6" into t1
   put "*" & return & "+" & return & "-" into t2
   put "1" & return & "2" & return & "3" & return & \
       "4" & return & "5" & return & "6" into t3
```

```
        mobilePick t1, 3, t2, 2, t3, 3
        --

        put char 1 of the result into t1
        put char 3 of the result into t2
        put char 5 of the result into t3
        --

        if t2 is 1 then
            answer t1 & " * " & t3 & " = " & (t1 * t3) with "Okay"
        else if t2 is 2 then
            answer t1 & " + " & t3 & " = " & (t1 + t3) with "Okay"
        else
            answer t1 & " - " & t3 & " = " & (t1 - t3) with "Okay"
        end if
    end openCard
```

Our source code has four basic areas. The first area is where we declare three local variables. The first variable (t1) is for the first number / number set; the second variable (t2) is for the mathematical operator; and the third variable (t3) is for the second number / number set.

The second section of source code populates the three columns of the picker menu. The first and third columns will have the numbers **1, 2, 3, 4, 5,** and **6**. The middle column will contain the following mathematical operator symbols: multiplication (*), addition (+), and subtraction (-). At the end of this section, a call is made to the mobilePick command. This is what instantiates the picker on mobile devices. The mobilePick command takes parameters in pairs, starting with the values and followed by the initial placeholder for that column. So, we have the first column identified as t1 with item 3 being displayed, the second column as t2 with the second data item being displayed, and t3 for the third column with the third item in that list being highlighted initially.

The next section of the code puts the output into local variables (t1, t2, and t3).

The final section uses an if...else branch to determine how to calculate the formula. The answer is provided in the form of a pop-up window.

Objective Complete-Mission Debriefing

This was a relatively straightforward user interface that can be created 100 percent via code. The picker menu interface is considered to be very user-friendly, so you should consider using it whenever it makes sense. The completed **Picker** card and functionality can be demonstrated by review of the following screenshots:

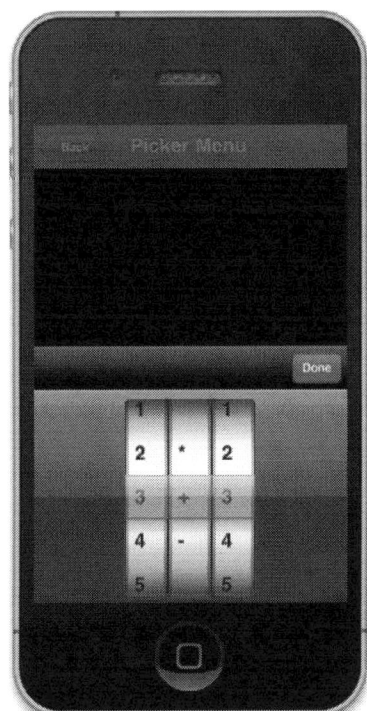

Creating a drop-down menu interface

In this section, we will create a drop-down menu interface on our Drop card. We will use the Menu Builder that is available via the Tools menu item.

Engage Thrusters

Next, we'll follow the seven steps detailed on the following pages in order to complete this task.

1. Navigate to the **Drop** card.

2. Select **Menu Builder** from the drop-down **Tools** menu in the main LiveCode menu system. You should see the **Menu Builder** main dialog window as shown in the following screenshot:

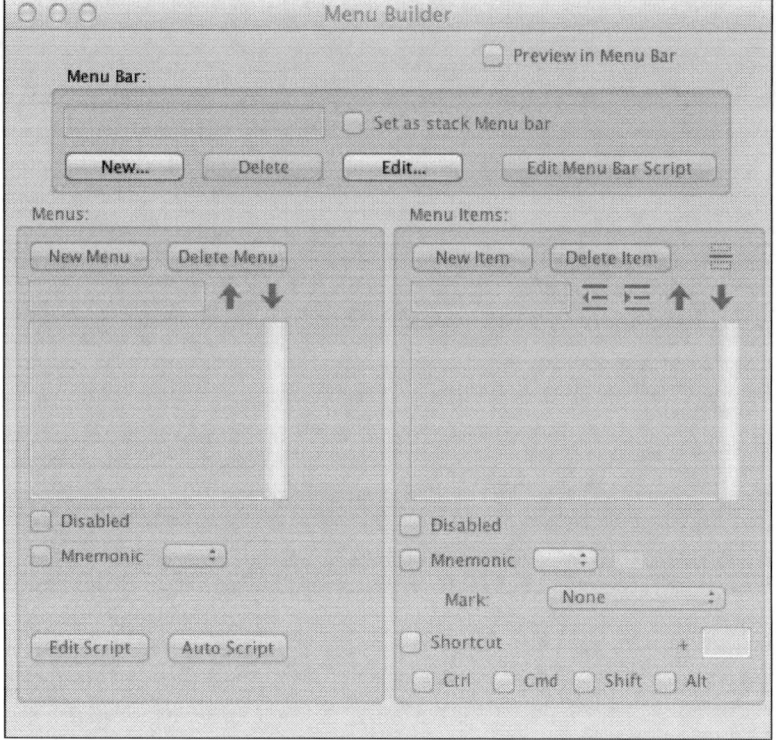

3. From the **Menu Builder** dialog window, select **New** and make the following entries on the pop-up form and change the Menus to Day, Month, and Year.

4. Using the **Menu Builder** dialog window, add menu items (Monday, Tuesday, Wednesday, Thursday, and Friday) to the **Day** menu. Refer to the following screenshot for details:

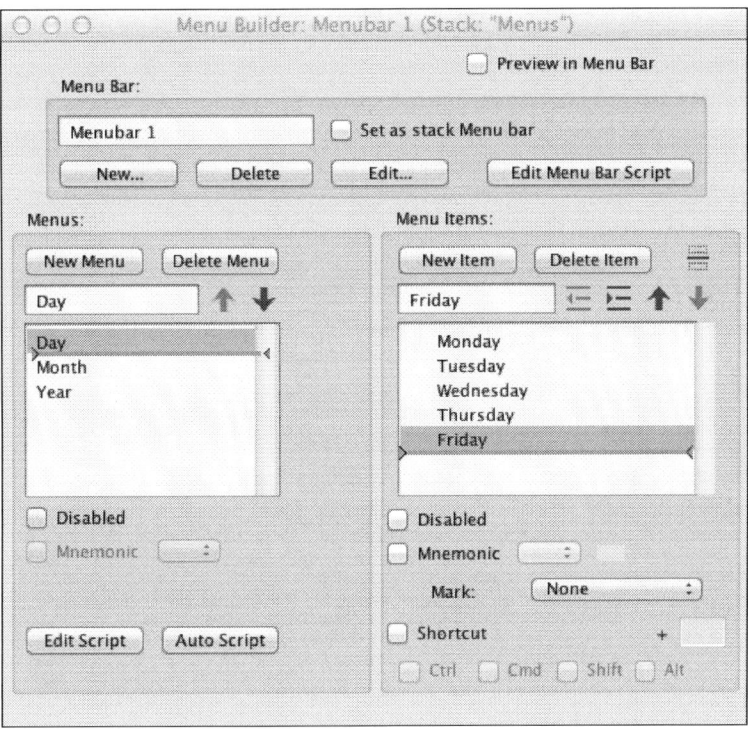

5. Enter menu items for the **Month** Menu. Enter all 12 months sequentially. Refer to the following screenshot for details:

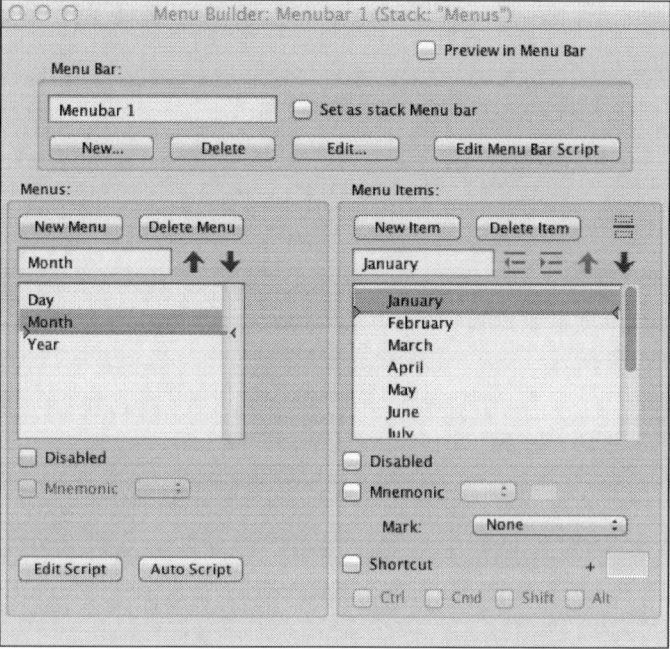

6. Enter menu items for the **Year** Menu. Enter `Before 1970`, `1970s`, `1980s`, `1990s`, `2000s`, and `After 2010`.

7. Test the app in the simulator. As you can see from the following screenshot, using LiveCode's **Menu Builder** can be somewhat problematic:

Objective Complete - Mission Debriefing

We completed our objective by using LiveCode's embedded **Menu Builder**. It became apparent that using drop-down menus is usually not appropriate for mobile devices. The **Menu Builder** is a powerful utility for creating drop-down menus. Unfortunately, it is not fully compatible with mobile devices.

Mission Accomplished

In this project, we developed a Menu of Menus mobile application using LiveCode. Our application featured the following menu types: **Swipe List**, **Pull-Down**, **Option**, **Combo Box**, **Pop-Up**, **Tab**, **Picker**, and **Drop-Down**. We made extensive use of the `MobGUI LiveCode` plugin to save time and help ensure our app had a familiar user interface schema.

The following screenshot shows the final project running in a simulator:

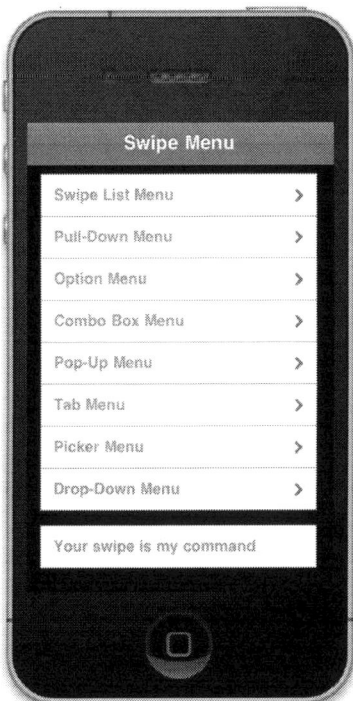

A Hotshot Challenge

For this Hotshot challenge, perform the following actions:

- On card 1 (**Swipe**), change the `Drop-Down Menu` label to `Hotshot Challenge`
- On Card 8 (**Drop-Down**), change the card so that it contains two or more menu types that work together in a creative and useful way

Good luck!

Project 5

Creating How Smart Am I? – A Quiz Game

Games are a very popular mobile application genre. Quizzes are a common technique used by educators and trainers to introduce materials and concepts to users and assess their knowledge. The gaming concept in a quiz game is that there are winning and losing conditions. LiveCode makes creating a quiz game for mobile devices relatively easy.

Mission Briefing

In this project, we will build a mobile application called **How Smart Am I?**. We'll use a single stack with six cards. The first card will be our main interface and each of the remaining cards will feature a different question format: true or false, multiple choice, sequencing, short answer, and picture-based. For each question card, we will create a question and answer data structure, display the questions, get and evaluate user answers, and provide feedback regarding the correct or incorrect nature of the user's answer.

We will use a landscape orientation for this application.

Here is an interface mockup of what the mobile app that we will build in this project will look like:

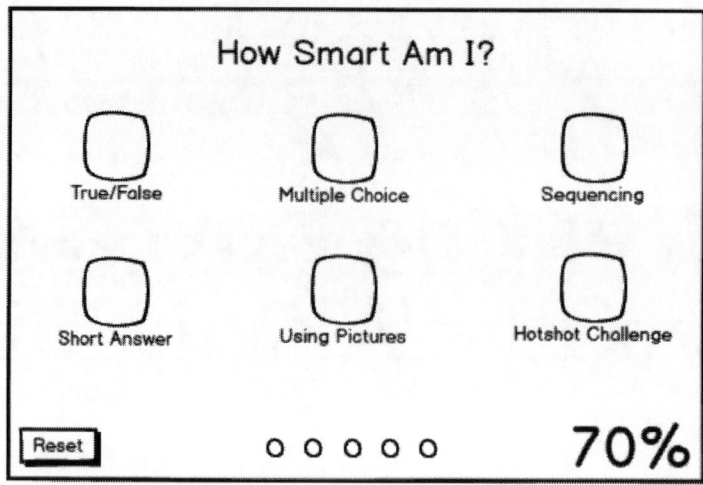

Why Is It Awesome?

The skills you learn while working on this project will help you design and develop your own mobile quiz app. More importantly, you will learn how to handle data and user input using LiveCode. These skills will help you develop a vast array of mobile applications that require data to be manipulated, evaluated, and otherwise processed.

Why is this a game? Quiz games might not have flashy animations and characters that interact with the user, but they are indeed games. Quiz games are an important type of mobile application and are in great demand.

Your Hotshot Objectives

To complete the How Smart Am I? project, we'll accomplish the following tasks:

- ▸ Creating the main stack
- ▸ Creating a true/false question card
- ▸ Creating a multiple choice question card
- ▸ Creating a sequencing question card
- ▸ Creating a short-answer question card
- ▸ Creating a picture question card
- ▸ Adding navigational scripting
- ▸ Adding scoring

Mission Checklist

You do not need plugins or additional software for LiveCode in order to accomplish this mission. You're all set, so let's get started.

Creating the main stack

Our first task is to create the main stack for our How Smart Am I? application. There will be six cards in our stack. As we create the main stack, refer to the interface mockup so you have a clear picture of what we are doing.

Engage Thrusters

1. Let's begin by creating a new main stack named HowSmart. Using the properties inspector, make the following customizations to the main stack:

    1. Change the size of the stack to 480 x 320 pixels. This will give us a landscape orientation.

    2. Set the name of the stack to HowSmart.

    3. Set the title of the stack to How Smart Am I?.

    4. Set the background color to black.

2. Rename the default card to Main.

3. Drag a Label field onto the **Main** card and make the following customizations using the properties inspector:

    1. Set the width to 470 and the height to 36.

    2. Set the location to 239, 22.

    3. Set the name of the field to Title.

    4. Set the text size to **24**.

    5. Center the text.

    6. Change the contents to How Smart Am I?.

    7. Set the foreground color to white.

    In the next six steps, we will create the six icons, one for each question type.

4. Drag a Rectangle Button onto the default card and make the following enhancements:

   1. Change the size of the button to 64 x 64 pixels.

   2. Set the location to 76, 102.

   3. Set the name of the button to true-false.

   4. Set the label of the button to True\nFalse.

[ When you use the \n escape sequence, it causes the remaining text to start on a new line.]

5. Drag a square button onto the default card and make the following enhancements:

   1. Change the size of the button to 64 x 64 pixels.

   2. Set the location to 238, 102.

   3. Set the name of the button to m-choice.

   4. Set the label of the button to Multiple\nChoice.

6. Drag a square button onto the default card and make the following enhancements:

   1. Change the size of the button to 64 x 64 pixels.

   2. Set the location to 400, 102.

   3. Set the name of the button to sequence.

   4. Set the label of the button to Sequence.

7. Drag a square button onto the default card and make the following enhancements:

   1. Change the size of the button to 64 x 64 pixels.

   2. Set the location to 76, 190.

   3. Set the name of the button to short-answer.

   4. Set the label of the button to Short\nAnswer.

8. Drag a square button onto the default card and make the following enhancements:

   1. Change the size of the button to 64 x 64 pixels.

   2. Set the location to 238, 190.

   3. Set the name of the button to pictures.

   4. Set the label of the button to Using\nPictures.

9. Drag a square button onto the default card and make the following enhancements:

   1. Change the size of the button to 64 x 64 pixels.

   2. Set the location to 400, 190.

   3. Set the name of the button to challenge.

   4. Set the label of the button to Hotshot\nChallenge.

So far, your interface should look like the following screenshot:

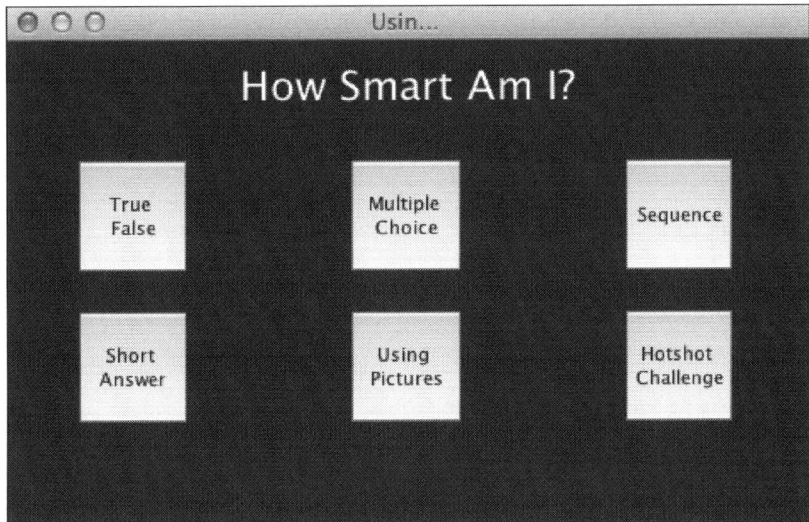

Next, let's continue building our main interface by adding the remaining three elements: the Reset button, progress indicators, and the grade label.

10. Drag a Rectangle Button onto the card and make the following modifications:

   1. Set the location to 55, 291.

   2. Set the name of the button to Reset.

   3. Set the label of the button to Reset.

11. Drag a Label field onto the card and make the following modifications:

   1. Set the location to 410, 291.

   2. Set the width to 100 and the height to 37.

   3. Set the name of the field to Score.

   4. Set the show focus border to false by deselecting it in the properties inspector.

5. Set the foreground color to white.

6. Set the text size to **24**.

12. Draw five oval graphics on the card with the following specifications:

1. Set **Opaque** to true.

2. Set the size to 28 x 28.

3. Set the foreground color to white.

4. Set the names to progress1, progress2, progress3, progress4, and progress5.

5. Set the location of graphic progress1 to 174, 291.

6. Set the location of graphic progress2 to 212, 291.

7. Set the location of graphic progress3 to 249, 291.

8. Set the location of graphic progress4 to 287, 291.

9. Set the location of graphic progress5 to 324, 291.

Objective Complete - Mini Debriefing

After completing the 12 steps in this section, your interface should look like the following screenshot. There are three main areas of our interface. First, is the header that only contains one label field. The second area contains six 64 x 64 buttons, each will open a new card. The last area is the footer, which contains three components: the **Reset** button, five progress graphics, and a label field to display the score.

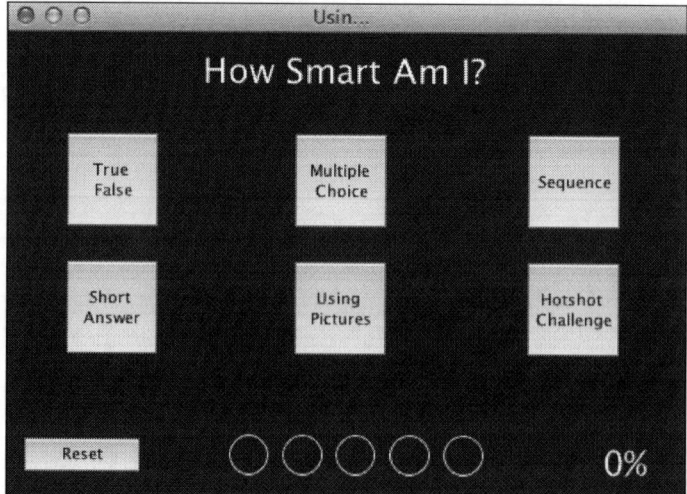

Classified Intel

The 12 steps in this task included creating six buttons that were very similar to each other. The only differences were the name, label, and location. There are also five identical oval graphics, identical in everyway except for name and location. In both these cases, there is great efficiency to be had in creating the first object in each group (buttons and graphics), replicating each one, and then making the necessary customizations.

Creating a true/false question card

In this section, we will create a new card for true/false questions. It will consist of a title label, question area, two buttons, and a position indicator.

Engage Thrusters

1. Create a new card and name it TF.

2. Copy the **Title** field from the Main card and paste it onto the new TF card. This will ensure the title field has a consistent format and location.

3. Drag a Rectangle Button onto the card and make the following modifications:

    1. Change the name to True.

    2. Change the display name to True.

    3. Set the size to 148 x 36.

    4. Set the location to 136, 214.

    5. Change the text size to **18**.

4. Drag a Rectangle Button onto the card and make the following modifications:

    1. Change the name to False.

    2. Change the display name to False.

    3. Set the size to 148 x 36.

    4. Set the location to 346, 214.

    5. Change the text size to **18**.

5. Drag a new Label field onto the bottom of the card and make the following modifications:

    1. Name the field `Progress`.
    2. Set the size to `436 x 32`.
    3. Set the location to `242, 294`.
    4. Change the text size to **18**.
    5. Change the text alignment to center.
    6. Change the foreground color to white.

Now that our user interface for the true/false questions is completed (as shown in the following screenshot), we can move on to programming the functionality of this card:

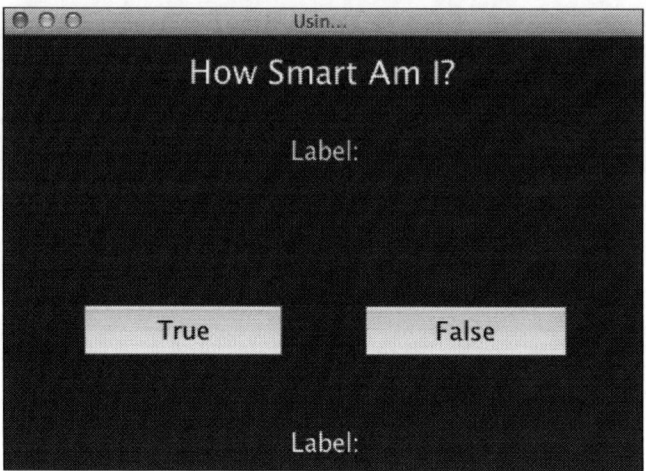

6. Add the following code in the TF card's script:

```
on preOpenCard
    global gNbr, gArray

    # Section 1
    put 1 into qNbr
    put empty into qText
    put empty into qAnswer
    # Section 2
    put "" into fld "Question"
    put "" into fld "Progress"
    # Section 3
     put "All houses have basements." into qArray["1"]["question"]
```

```
        put "F" into qArray["1"]["answer"]
        put "This simply is not true." into qArray["1"]["feedback"]
        --
        put "Dogs eat grapes." into qArray["2"]["question"]
        put "F" into qArray["2"]["answer"]
        put "Actually, grapes are bad for dogs." into qArray["2"]
["feedback"]
        --
        put "Ink can be used for writing." into qArray["3"]["question"]
        put "T" into qArray["3"]["answer"]
        put "Inks are commonly used in pens for writing." into
qArray["3"]["feedback"]
end preOpenCard
```

This code declares two variables, one each for the question number (qNbr) and the question array (qArray). The rest of the code is divided into sections, each with a # `Section number` comment line preceding its code.

In section 1 after declaring the variables, our code resets qNbr to 1 and puts `empty` into qText and qAnswer.

In section 2 the second section of code clears out the **Question** and **Progress** label fields.

In section 3 of our code, we are putting our three true/false questions into an array called qArray.

7. Now, we can program the card to display the first question. Add the following code to the TF card:

```
on openCard
    global qNbr, qArray

    put qArray[qNbr]["question"] into fld "Question"
    put "Question " & qNbr & " of 3" into fld "Progress"
end openCard
```

This code pulls the first question from the qArray array and updates both the **Question** and **Progress** fields.

8. Add the following code to the **True** button's script:

```
on mouseUp
    global qNbr, qText, qAnswer, qArray

    # Section 1
    if qArray[qNbr]["answer"] is "T" then
        if qNbr < 3 then
            answer "Very Good." with "Next" titled "Correct"
```

```
        else
            answer "Very Good." with "Okay" titled "Correct"
        end if
    else
        if qNbr < 3 then
            answer qArray[qNbr]["feedback"] with "Next" titled "Wrong
Answer"
        else
            answer qArray[qNbr]["feedback"] with "Okay" titled "Wrong
Answer"
        end if
    end if

    # Section 2
    if qNbr < 3 then
        add 1 to qNbr
        nextQuestion
    else
        go to card "Main"
    end if

end mouseUp
```

In section 1 of this code, you can see that we first evaluate if the question's answer is T (true). We know that there are only three questions, so we will either present the user with a **Next** or **Okay** button, as appropriate. When we provide results to the user, we either tell them **Very Good** or provide feedback from qArray.

9. Next, we need to script the **False** button. You should copy the code from the True button and then modify it to match the following code:

```
on mouseUp
    global qNbr, qText, qAnswer, qArray

    # Section 1
    if qArray[qNbr]["answer"] is "F" then
        if qNbr < 3 then
            answer "Very Good." with "Next" titled "Correct"
        else
            answer "Very Good." with "Okay" titled "Correct"
        end if
    else
```

```
        if qNbr < 3 then
            answer qArray[qNbr]["feedback"] with "Next" titled "Wrong
Answer"
        else
            answer qArray[qNbr]["feedback"] with "Okay" titled "Wrong
Answer"
        end if
    end if

    # Section 2
    if qNbr < 3 then
        add 1 to qNbr
        nextQuestion
    else
        go to card "Main"
    end if

end mouseUp
```

10. Both the **True** and **False** button scripts call a command named `nextQuestion`, which we have not written yet. Let's do that now with the following code:

```
command nextQuestion
    global qNbr, qArray

    put qArray[qNbr]["question"] into fld "Question"
    put "Question " & qNbr & " of 3" into fld "Progress"
end nextQuestion
```

You might recognize this code. This is the same code we used in step 8. Instead of duplicating the code, let's update the `openCard` script to simply call the `nextQuestion` command. We can accomplish this with the following code:

```
on openCard
    nextQuestion
end openCard
```

Objective Complete - Mini Debriefing

If you followed the 10 steps in this task, you will have a fully functioning true/false question interface. When a question is fully populated on the screen, it should look like the following screenshot:

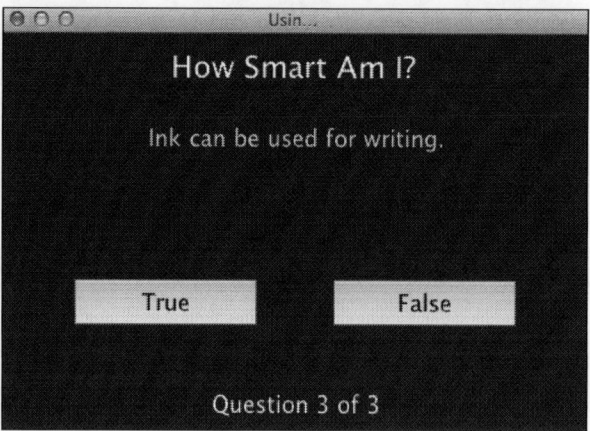

Creating a multiple choice question card

In this section, we will create a new card for multiple choice questions. It will consist of a title label, question area, four buttons, four answer choices, and a position indicator.

Engage Thrusters

1. Create a new card and name it MC.

2. Copy the **Title** label from the Main card and paste it onto the new MC card. This will ensure the title label field has a consistent format and location.

3. Copy the **Question** label from the TF card and paste it onto the new MC card.

4. Copy the **Progress** label from the TF card and paste it onto the new MC card.

5. Drag a Rectangle Button onto the card and make the following modifications:

   1. Change the name to b1.

   2. Change the display name to A.

   3. Set the size to 36 x 36.

   4. Set the location to 51, 189.

   5. Change the text size to **18**.

6. Drag a Rectangle Button onto the card and make the following modifications:

    1. Change the name to b2.

    2. Change the display name to B.

    3. Set the size to 36 x 36.

    4. Set the location to 51, 236.

    5. Change the text size to **18**.

7. Drag a Rectangle Button onto the card and make the following modifications:

    1. Change the name to b3.

    2. Change the display name to C.

    3. Set the size to 36 x 36.

    4. Set the location to 273, 189.

    5. Change the text size to **18**.

8. Drag a Rectangle Button onto the card and make the following modifications:

    1. Change the name to b4.

    2. Change the display name to D.

    3. Set the size to 36 x 36.

    4. Set the location to 273, 236.

    5. Change the text size to **18**.

9. Drag a Label field onto the card and make the following modifications:

    1. Change the name to b1.

    2. Set the size to 182 x 42.

    3. Set the location to 161, 189.

    4. Change the text size to **14**.

    5. Left-align the text.

10. Drag a Label field onto the card and make the following modifications:

    1. Change the name to b2.

    2. Set the size to 182 x 42.

    3. Set the location to 161, 237.

    4. Change the text size to **14**.

    5. Left-align the text.

11. Drag a Label field onto the card and make the following modifications:

    1. Change the name to b3.

    2. Set the size to 182 x 42.

    3. Set the location to 383, 189.

    4. Change the text size to **14**.

    5. Left-align the text.

12. Drag a Label field onto the card and make the following modifications:

    1. Change the name to b4.

    2. Set the size to 182 x 42.

    3. Set the location to 383, 237.

    4. Change the text size to **14**.

    5. Left-align the text.

 While using multiple choice question sets, users will want to be able to click on the button and the text, so your user interface should take that into consideration.

13. Let's next code the four label fields that will hold the answers to each question. We merely want to pass the "mouseUp" message to the corresponding button. Place the following code into each of the four label fields:

```
on mouseUp
    send "mouseUp" to btn(short name of me)
end mouseUp
```

We are able to use the exact same code for each of the four label fields because we gave the labels the same names as their corresponding buttons. LiveCode knows the difference between a label named b1 and a button named b1.

14. Add the following code to the MC card's script:

```
on preOpenCard
    global qNbr, qArray

    # Section 1
    put 1 into qNbr
    # Section 2
    put "" into fld "Question"
    put "" into fld "b1"
    put "" into fld "b2"
    put "" into fld "b3"
```

```
    put "" into fld "b4"
    put "" into fld "Progress"
    # Section 3
    put "Which is not an automotive manufacturer?" into qArray["1"]
["question"]
    put "b4" into qArray["1"]["correct"]
    put "Ford" into qArray["1"]["answer1"]
    put "Audi" into qArray["1"]["answer2"]
    put "Chevy" into qArray["1"]["answer3"]
    put "Kiap" into qArray["1"]["answer4"]
    --
    put "Which is the smallest dog breed?" into qArray["2"]
["question"]
    put "b1" into qArray["2"]["correct"]
    put "Corgi" into qArray["2"]["answer1"]
    put "Husky" into qArray["2"]["answer2"]
    put "Shar Pei" into qArray["2"]["answer3"]
    put "Irish Setter" into qArray["2"]["answer4"]
    --
    put "Which U.S. state is the furthest south?" into qArray["3"]
["question"]
    put "b2" into qArray["3"]["correct"]
    put "Washington" into qArray["3"]["answer1"]
    put "Texas" into qArray["3"]["answer2"]
    put "New York" into qArray["3"]["answer3"]
    put "Connecticut" into qArray["3"]["answer4"]
end preOpenCard
```

This code is similar to what we used for the TC card. The difference here is the structure of the question set array. We now have a question, correct answer code, and four answers in each row of data. We will use b1, b2, b3, and b4 for correct answer codes, since those are also the names of our buttons.

15. Next, we need to write our code so that we can sequence between questions. Here is the code to accomplish that:

```
on openCard
    nextQuestion
end openCard

command nextQuestion
    global qNbr, qArray

    put qArray[qNbr]["question"] into fld "Question"
    put qArray[qNbr]["answer1"] into fld "b1"
    put qArray[qNbr]["answer2"] into fld "b2"
```

```
      put qArray[qNbr]["answer3"] into fld "b3"
      put qArray[qNbr]["answer4"] into fld "b4"
      put "Question " & qNbr & " of 3" into fld "Progress"
   end nextQuestion
```

As you can see, we simply modified the `nextQuestion` code from the TF card to reflect the new question set data structure.

16. The next thing for us to do is to add code so that we can evaluate our user's answers. We will accomplish this by writing an `evaluateMC` command. Put the following code at the card level:

```
command evaluateMC theGuess
   global qNbr, qArray

   # Section 1
   if qArray[qNbr]["correct"] is theGuess then
      if qNbr < 3 then
         answer "Very Good." with "Next" titled "Correct"
      else
         answer "Very Good." with "Okay" titled "Correct"
      end if
   else
      if qNbr < 3 then
         answer "That is not correct" with "Next" titled "Wrong
Answer"
      else
         answer "That is not correct" with "Okay" titled "Wrong
Answer"
      end if
   end if

   # Section 2
   if qNbr < 3 then
      add 1 to qNbr
      nextQuestion
   else
      go to card "Main"
   end if
end evaluateMC
```

Again, you can see that this code is a slight modification of the code we used for the **True** and **False** buttons on the TF card. We made a few minor modifications and excluded specific feedback.

17. The last thing for us to do is to attach code to each of the four buttons (**b1**, **b2**, **b3**, and **b4**) so we can evaluate our users' answers. We will add the following code to pass the selected button's short name to the evaluateMC command we created in the previous step. Add the following code to each of the four buttons:

```
on mouseUp
    evaluateMC(the short name of me)
end mouseUp
```

Objective Complete - Mini Debriefing

If you have followed the 17 steps in this task, you will have a fully functioning true/false question interface. When a question is fully populated on the screen, it should look like the following screenshot:

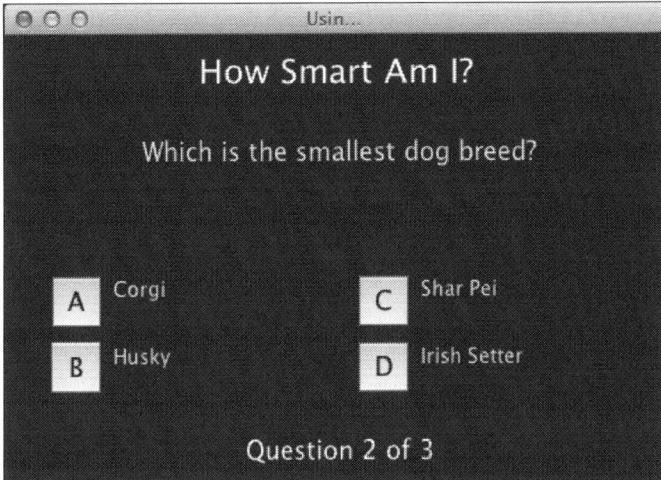

Creating a sequencing question card

In this section, we will create a new card for multiple choice questions. It will consist of a title label, question area, four buttons, four answer choices, and a position indicator.

Engage Thrusters

1. Create a new card and name it Sequencing.

2. Copy the **Title** label from the Main card and paste it onto the new Sequencing card. This will ensure the **Title** label field has a consistent format and location.

3. Copy the **Question** label from the MC card and paste it onto the new Sequencing card.

4. Copy the Progress label from the MC card and paste it onto the new Sequencing card.

5. Change the contents of the label field **Questions** to Drag the numbers over the steps below to show proper sequence. For the sequencing question type, we will have one persistent question text for all three sequencing questions. Change the size to 436 x 56 and the location to 240, 24.

6. Draw a rectangular graphic on the card with the following characteristics:

    1. Change the name to rect1.

    2. Set the line size under **Border** to 2.

    3. Set the foreground color to yellow.

    4. Set the background color to gray.

    5. Set **Opaque** to true.

    6. Set the size to 108 x 66.

    7. Set the location to 64, 181.

7. Replicate graphic rect1 and make the following modifications to the new graphic:

    1. Change the name to rect2.

    2. Set the location to 181, 181.

8. Replicate graphic rect1 and make the following modifications to the new graphic:

    1. Change the name to rect3.

    2. Set the location to 299, 181.

9. Replicate graphic rect1 and make the following modifications to the new graphic:

    3. Change the name to rect4.

    4. Set the location to 416, 181.

10. Drag four Label fields onto the card with the following characteristics:

    1. Set the size to 100 x 58.

    2. Set the text size to **14**.

    3. Center the text.

    4. Disable the **Don't Wrap** feature.

    5. Change the names to label1, label2, label3, and label4.

    6. Set the location to 64, 181 (label1), 180, 181 (label2), 298, 181 (label3), and 418, 181 (label4).

11. Select graphic `rect1` and field `label1`. Combine the two objects into a group named `grp1`.

12. Select graphic `rect2` and field `label2`. Combine the two objects into a group named `grp2`.

13. Select graphic `rect3` and field `label3`. Combine the two objects into a group named `grp3`.

14. Select graphic `rect4` and field `label4`. Combine the two objects into a group named `grp4`.

15. Drag a Rectangle Button onto the card and make the following modifications:

    1. Change the name to `s1`.
    2. Change the display name to `1`.
    3. Set the size to `35 x 35`.
    4. Set the location to `45, 263`.
    5. Change the text size to **18**.

16. Drag a Rectangle Button onto the card and make the following modifications:

    1. Change the name to `s2`.
    2. Change the display name to `2`.
    3. Set the size to `35 x 35`.
    4. Set the location to `95, 263`.
    5. Change the text size to **18**.

17. Drag a Rectangle Button onto the card and make the following modifications:

    1. Change the name to `s3`.
    2. Change the display name to `3`.
    3. Set the size to `35 x 35`.
    4. Set the location to `145, 263`.
    5. Change the text size to **18**.

18. Drag a Rectangle Button onto the card and make the following modifications:

    1. Change the name to `s4`.
    2. Change the display name to `4`.
    3. Set the size to `35 x 35`.
    4. Set the location to `195, 263`.
    5. Change the text size to **18**.

19. Drag a Rectangle Button onto the card and make the following modifications:

    1. Change the name to `Submit`.

    2. Change the display name to `Submit`.

    3. Set the location to `419, 255`.

20. Drag a Label field onto the card with the following specifications:

    1. Change the name to `category`.

    2. Set the foreground color to red.

    3. Set the size to `458 x 31`.

    4. Set the location to `241, 121`.

    5. Change the text size to **18**.

    6. Bold and center the text.

21. Add the following code to buttons **s1**, **s2**, **s3**, and **s4**:

```
on mouseDown
    grab me
end mouseDown
```

    This code will allow the users to move the four buttons.

22. Next, let's add our `preOpenCard` script:

```
on preOpenCard
    global qNbr, qArray

    # Section 1
    put 1 into qNbr
    # Section 2
    put "" into fld "category"
    put "" into fld "label1"
    put "" into fld "label2"
    put "" into fld "label3"
    put "" into fld "label4"
    put "" into fld "progress"
    # Section 3
    put "Driving a car" into qArray["1"]["category"]
    put "Visual Inspection" into qArray["1"]["s1"]
    put "Seat Belt" into qArray["1"]["s2"]
    put "Start Engine" into qArray["1"]["s3"]
    put "Drive" into qArray["1"]["s4"]
    --

    put "Primary Schools" into qArray["2"]["category"]
```

```
      put "Kindergarten" into qArray["2"]["s1"]
      put "Elementary" into qArray["2"]["s2"]
      put "Middle School" into qArray["2"]["s3"]
      put "High School" into qArray["2"]["s4"]
      --
      put "Life Stages" into qArray["3"]["category"]
      put "Birth" into qArray["3"]["s1"]
      put "Youth" into qArray["3"]["s2"]
      put "Adult" into qArray["3"]["s3"]
      put "Elderly" into qArray["3"]["s4"]
   end preOpenCard
```

Section 1 of the code simply sets the qNbr counter to 1. Section 2 clears the five on screen label fields. Section 3 populates the qArray question set.

23. Our next step is to program the nextQuestion feature. Here is that code:

```
on openCard
   nextQuestion
end openCard

command nextQuestion
   global qNbr, qArray

   # Section 1
   put qArray[qNbr]["category"] into fld "category"
   put qArray[qNbr]["s1"] into fld "label1"
   put qArray[qNbr]["s2"] into fld "label2"
   put qArray[qNbr]["s3"] into fld "label3"
   put qArray[qNbr]["s4"] into fld "label4"
   put "Question " & qNbr & " of 3" into fld "Progress"

   # Section 2
   set the loc of btn "s1" to 45,263
   set the loc of btn "s2" to 95,263
   set the loc of btn "s3" to 145,263
   set the loc of btn "s4" to 195,263
end nextQuestion
```

In section 1 of this code, we load the next set of data from the array and populate the label fields. In section 2 of this code, we are resetting the original locations of the buttons **s1**, **s2**, **s3**, and **s4**.

24. Our final step is to program the **Submit** button so that it evaluates the order selected by the user. Here is the code you will need to enter:

```
on mouseUp
    global qNbr, qArray
    local tResult

    # Section 1
    if the loc of btn "s1" is within the rect of grp "grp1" AND \
        the loc of btn "s2" is within the rect of grp "grp2" AND \
        the loc of btn "s3" is within the rect of grp "grp3" AND \
        the loc of btn "s4" is within the rect of grp "grp4" then
        put "correct" into tResult
    else
        put "incorrect" into tResult
    end if

    #Section 2
    switch tResult
        case "correct"
            if qNbr < 3 then
            answer "Very Good." with "Next" titled "Correct"
        else
            answer "Very Good." with "Okay" titled "Correct"
        end if
        break
    case "incorrect"
        if qNbr < 3 then
            answer "That is not correct" with "Next" titled "Wrong
Answer"
        else
            answer "That is not correct" with "Okay" titled "Wrong
Answer"
        end if
        break
    end switch

    # Section 3
    if qNbr < 3 then
        add 1 to qNbr
        nextQuestion
    else
        go to card "Main"
    end if
end mouseUp
```

In section 1 of the code, we are evaluating to see if the sequence buttons (**s1**, **s2**, **s3**, and **s4**) are contained within (on top of) the appropriate groups (**grp1**, **grp2**, **grp3**, and **grp4**). Depending upon the evaluation results, we will either put `correct` or `incorrect` into the local variable `tResult`.

Section 2 of our code, contains a switch statement that displays a feedback pop-up dialog to the user with either **Next** or **Okay**, depending upon which question number the user is on.

Section 3's code routes the user either to the next question or back to the main card once they have answered all three questions.

Objective Complete - Mini Debriefing

We successfully coded our sequencing quiz card. We used a simple interface that requires the users to drag-and-drop four buttons to indicate the proper sequence. Mobile device users use their fingers to interact with mobile apps, so our implementation of drag-and-drop objects is ideally suited for this app.

Your user interface should resemble the following screenshot:

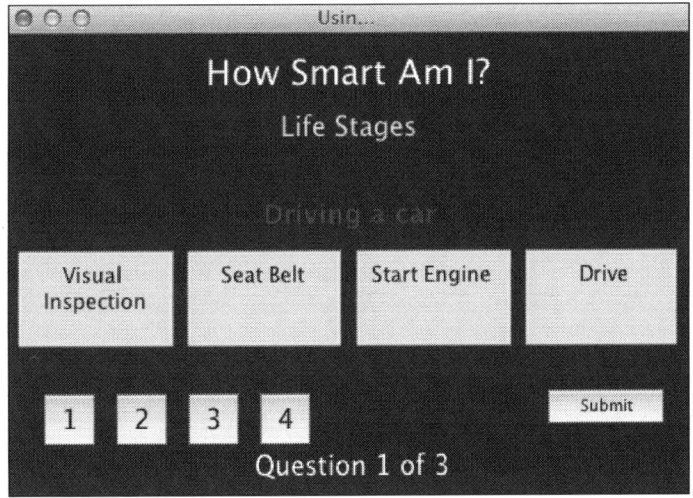

Creating a short-answer question card

For this task, we will create a card to host an interface for a short-answer question. This type of question allows the user to input their answers via the keyboard. Evaluating this type of answer can be especially challenging, since there could be several correct answers and users are prone to make spelling mistakes.

Engage Thrusters

1. Create a new card and name it SA.

2. Copy the **Title** label from the Main card and paste it onto the new SA card. This will ensure the title label field has a consistent format and location.

3. Copy the **Question** label from the TF card and paste it onto the new SA card.

4. Copy the **Progress** label from the TF card and paste it onto the new SA card.

5. Copy the **Submit** button from the Sequencing card and paste it onto the new SA card.

6. Drag a text entry field onto the card and make the following modifications:

    1. Change the name to answer.

    2. Set the size to 362 by 46.

    3. Set the location to 237, 185.

    4. Change the text size to **14**.

7. We are now ready to program our interface. Enter the following code at the card level:

```
on preOpenCard
    global qNbr, qArray

    # Section 1
    put 1 into qNbr
    # Section 2
    put "" into fld "question"
    put "" into fld "answer"
    put "" into fld "progress"
    # Section 3
    put "What farm animal eats shrubs, can be eaten, and are
smaller than cows?" into qArray["1"]["question"]
    put "goat" into qArray["1"]["answer"]
    --
```

```
   put "What is used in pencils for writing?" into qArray["2"]
["question"]
   put "lead" into qArray["2"]["answer"]
   --
   put "What programming language are you learning" into
qArray["3"]["question"]
   put "livecode" into qArray["3"]["answer"]
end preOpenCard
```

In section 1 of this code, we reset the question counter (qNbr) variable to 1.

Section 2 contains the code to clear the question, answer, and progress fields.

Section 3 populates the question/answer array (qArray). As you can see, this is the simplest array we have used. It only contains a question and answer pairing for each row.

8. Our last step for the short answer question interface is to program the **Submit** button. Here is the code for that button:

```
on mouseUp
   global qNbr, qArray
   local tResult

   # Section 1
   if the text of fld "answer" contains qArray[qNbr]["answer"]
then
      put "correct" into tResult
   else
      put "incorrect" into tResult
   end if

   #Section 2
   switch tResult
     case "correct"
       if qNbr < 3 then
         answer "Very Good." with "Next" titled "Correct"
       else
         answer "Very Good." with "Okay" titled "Correct"
       end if
       break
     case "incorrect"
       if qNbr < 3 then
         answer "The correct answer is: " & \
             qArray[qNbr]["answer"] & "." \
             with "Next" titled "Wrong Answer"
       else
```

```
            answer "The correct answer is: " & \
                qArray[qNbr]["answer"] & "." \
                with "Okay" titled "Wrong Answer"
        end if
        break
    end switch

    # Section 3
    if qNbr < 3 then
        add 1 to qNbr
        nextQuestion
    else
        go to card "Main"
    end if
end mouseUp
```

Our **Submit** button script is divided into three sections. The first section (section 1) checks to see if the answer contained in the array (qArray) is part of the answer the user entered. This is a simple string comparison and is not case sensitive.

Section 2 of this button's code contains a switch statement based on the local variable tResult. Here, we provide the user with the actual answer if they do not get it right on their own.

The final section (section 3) navigates to the next question or to the main card, depending upon which question set the user is on.

Objective Complete - Mini Debriefing

We have successfully coded our short answer quiz card. Our approach was to use a simple question and data input design with a **Submit** button.

Your user interface should resemble the following screenshot:

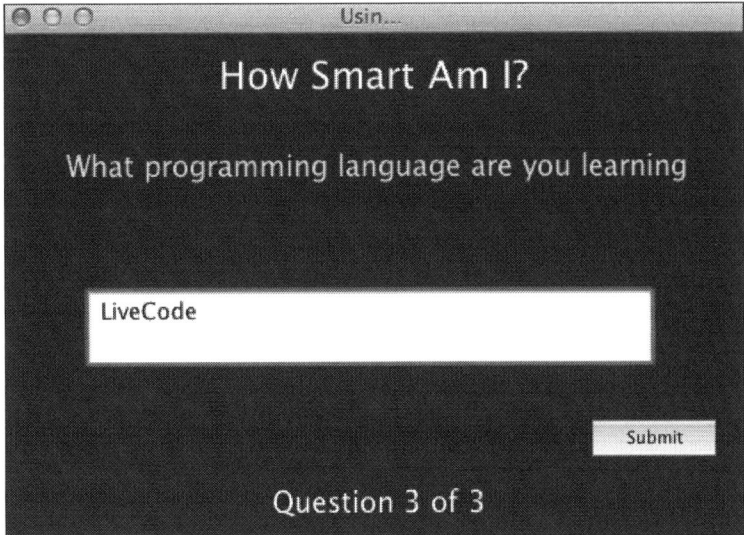

Creating a picture question card

Using pictures as part of a quiz, poll, or other interface can be fun for the user. It might also be more appropriate than simply using text. Let's create a card that uses pictures as part of a quiz.

Engage Thrusters

1. Create a new card and name it `Pictures`.

2. Copy the **Title** label from the Main card and paste it onto the new Pictures card. This will ensure the title label field has a consistent format and location.

3. Copy the **Question** label from the TF card and paste it onto the new Pictures card.

4. Copy the **Progress** label from the TF card and paste it onto the new Pictures card.

5. Drag a Rectangle Button onto the card and make the following customizations:

   1. Change the name to `picture1`.

   2. Set the size to `120 x 120`.

   3. Set the location to `128, 196`.

6.   Drag a second Rectangle Button onto the card and make the following customizations:

    1.   Change the name to `picture2`.

    2.   Set the size to `120 x 120`.

    3.   Set the location to `336, 196`.

Upload the following listed files into your mobile application's **Image Library**. This LiveCode function is available by selecting the **Development** pull-down menu, then selecting **Image Library**. Near the bottom of the **Image Library** dialog is an **Import File** button. Once your files are uploaded, take note of the ID numbers assigned by LiveCode:

- `q1a1.png`
- `q1a2.png`
- `q2a1.png`
- `q2a2.png`
- `q3a1.png`
- `q3a2.png`

7.   With our interface fully constructed, we are now ready to add LiveCode script to the card. Here is the code you will enter at the card level:

```
on preOpenCard
    global qNbr, qArray

    # Section 1
    put 1 into qNbr
    set the icon of btn "picture1" to empty
    set the icon of btn "picture2" to empty

    # Section 2
    put "" into fld "question"
    put "" into fld "progress"

    # Section 3
    put "Which puppy is real?" into qArray["1"]["question"]
    put "2175" into qArray["1"]["pic1"]
    put "2176" into qArray["1"]["pic2"]
    put "q1a1" into qArray["1"]["answer"]
    --
    put "Which puppy looks bigger?" into qArray["2"]["question"]
    put "2177" into qArray["2"]["pic1"]
```

```
      put "2178" into qArray["2"]["pic2"]
      put "q2a2" into qArray["2"]["answer"]
      --
      put "Which scene is likely to make her owner more upset?" into
   qArray["3"]["question"]
      put "2179" into qArray["3"]["pic1"]
      put "2180" into qArray["3"]["pic2"]
      put "q3a1" into qArray["3"]["answer"]
end preOpenCard
```

In section 1 of this code, we set the qNbr to 1. This is our question counter. We also ensure that there is no image visible in the two buttons. We do this by setting the icon of the buttons to empty.

In section 2, we empty the contents of the two onscreen fields (**Question** and **Progress**).

In the third section, we populate the question set array (qArray). Each question has an answer that corresponds with the filename of the images you added to your stack in the previous step. The ID numbers of the six images you uploaded are also added to the array, so you will need to refer to your notes from step 7.

8. Our next step is to program the **picture1** and **picture2** buttons. Here is the code for the picture1 button:

```
on mouseUp
   global qNbr, qArray

   # Section 1
   if qArray[qNbr]["answer"] contains "a1" then
      if qNbr < 3 then
         answer "Very Good." with "Next" titled "Correct"
      else
         answer "Very Good." with "Okay" titled "Correct"
      end if
   else
      if qNbr < 3 then
         answer "That is not correct." with "Next" titled "Wrong
Answer"
      else
         answer "That is not correct."  with "Okay" titled "Wrong
Answer"
      end if
   end if

   # Section 2
   if qNbr < 3 then
```

```
        add 1 to qNbr
        nextQuestion
    else
      go to card "Main"
    end if

end mouseUp
```

In section 1 of our code, we check to see if the answer from the array contains a1, which indicates that the picture on the left is the correct answer. Based on the answer evaluation, one of two text feedbacks is provided to the user. The name of the button on the feedback dialog is either **Next** or **Okay**, depending upon which question set the user is currently on. The second section of this code routes the user to either the main card (if they finished all three questions) or to the next question.

9. Copy the code you entered in the picture1 button and paste it onto the picture2 button. Only one piece of code needs to change. On the first line of the section 1 code, change the string from a1 to a2. That line of code should be as follows:

```
if qArray[qNbr]["answer"] contains "a2" then
```

Objective Complete - Mini Debriefing

In just 9 easy steps, we created a picture-based question type that uses images we uploaded to our stack's image library and a question set array. Your final interface should look similar to the following screenshot:

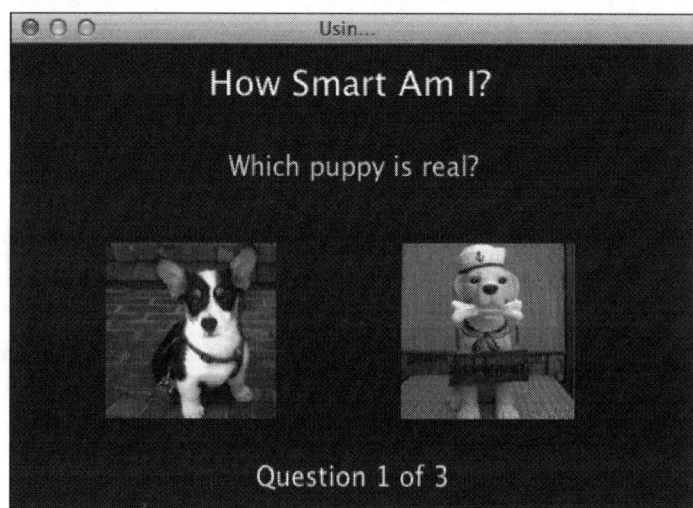

Adding navigational scripting

In this task, we will add scripts to the interface buttons on the Main card.

Engage Thrusters

1. Navigate to the Main card.

2. Add the following script to the **true-false** button:

    ```
    on mouseUp
        set the disabled of me to true
        go to card "TF"
    end mouseUp
    ```

3. Add the following script to the **m-choice** button:

    ```
    on mouseUp
        set the disabled of me to true
        go to card "MC"
    end mouseUp
    ```

4. Add the following script to the **sequence** button:

    ```
    on mouseUp
        set the disabled of me to true
        go to card "Sequencing"
    end mouseUp
    ```

5. Add the following script to the **short-answer** button:

    ```
    on mouseUp
        set the disabled of me to true
        go to card "SA"
    end mouseUp
    ```

6. Add the following script to the **pictures** button:

    ```
    on mouseUp
        set the disabled of me to true
        go to card "Pictures"
    end mouseUp
    ```

7. The last step in this task is to program the **Reset** button. Here is the code for that button:

```
on mouseUp
    global theScore, totalQuestions, totalCorrect

    # Section 1
    set the disabled of btn "true-false" to false
    set the disabled of btn "m-choice" to false
    set the disabled of btn "sequence" to false
    set the disabled of btn "short-answer" to false
    set the disabled of btn "pictures" to false

    # Section 2
    set the backgroundColor of grc "progress1" to empty
    set the backgroundColor of grc "progress2" to empty
    set the backgroundColor of grc "progress3" to empty
    set the backgroundColor of grc "progress4" to empty
    set the backgroundColor of grc "progress5" to empty

    # Section3
    put 0 into theScore
    put 0 into totalQuestions
    put 0 into totalCorrect
    put theScore & "%" into fld "Score"
end mouseUp
```

There are three sections to this code. In section 1, we are enabling each of the buttons. In the second section, we are clearing out the background color of each of the five progress circles in the bottom-center of the screen. In the final section, section 3, we reset the score and the score display.

Objective Complete - Mini Debriefing

That is all there was to this task, seven easy steps. There are no visible changes to the mobile application's interface.

Adding scoring

For our project's final task, we will add scoring to our mobile application. This will require us to edit all six cards.

Engage Thrusters

1. We want to ensure that the scoring is set to zero each time the application is run. So, we'll add the following code at the stack level:

```
on openStack
    global theScore, totalQuestions, totalCorrect

    put 0 into theScore
    put 0 into totalQuestions
    put 0 into totalCorrect
end openStack
```

2. Each time the user is taken back to the Main card, we want to recalculate the score. Here is the code to accomplish that. Put this code at the card level on the Main card:

```
on openCard
    global theScore, totalQuestions, totalCorrect

    put totalCorrect / totalQuestions into theScore
    put theScore * 100 into theScore
    put format("%2d", theScore) & "%" into fld "Score"
end openCard
```

Next, we want to track scores for each question type. We will make similar scripting edits and additions to each of the question type cards. To ensure we do not make any errors, we will have one step for each question type.

3. Perform the following operations on the TF card:

   1. Add `global tQ, tC` to the `on preOpenCard` script. The `tQ` variable will hold the total number of questions for this question type. The `tC` variable will hold the total number of correctly answered questions for this question type.

   2. Add the following lines of code to section 1 of the `on preOpenCard` script:

```
put 0 into tQ
put 0 into tC
```

3. Add global tQ, tC to the on mouseUp script of the **True** button.

4. Edit section 1 of the on mouseUp script of the **True** button.

```
# Section 1
   add 1 to tQ
   if qArray[qNbr]["answer"] is "T" then
      if qNbr < 3 then
         answer "Very Good." with "Next" titled "Correct"
      else
         answer "Very Good." with "Okay" titled "Correct"
      end if
      add 1 to tC
   else
      if qNbr < 3 then
         answer qArray[qNbr]["feedback"] with "Next" titled
"Wrong Answer"
      else
         answer qArray[qNbr]["feedback"] with "Okay" titled
"Wrong Answer"
      end if
   end if
```

In section 1, we merely added two lines, one each to increment the tQ and tC variables.

5. Add global tQ, tC to the on mouseUp script of the **False** button.

6. Edit section 1 of the on mouseUp script of the **False** button.

```
# Section 1
   add 1 to tQ
   if qArray[qNbr]["answer"] is "F" then
      if qNbr < 3 then
         answer "Very Good." with "Next" titled "Correct"
      else
         answer "Very Good." with "Okay" titled "Correct"
      end if
      add 1 to tC
   else
      if qNbr < 3 then
         answer qArray[qNbr]["feedback"] with "Next" titled
"Wrong Answer"
      else
         answer qArray[qNbr]["feedback"] with "Okay" titled
"Wrong Answer"
      end if
   end if
```

In section 1, we merely added two lines, one each to increment the `tQ` and `tC` variables.

7. Next, we will create a score calculation by adding the following code at the stack level:

```
command exitOperations theProgressBar
    global theScore, totalQuestions, totalCorrect
    global tQ, tC

    # Section 1
    put totalQuestions + tQ into totalQuestions
    put totalCorrect + tC into totalCorrect

    # Section 2
    if (tC / tQ) > .69 then
        set the backgroundColor of grc theProgressBar on card
"Main" to green
    else
        set the backgroundColor of grc theProgressBar on card
"Main" to red
    end if

    # Section 3
    go to card "Main"
end exitOperations
```

In section 1 of this code, we add the questions and correct answers to the global variables. In section 2, we first calculate how the player scored with the questions presented on this card. If the player scored 70 percent or better, the corresponding progress indicator on the Main card will be filled in (using the foreground color) with green; otherwise, the fill color will be red.

Our next step is to make calls to the `exitOperations` code. We will do this by replacing the `go to card "Main"` code in both the **True** and **False** button scripts with `exitOperations("Progress1")`.

4. Perform the following operations on the MC card:

   1. Add `global tQ, tC` to the on `preOpenCard` script.

   2. Add the following lines of code to section 1 of the `on preOpenCard` script:
      ```
      put 0 into tQ
      put 0 into tC
      ```

   3. Add `global tQ, tC` to the `evaluateMC` script.

4. Edit section 1 of the on `mouseUp` script of the `evaluateMC` script.

```
# Section 1
add 1 to tQ
if qArray[qNbr]["correct"] is theGuess then
    if qNbr < 3 then
        answer "Very Good." with "Next" titled "Correct"
    else
        answer "Very Good." with "Okay" titled "Correct"
    end if
    add 1 to tC
else
    if qNbr < 3 then
        answer "That is not correct" with "Next" titled
"Wrong Answer"
    else
        answer "That is not correct" with "Okay" titled
"Wrong Answer"
    end if
end if
```

Our next step is to make calls to the `exitOperations` code. We will do this by replacing the `go to card "Main"` code in section 2 of the `evaluateMC` script with `exitOperations("Progress2")`.

5. Perform the following operations on the Sequencing card:

   1. Add global `tQ, tC` to the on `preOpenCard` script.

   2. Add the following lines of code to section 1 of the on `preOpenCard` script:

   ```
   put 0 into tQ
   put 0 into tC
   ```

   3. Add global `tQ, tC` to the on `mouseUp` script of the **Submit** button.

   4. Edit section 1 of the on `mouseUp` script of the **Submit** button.

   ```
   # Section 1
   add 1 to tQ
   if the loc of btn "s1" is within the rect of grp "grp1"
   AND \
           the loc of btn "s2" is within the rect of grp
   "grp2" AND \
           the loc of btn "s3" is within the rect of grp
   "grp3" AND \
           the loc of btn "s4" is within the rect of grp
   "grp4" then
   ```

```
            put "correct" into tResult
            add 1 to tC
        else
            put "incorrect" into tResult
        end if
```

Our next step is to make calls to the exitOperations code. We will do this by replacing the go to card "Main" code in section 3 of the on mouseUp script of the Submit button with exitOperations("Progress3").

6. Perform the following operations on the SA card:

   1. Add global tQ, tC to the on preOpenCard script.

   2. Add the following lines of code to section 1 of the on preOpenCard script:

      ```
      put 0 into tQ
      put 0 into tC
      ```

   3. Add global tQ, tC to the on mouseUp script of the **Submit** button.

   4. Edit section 1 of the on mouseUp script of the **Submit** button.

      ```
      # Section 1
          add 1 to tQ
          if the text of fld "answer" contains qArray[qNbr]
      ["answer"] then
              put "correct" into tResult
              add 1 to tC
          else
              put "incorrect" into tResult
          end if
      ```

   Our next step is to make calls to the exitOperations code. We will do this by replacing the go to card "Main" code in section 3 of the on mouseUp script of the **Submit** button with exitOperations("Progress4").

7. Perform the following operations on the Pictures card:

   1. Add global tQ; tC to the on preOpenCard script.

   2. Add the following lines of code to section 1 of the on preOpenCard script:

      ```
      put 0 into tQ
      put 0 into tC
      ```

   3. Add global tQ, tC to the on mouseUp script of the picture1 button.

4. Edit section 1 of the on mouseUp script of the picture1 button.

```
# Section 1
   add 1 to tQ
   if qArray[qNbr]["answer"] contains "a1" then
      add 1 to tC
      if qNbr < 3 then
         answer "Very Good." with "Next" titled "Correct"
      else
         answer "Very Good." with "Okay" titled "Correct"
      end if
   else
      if qNbr < 3 then
         answer "That is not correct." with "Next" titled
"Wrong Answer"
      else
         answer "That is not correct."  with "Okay" titled
"Wrong Answer"
      end if
   end if
```

5. Replace the go to card "Main" code in section 2 of the on mouseUp script of the picture1 button with exitOperations("Progress5").

6. Add global tQ, tC to the on mouseUp script of the picture2 button.

7. Edit section 1 of the on mouseUp script of the picture2 button.

```
# Section 1
add 1 to tQ
if qArray[qNbr]["answer"] contains "a2" then
   add 1 to tC
   if qNbr < 3 then
      answer "Very Good." with "Next" titled "Correct"
   else
      answer "Very Good." with "Okay" titled "Correct"
   end if
else
   if qNbr < 3 then
      answer "That is not correct." with "Next" titled
"Wrong Answer"
   else
      answer "That is not correct."  with "Okay" titled
"Wrong Answer"
   end if
end if
```

8. Replace the `go to card "Main"` code in section 2 of the `on mouseUp` script of the picture1 button with `exitOperations("Progress5")`.

Objective Complete - Mini Debriefing

Our scoring system is complete. Now, each section is scored separately (indicated by color) and we have a comprehensive scoring system.

Mission Accomplished

In this project, we developed a somewhat complex **How Smart Am I?** mobile application that featured five specific question types: true/false, multiple choice, sequencing, short answer, and picture-based.

The following screenshot shows how we do the following:

▶ Disable buttons once we have completed the corresponding section

▶ How the color codes along the bottom indicate progress

▶ How the overall score is displayed in the bottom-right corner of the screen

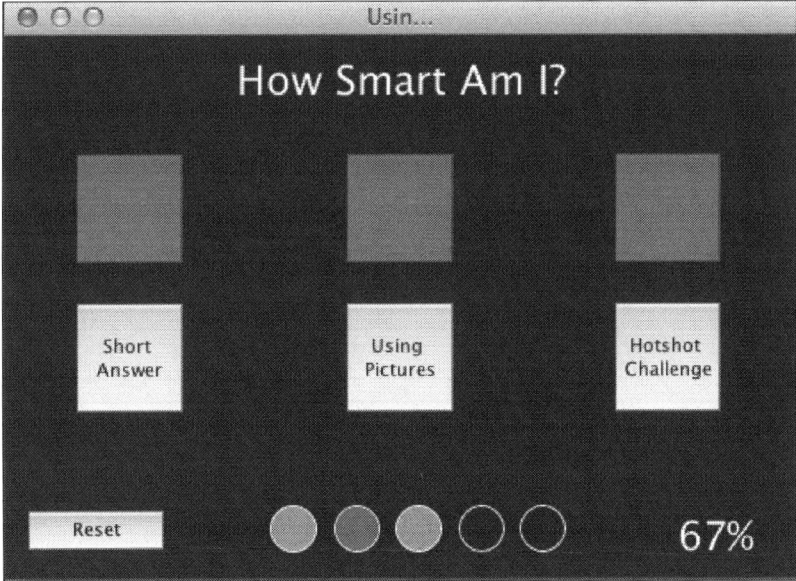

A Hotshot Challenge

For this Hotshot challenge, perform the following actions:

1. Create a Challenge card and link the **Hotshot Challenge** button on the Main card to it.

2. On your new card, program a question type of your choice.

3. Ensure you update the scoring system to incorporate your new question type.

4. Finally, add a progress indicator at the bottom of the Main card and update the appropriate functionality.

Good luck and have fun!

Project 6

Creating the Find the Bananas Game

This project consists of designing and developing a **Find the Bananas** game that is based on the classic three-shell game of chance, which is often referred to as **shell game** or **Thimblerig**. Historically, this game is played with three shells and a pea. It is viewed by most as a game of chance or a gambling game. In practice, the game is often employed as a confidence trick to fraudulently take people's money. There will be no fraud in our game, just honest fun.

Mission Briefing

Our version of the shell game will consist of three coconut halves instead of shells and a bunch of bananas instead of a pea. Where else would you expect to find bananas but under a coconut? The object of the game will be for the user to correctly guess which coconut half is hiding the bananas. The game will have an endless number of rounds, each one scoring higher than the last.

The interface will consist of a title, three game spot buttons, an information icon, a label for the current round number, a label for points, and three banana icons which indicate how many lives the player has remaining.

The following diagram is an interface mockup of what the mobile app that we will build in this project will look like:

Why Is It Awesome?

By working through this project, you will gain an understanding, and hands-on experience, of how to effectively use images in a mobile application using LiveCode. You'll also gain experience with developing a complete game with just one LiveCode card.

This type of simplicity of design has two major purposes. First, it is likely to result in smaller application file sizes, which should result in the application running faster. Secondly, simple interfaces are good from a usability perspective.

 Usability refers to the ability for a mobile application to be used for its intended purpose effectively by the user. When a mobile application is intuitively designed, it means that users can immediately start using the application without having to refer to help or instructions.

Your Hotshot Objectives

To complete the Find the Bananas project, we'll accomplish the following tasks:

- ▸ Creating the main stack
- ▸ Creating the user interface
- ▸ Importing and optimizing the images
- ▸ Programming the game
- ▸ Adding a scoring schema

Creating the main stack

We'll start by creating the main stack for our Find the Bananas game. For this application, we will only have one stack and a single card.

Engage Thrusters

1. Let's begin by creating a new main stack named `Bananas`. Using the properties inspector, make the following customizations to the main stack:

    1. Change the size of the stack to `480 x 320` pixels. This will give us a landscape orientation.

    2. Set the name of the stack to `Bananas`.

    3. Set the title of the stack to `Find the Bananas`.

    4. Set the background color to white.

2. Rename the default card to `Main`.

Objective Complete - Mini Debriefing

Since we will only have one stack and one card for this application, we can quickly accomplish this task. In the next task, we will create the user interface.

Creating the user interface

For this task, we will create the user interface. The game's interface will consist of four labels, three buttons, and three images. The labels are:

- Game title
- Information icon
- Points display
- Round (level) display

The three buttons will represent the three game spots.

The three images will consist of three small banana bunches.

As you work through the steps in this task, refer back to the interface mockup so you have a clear picture of what we are doing.

Engage Thrusters

1. Drag a Label field onto the **Main** card and make the following customizations using the properties inspector:

    1. Set the width to 470 and the height to 36.

    2. Set the location to 239, 22.

    3. Set the name of the field to Title.

    4. Set the text size to **24**.

    5. Center-align the text.

    6. Change the contents to Find the Bananas.

    7. Set the foreground color to black.

2. Drag a Label field onto the **Main** card and make the following customizations using the properties inspector:

    1. Set the width to 42 and the height to 58.

    2. Set the location to 25, 289.

    3. Set the name of the field to Information.

    4. Set the text size to **36**.

    5. Center-align the text.

    6. Italicize the text.

    7. Change the contents to i.

    8. Set the foreground color to black.

3. Drag a Label field onto the card **Main** and make the following customizations using the properties inspector:

    1. Set the width to 188 and the height to 29.

    2. Set the location to 200, 290.

    3. Set the name of the field to Level.

    4. Set the text size to **18**.

    5. Left-align the text.

    6. Change the contents to Current Run: 0.

    7. Set the foreground color to black.

4. Drag a Label field onto the **Main** card and make the following customizations using the properties inspector:

    1. Set the width to `188` and the height to `29`.

    2. Set the location to `200, 266`.

    3. Set the name of the field to `Score`.

    4. Set the text size to **18**.

    5. Left-align the text.

    6. Change the contents to `Score: 0`.

    7. Set the foreground color to black.

5. Drag a Rectangle Button onto the card and make the following customizations using the properties inspector:

    1. Set the width to `120` and the height to `120`.

    2. Set the location to `90, 136`.

    3. Set the name of the button to `spot1`.

    4. Set **Show name** to false.

    5. Set **Opaque** to false.

    6. Set **Three D** to false.

    7. Set **Border** to false.

    8. Set the **Hilite border** to false by ensuring the **Hilite border** checkbox is unchecked.

6. Drag a Rectangle Button onto the card and make the following customizations using the properties inspector:

    1. Set the width to `120` and the height to `120`.

    2. Set the location to `240, 136`.

    3. Set the name of the field to `spot2`.

    4. Set the **Show name** to false.

    5. Set the **Opaque** to false.

    6. Set the **Three D** to false.

    7. Set the **Border** to false.

    8. Set the **Hilite border** to false.

7. Drag a Rectangle Button onto the card and make the following customizations using the properties inspector:

   1. Set the width to 120 and the height to 120.

   2. Set the location to 390, 136.

   3. Set the name of the field to spot3.

   4. Set the **Show name** to false.

   5. Set the **Opaque** to false.

   6. Set the **Three D** to false.

   7. Set the **Border** to false.

   8. Set the **Hilite border** to false.

8. Drag an Image Area object onto the card and make the following customizations using the properties inspector:

   1. Set the width to 40 and the height to 40.

   2. Set the location to 362, 288.

   3. Set the name of the field to loss1.

9. Drag an Image Area object onto the card and make the following customizations using the properties inspector:

   1. Set the width to 40 and the height to 40.

   2. Set the location to 406, 288.

   3. Set the name of the field to loss2.

10. Drag an Image Area object onto the card and make the following customizations using the properties inspector:

    1. Set the width to 40 and the height to 40.

    2. Set the location to 450, 288.

    3. Set the name of the field to loss3.

Objective Complete - Mini Debriefing

After completing the 10 steps in this section, your interface should look similar to the following image. There are only three types of objects for this interface: labels, buttons, and images. Our interface consists of four labels, three buttons, and three images.

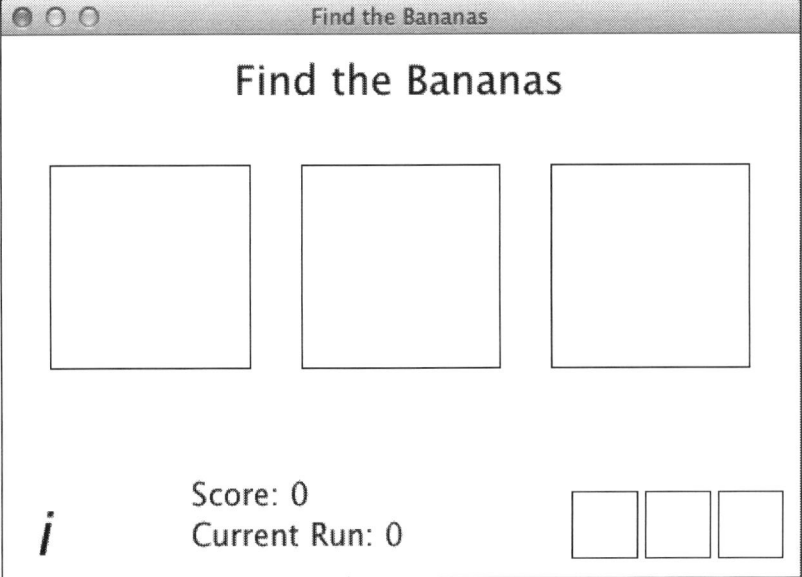

Classified Intel

We are using a single button for each game spot, each capable of showing any of the three game images. Depending on the game state, each of those game spots (spot1, spot2, and spot3) could display a coconut half with the open end down, a coconut half with the open end exposed, or the bunch of bananas. This keeps our total number of objects low.

Importing and optimizing the images

In this task, we will import our images files and ensure they are optimized for our mobile application. In the last task, we created three buttons sized 120 x 120 and three image objects sized 40 x 40.

The three buttons will either display a coconut half with the open end facing down, a coconut half with the open end facing up, or the bunch of bananas. Before the user guesses which coconut half the bananas are hiding under, all three game spots (spot1, spot2, and spot3) will show the coconut half with the open end facing down. When the user taps on one of the buttons, it will either display the coconut half with the open end facing up or the bunch of bananas.

The three images will show a bunch of bananas. Each time the player fails to find the bananas, one of the banana bunches will be hidden using the set the visible of img <image name> to false syntax.

Engage Thrusters

1. Using LiveCode's drop-down menu system, navigate to **File | Import As Control | Image File**. Select the `bananas.png`, `coconut-down.png`, `coconut-up.png`, and `loss.png files`, in that order.

2. For each of the images, set the location to `544, 166`. This puts the images out of the viewable area of the mobile device.

3. For each of the images, set **Lock size and position** to true. This setting is available on the **Size and Position** area of the properties inspector.

4. Verify that the object IDs for the four imported images match the table below. If the image IDs do not match, edit them using the properties inspector so that they match precisely. If you have any problems assigning these Object IDs, simply keep track of the IDs you use and make any necessary changes in subsequent steps so that your code is referencing the proper IDs.

Object ID	Image File
1021	bananas.png
1022	coconut_down.png
1023	coconut_up.png
1024	loss.png

5. Using the message box, issue the command `set the icon of btn "spot1" to 1022`. This will display the coconut-down image (ID 1022) in the first game spot.

6. Using the message box, issue the command `set the icon of btn "spot2" to 1021`. This will display the bananas image (ID 1021) in the first game spot.

7. Using the message box, issue the command `set the icon of btn "spot3" to 1023`. This will display the coconut-up image (ID 1023) in the first game spot.

8. Make the following modifications to the `loss1` image:

    1. Set the source to `loss.png`.

    2. Set the **Show Border** to false.

9. Make the following modifications to the `loss2` image:

    1. Set the source to `loss.png`.

    2. Set the **Show Border** to false.

10. Make the following modifications to the `loss3` image:

    1. Set the source to `loss.png`.

    2. Set the **Show Border** to false.

Objective Complete - Mini debriefing

If you examine the images files that you imported, each of them was the exact same size as the object that is set to display them. By ensuring the images were optimized (set at the correct size) before importing them, we do not need LiveCode to resize them. This also ensures that the images are displayed how we want them, without losing any aspect or gaining any pixilation.

After you complete the preceding 10 steps, your interface should look like the following screenshot:

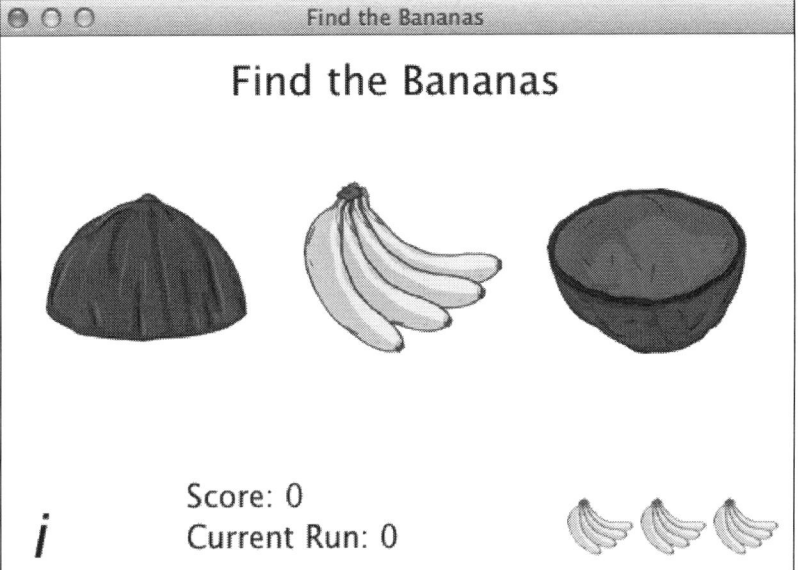

Classified Intel

Although each of the images we imported can be used in three different spots each, we only have one copy of each image. Instead of putting three copies of each image in each spot they could possibly be displayed in the game, we merely reference the image's ID to display it. This keeps the mobile application's size down and helps the application be more efficient.

Programming the game

We are now ready to program the game. There are only four programmable objects for this application: the three buttons (spot1, spot2, and spot3) and the information label. Most of our code will be placed at the card level.

Engage Thrusters

1. Add the following code to the **Main** card:

```
command setupGame
    global gScore, gLevel, gLoss, gAnswer

    # Section 1
    put 0 into gScore
    put 0 into gLevel
    put 0 into gLoss
    put 0 into gAnswer
    # Section 2
    set the icon of btn "spot1" to 1022
    set the icon of btn "spot2" to 1022
    set the icon of btn "spot3" to 1022
    # Section 3
    set the text of fld "Score" to "Score: 0"
    set the text of fld "Level" to "Current Run: 0"
    # Section 4
    set the vis of img "loss1" to true
    set the vis of img "loss2" to true
    set the vis of img "loss3" to true
end setupGame
```

In section 1 of the preceding code, we are resetting the values of four global variables (gScore, gLevel, gLoss, and gAnswer) by putting 0 (zero) into each variable.

Section 2 contains the necessary code to display the coconut half image with the open end facing down into each of the three spots (buttons spot1, spot2, and spot3).

The next section, section 3, is where we reset the two label fields to display the current score and level information.

In the final section, section 4, we ensure all three loss images (loss1, loss2, and loss3) are visible.

2. Add the following code to the **Main** card:

```
on openCard
    setupGame
end openCard
```

This code simply makes a call to the command setupGame script each time the card is initially opened. We handle the game's setup in its own code set so that we can invoke it if the game is over and the player wishes to replay.

3. Next, we will program a `resetCoconuts` script so that we can easily put an image of the coconut half with the open end face down into each of the three game spots. Enter the following code at the card level:

```
command resetCoconuts
    set the icon of btn "spot1" to 1022
    set the icon of btn "spot2" to 1022
    set the icon of btn "spot3" to 1022
end resetCoconuts
```

This is the same code found in section 2 of the code we entered in step 2. So, let's replace that code in the `setupGame` script with `resetCoconuts`. Your new `setupGame` code should be as the following code (note the only difference is in section 2):

```
command setupGame
    global gScore, gLevel, gLoss, gAnswer

    # Section 1
    put 0 into gScore
    put 0 into gLevel
    put 0 into gLoss
    put 0 into gAnswer
    # Section 2
    resetCoconuts
    # Section 3
    set the text of fld "Score" to "Score: 0"
    set the text of fld "Level" to "Current Run: 0"
    # Section 4
    set the vis of img "loss1" to true
    set the vis of img "loss2" to true
    set the vis of img "loss3" to true
end setupGame
```

4. Our next step is to program a `getAnswer` script so that we can generate a new answer (which spot the bananas are in). Here is the code you will enter at the card level:

```
command getAnswer
    global gAnswer

    set the randomSeed to the seconds
    put random(3) into gAnswer
end getAnswer
```

In our `getAnswer` script, we start by setting the `randomSeed` to `seconds`. This ensures we will have a truly random result each time a new answer is requested. Then, we simply generate a random number from 1 to 3 and put it into the global `gAnswer` variable.

5. Now, we can write a script to process the answer. Here is the code you will enter at the card level:

```
command processAnswer theGuess
    global gScore, gLevel, gLoss, gAnswer


    # User found the bananas
    answer "Good Guessing! Your score has been updated. Continue
playing?" with "Yes" and "No" titled "You found the bananas!"
        if it is "Yes" then
            add 1 to gLevel
            set the text of fld "Level" to "Current Run: " & gLevel
            --
            resetCoconuts
            getAnswer
        else
            quit
        end if
    else
        # User did not find the bananas
        addLoss
    end if

end processAnswer
```

The `processAnswer` takes `theGuess` as a parameter, which will be passed from one of the three game buttons. There are two conditions that can exist: the user guessed the answer correctly or incorrectly. The first section of our code handles the correct case.

When the user correctly finds the bananas, we prompt the user to congratulate them on their correct guess and see if they want to continue or not. If they do not want to continue, we exit the game. Otherwise, we increment the level and update the level display.

The last thing we do for correct guesses, assuming the user wants to continue, is to make calls to the `resetCoconuts` and `getAnswer` commands.

In the event that the user does not find the bananas, we simply make a call to the `addLoss` command's script, which we will write in the next step.

6. If a user fails to find the bananas, the `addLoss` command's script will be invoked. Here is that code (add this to the card level):

```
command addLoss
   global gLoss

   add 1 to gLoss

   switch gLoss
      case "1"
         set the vis of img "loss1" to false
         answer "No bananas there." with "Okay" titled "No Bananas
for You!"
         resetCoconuts
         getAnswer
         break
      case "2"
         set the vis of img "loss2" to false
         answer "No bananas there." with "Okay" titled "No Bananas
for You!"
         resetCoconuts
         getAnswer
         break
      case "3"
         set the vis of img "loss3" to false
         answer "Game Over." with "Quit" and "Try Again" titled
"No Bananas for You!"
         if it is "Quit" then
            quit
         else
            setupGame
            getAnswer
         end if
         break
   end switch
end addLoss
```

This script is only executed if the user fails to find the bananas. The first thing we do is to increment `gLoss`. Next, we use a `switch` statement so we can handle each case differently.

On the user's first incorrect guess, we will make the first bunch of bananas (`loss1`) invisible. Then, we provide the user with feedback and make calls to the `resetCoconuts` and `getAnswer` scripts.

When the user fails to find the bananas for the second time, we make the second bunch of bananas (loss2) invisible. Then, we provide the user with feedback and make calls to the resetCoconuts and getAnswer scripts.

After the user's third incorrect answer, we make the third bunch of bananas (loss3) invisible. Then, we provide the user with feedback and ask if they want to quit or try again. If they want to try again, we make calls to the setupGame and getAnswer scripts.

7. Next, we need to program each of the three buttons (spot1, spot2, and spot3). Here is the code for the spot1 button:

```
on mouseUp
    global gAnswer

    if gAnswer is 1 then
        set the icon of me to 1021
    else
        set the icon of me to 1023
    end if
    processAnswer(1)
end mouseUp
```

With this on mouseUp script, we check to see if the user correctly guessed the answer. If they found the bananas, then they are displayed (ID 1021). Otherwise, the coconut half with the open end up (ID 1023) is displayed. Next, a call to the processAnswer() script is made with the number 1 passed to it. This makes the processAnswer() script aware of which button sent the message.

8. The following code is for the spot2 button:

```
on mouseUp
    global gAnswer

    if gAnswer is 2 then
        set the icon of me to 1021
    else
        set the icon of me to 1023
    end if
    processAnswer(2)
end mouseUp
```

With this on mouseUp script, we check to see if the user correctly guessed the answer. If they found the bananas, then they are displayed (ID 1021). Otherwise, the coconut half with the open end up (ID 1023) is displayed. Next, a call to the processAnswer() script is made with the number 2 passed to it. This makes the processAnswer() script aware of which button sent the message.

9. The following code is for the `spot3` button:

```
on mouseUp
   global gAnswer

   if gAnswer is 3 then
      set the icon of me to 1021
   else
      set the icon of me to 1023
   end if
   processAnswer(3)
end mouseUp
```

With this `on mouseUp` script, we check to see if the user correctly guessed the answer. If they found the bananas, then they are displayed (ID 1021). Otherwise, the coconut half with the open end up (ID 1023) is displayed. Next, a call to the `processAnswer()` script is made with the number 3 passed to it. This makes the `processAnswer()` script aware of which button sent the message.

Objective Complete - Mini Debriefing

That was a lot of code for a simple game. As you have seen, there can be a lot of finite details that go into programming a mobile application, even with a scripting language such as LiveCode.

Once you have completed the preceding nine steps, you will have a fully functioning game. Your interface should be similar to the following screenshot:

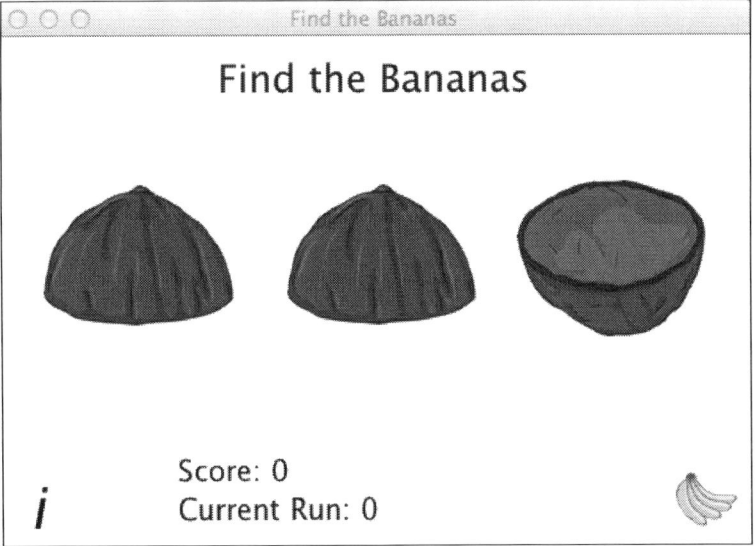

Adding a scoring schema

A game is not really a game without some sort of scoring. To add a scoring schema to our game, we will simply add a few lines of code to our `processAnswer()` script.

Engage Thrusters

Add the following lines of code to the `processAnswer()` script just after the `if theGuess is gAnswer then` line of code:

```
if gLevel is 0 then
   add 50 to gScore
   else
   add (100 * gLevel) to gScore
   end if
   set the text of fld "Score" to "Score: " & gScore
```

When the user correctly finds the bananas, we need to check to see if it is the first time they guessed correctly. If it is, then the `gLevel` will still be 0 and the `add (100 * gLevel) to gScore` statement will result in 0 points. So, if `gLevel` is 0, we will award the user 50 points. After awarding the appropriate points, we update the score display.

The following complete `processAnswer()` script is to help you ensure you added the new six lines of code in the right location:

```
command processAnswer theGuess
   global gScore, gLevel, gLoss, gAnswer

   # User found the bananas
   if theGuess is gAnswer then
   if gLevel is 0 then
   add 50 to gScore
   else
   add (100 * gLevel) to gScore
   end if
   set the text of fld "Score" to "Score: " & gScore
   --
   answer "Good Guessing! Your score has been updated. Continue
      playing?" with "Yes" and "No" titled "You found the bananas!"
   if it is "Yes" then
   add 1 to gLevel
   set the text of fld "Level" to "Current Run: " & gLevel
   --
   resetCoconuts
```

```
    getAnswer
  else
    quit
    end if
    else
    # User did not find the bananas
    addLoss
    end if

  end processAnswer
```

Objective Complete - Mini Debriefing

Our scoring schema has been fully implemented. Users will now see their score as they progress through the game.

Mission Accomplished

In this project, we developed a simple Find the Bananas mobile application using a single stack and a single card. Moreover, we only used a total of four label fields, three buttons, and three image objects. We explored how to use references to images so that they can be displayed more than once simultaneously without sacrificing application size.

The following screenshot shows the completed game with a high score of 5,550 on Level 11:

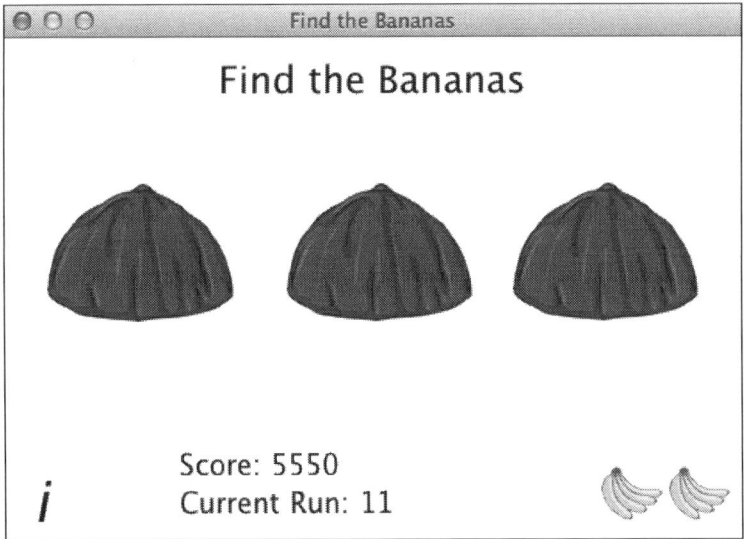

A Hotshot Challenge

Your Hotshot challenge for this project has two components:

▸ Program the information label field that is located in the lower left corner of the application screen. Simply add a dialog box that explains the scoring system.

▸ Implement a high score feature to this game.

That's it; have fun!

Project 7

Creating the Jungle Dance Party Mobile App

In this project, we will create the **Jungle Dance Party** app. We will present the user with three animals and provide them with the opportunity to make each of them have a little fun, one at a time. There is no scoring, no way to win, and no way to lose. Our mobile app will simply provide our users with an opportunity to have a little fun while we show off our animation skills.

Mission Briefing

Our mobile app will consist of one stack and four cards. The first card will be our main interface screen that will present the user with animal selections. The remaining three cards will be for the animal animations, one card per animal.

When one of the animals is selected from the main card, our app will open the appropriate card, and after a forced 2-second delay, we will animate the animal until the user elects to go back to the main card.

Here is a mockup of our app's main interface:

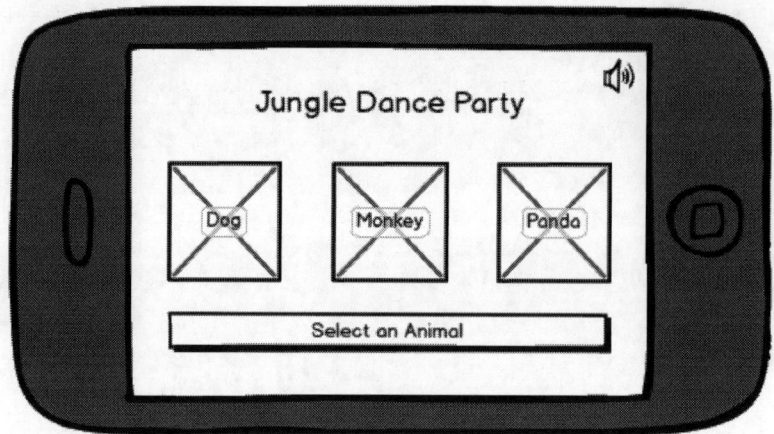

Why Is It Awesome?

As you work through this project, you will gain experience in creating a basic animation of objects. We will design our app from start to finish to include a main interface and three additional cards to hold the individual animal animations.

We will employ a simple sequence of image swapping to animate our three animals. This technique is common in most games and LiveCode makes the development process easy.

Your Hotshot Objectives

To complete the **Jungle Dance Party** project, we'll accomplish the following tasks:

- ▶ Creating the main stack
- ▶ Creating the user interface
- ▶ Creating the Dog card
- ▶ Creating the Monkey card
- ▶ Creating the Panda card
- ▶ Programming the application
- ▶ Adding optional sound

Creating the main stack

Our first task is to create the main stack for our **Jungle Animal Party** mobile app. For this application, we will only have one stack and four cards. First, we will create the main stack.

Engage Thrusters

1. Let's begin by creating a new main stack named `Jungle`. Using the properties inspector, make the following customizations to the main stack:

    1. Change the size of the stack to `480 x 320` pixels. This will give us a landscape orientation.

    2. Set the name of the stack to `Jungle`.

    3. Set the title of the stack to `Jungle Dance Party`.

    4. Set the background color to white.

2. Rename the default card to `Main`.

Objective Complete - Mini Debriefing

When we created the main stack, LiveCode created a default card for us. In our next task, we will configure the default card to house our main user interface.

Creating the user interface

For this task, we will create the user interface. The game's interface will consist of a title label, a sound icon, three image objects (one for each animal), and a footer label.

As you work through the steps in this task, refer back to the interface mockup so that you have a clear picture of what we are doing.

Engage Thrusters

1. Drag a Label field onto the Main card and make the following customizations using the properties inspector:

    1. Set the width to 470 and the height to 36.

    2. Set the location to 239, 39.

    3. Set the name of the field to Title.

    4. Set the text size to **24**.

    5. Center the text.

    6. Change the contents to Jungle Dance Party.

    7. Set the text (foreground color) to black.

2. Drag a Label field onto the Main card and make the following customizations using the properties inspector:

    1. Set the width to 188 and the height to 29.

    2. Set the location to 239, 266.

    3. Set the name of the field to Footer.

    4. Set the text size to **18**.

    5. Center the text.

    6. Change the contents to Select an Animal.

    7. Set the foreground color to black.

3. Drag a Rectangle Button onto the card and make the following customizations using the properties inspector:

    1. Set the width to 30 and the height to 30.

    2. Set the location to 459, 21.

    3. Set the name of the field to sound.

    4. Using the **Icons & Border** section of the properties inspector, click on the wand icon to the right of the **Icon** label and field. Next, in the **Image library:** drop-down list, select **MetaCard Compatible Icons**. Scroll until you find the large sound icon. Select that icon. You will see that this resulted in the icon of the button being set to image ID 394.

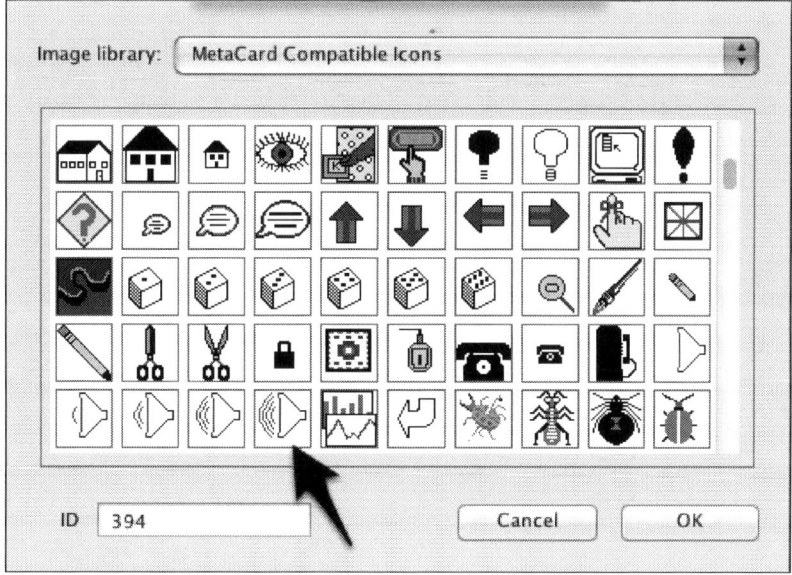

5. Set **Show name** to false.

6. Set **Opaque** to false.

7. Set **Three D** to false.

8. Set **Border** to false.

9. Set **Hilite Border** to false.

4. Drag a Rectangle Button onto the card and make the following customizations using the properties inspector:

    1. Set the width to `120` and the height to `120`.

    2. Set the location to `90, 136`.

    3. Set the name of the button to `dog`.

    4. Import the `dog_120x120.png` image as an object. Set the location of the image to `692, 188`. Lock the location. Then, set the icon of the **dog** button to the image.

> When we set the location of objects outside the visible area of a card, we are essentially keeping it handy (on the card) and ensuring that the object is not visible. This gives us great control over what the user sees on the screen.

5. Set **Show name** to false.

6. Set **Opaque** to false.

7. Set **Three D** to false.

8. Set **Border** to false.

9. Set **Hilite Border** to false.

5. Drag a Rectangle Button onto the card and make the following customizations using the properties inspector:

    1. Set the width to 120 and the height to 120.

    2. Set the location to 240, 136.

    3. Set the name of the field to monkey.

    4. Import the monkey_120x120.png image as an object. Set the location of the image to 692, 188. Lock the location. Then, set the icon of the **monkey** button to the image.

    5. Set **Show name** to false.

    6. Set **Opaque** to false.

    7. Set **Three D** to false.

    8. Set **Border** to false.

    9. Set **Hilite Border** to false.

6. Drag a Rectangle Button onto the card and make the following customizations using the properties inspector:

    1. Set the width to 120 and the height to 120.

    2. Set the location to 390, 136.

    3. Set the name of the field to panda.

    4. Import the panda_120x120.png image as an object. Set the location of the image to 692, 188. Lock the location. Then, set the icon of the **panda** button to the image.

    5. Set **Show name** to false.

    6. Set **Opaque** to false.

    7. Set **Three D** to false.

    8. Set **Border** to false.

    9. Set **Hilite Border** to false.

Objective Complete - Mini Debriefing

After completing the six steps in this task, your interface should look similar to the following screenshot. There are only three types of objects for this interface: labels, buttons, and images. Our interface consists of two labels, four buttons, and three images. Note that, the images are used as button icons. We placed and locked the original images off of the visible screen.

Classified Intel

We uploaded three images, one for each animal. Because our original images are of the same size as our buttons (120 x 120), our interface is considered to be optimized. It is worth the time to format the images (and other objects) before importing them into LiveCode as objects.

Creating the Dog card

With our interface complete, we are ready to create a card for each animal. We'll start with the dog. Our card will contain a series of images that we will display in sequence and a button for the user to navigate back to the main card.

The following image shows the 10 individual frames of the dog playing with his ball:

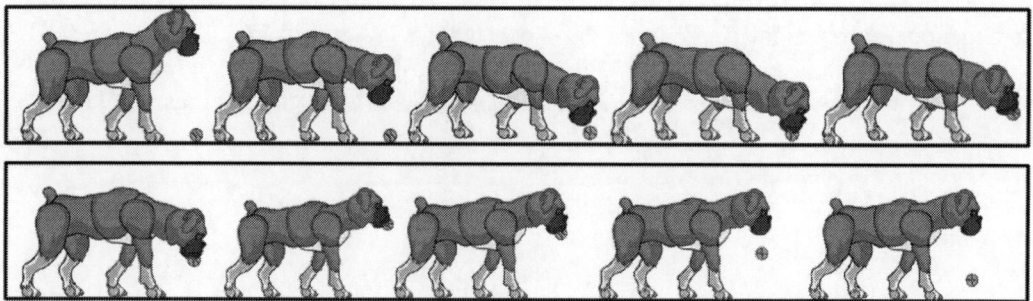

Engage Thrusters

1. Create a new card and name it Dog.

2. Drag a Rectangle Button onto the card and make the following modifications to the default button settings:

    1. Set the width to 82 and the height to 23.

    2. Set the location to 240, 301.

    3. Set the name of the button to Enough.

3. Import the dog1.png, dog2.png, dog3.png, dog4.png, dog5.png, dog6.png, dog7.png, dog8.png, dog9.png, and dog10.png files.

4. Place the 10 image files in the center of the screen.

5. With all 10 image files selected, align the images to the left.

6. With all 10 image files selected, align the images to the bottom.

7. Rename each of the 10 dog images so that they only contain dog and the image number, no period or file extension. So, the image names should be dog1, dog2, dog3, dog4, dog5, dog6, dog7, dog8, dog9, and dog10.

Objective Complete - Mini Debriefing

In just seven steps, we created the Dog card and prepared it for animation. Once you complete the steps, your card will contain 10 dog images overlaid on each other, and an **Enough** button. Your card should look similar to the following screenshot:

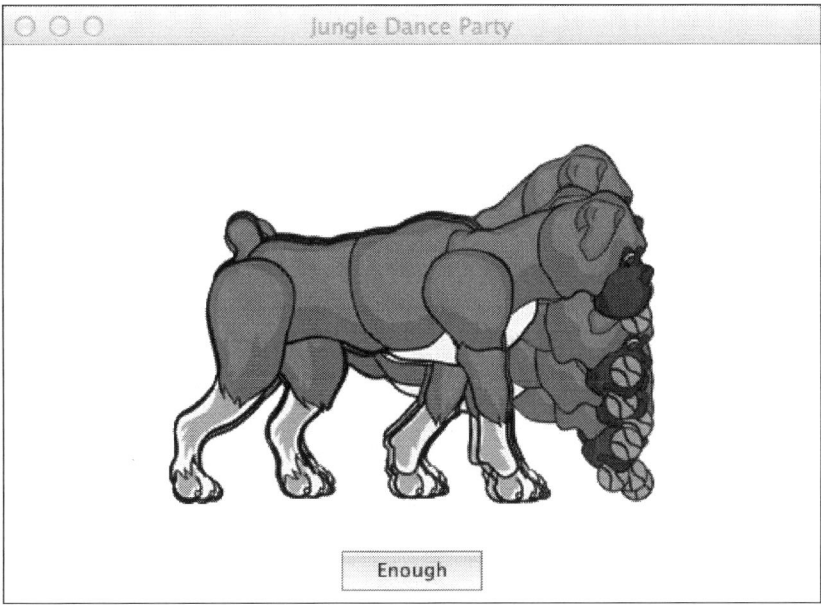

Creating the Monkey card

Next, we will create a card for the monkey animation. You will note a lot of similarities in this task from what you accomplished with the Dog card. Our Monkey card will contain five images that we will display in sequence and a button for the user to navigate back to the main card.

The following image shows five individual frames of the monkey dancing:

Engage Thrusters

1. Create a new card and name it `Monkey`.

2. Drag a Rectangle Button onto the card and make the following modifications to the default button settings:

    1. Set the width to `82` and the height to `23`.

    2. Set the location to `240, 301`.

    3. Set the name of the button to `Enough`.

3. Import the `monkey1.png`, `monkey2.png`, `monkey3.png`, `monkey4.png`, `monkey5.png` files.

4. Place the five image files in the center of the screen.

5. With all the five image files selected, align the images to the center.

6. With all the five image files selected, align the images to the middle.

7. Rename each of the five monkey images so that they only contain `monkey` and the image number, no period or file extension. So, the image names should be `monkey1`, `monkey2`, `monkey3`, `monkey4`, and `monkey5`.

Objective Complete - Mini Debriefing

Our Monkey card is now ready for animation. We will program the animation in a later task. After you complete the seven steps listed in this task, your card will contain five monkey images overlaid on each other, and an **Enough** button. Your card should look similar to the following screenshot:

Creating the Panda card

We are now ready to create our last card, the **Panda** card. There are eight images in the panda animation sequence. We will put all eight of those images on the Panda card as well as a button named Enough. Like with the last two cards, our **Enough** button will be used to navigate back to the main card.

The following image shows eight individual frames of the panda walking:

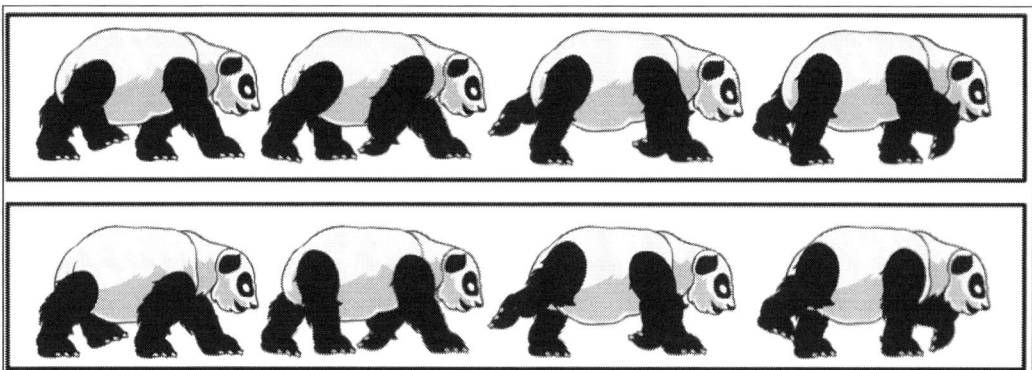

Engage Thrusters

1. Create a new card and name it `Panda`.

2. Drag a Rectangle Button onto the card and make the following modifications to the default button settings:

    1. Set the width to `82` and the height to `23`.

    2. Set the location to `240, 301`.

    3. Set the name of the button to `Enough`.

3. Import the `panda1.png, panda2.png, panda3.png, panda4.png, panda5.png, panda6.png, panda7.png,` and `panda8.png` files.

4. Place the eight image files in the center of the screen.

5. With all eight image files selected, align the images to the center.

6. With all eight image files selected, align the images to the bottom.

7. Rename each of the eight panda images so that they only contain `panda` and the image number, no period or file extension. So, the image names should be `panda1, panda2, panda3, panda4, panda5, panda6, panda7,` and `panda8`.

Objective Complete - Mini Debriefing

After you complete the seven steps listed in this task, your card will contain eight panda images overlaid on each other and an **Enough** button. Your card should look similar to the following screenshot:

Programming the application

All the pieces are in place now. You created the stack, the four cards, and all the required objects for the Jungle Dance Party. All that is left is to program the application. We will start with programming the navigation between cards, and then we will program the individual animation sequences.

Engage Thrusters

1. Add the following LiveCode script to the **dog** button on the main card:

    ```
    on mouseUp
        go to card "Dog"
    end mouseUp
    ```

2. Add the following LiveCode script to the **monkey** button on the main card:

    ```
    on mouseUp
        go to card "Monkey"
    end mouseUp
    ```

3. Add the following LiveCode script to the **panda** button on the main card:

```
on mouseUp
    go to card "Panda"
end mouseUp
```

4. Add the following LiveCode script to the **Enough** button on the Dog card:

```
on mouseUp
    go to card "Main"
end mouseUp
```

5. Add the following LiveCode script to the **Enough** button on the Monkey card:

```
on mouseUp
    go to card "Main"
end mouseUp
```

6. Add the following LiveCode script to the **Enough** button on the Panda card:

```
on mouseUp
    go to card "Main"
end mouseUp
```

Next, we will prepare each of the animal cards by writing `preOpenCard` commands.

7. Add the following code to the Dog card. This will ensure that the only visible image is the first image in the animation sequence.

```
on preOpenCard
    set the vis of img "dog1" to true
    set the vis of img "dog2" to false
    set the vis of img "dog3" to false
    set the vis of img "dog4" to false
    set the vis of img "dog5" to false
    set the vis of img "dog6" to false
    set the vis of img "dog7" to false
    set the vis of img "dog8" to false
    set the vis of img "dog9" to false
    set the vis of img "dog10" to false
end preOpenCard
```

8. Add the following code to the Monkey card. This will make the first image visible and the others not visible.

```
on preOpenCard
    set the vis of img "monkey1" to true
    set the vis of img "monkey2" to false
    set the vis of img "monkey3" to false
    set the vis of img "monkey4" to false
    set the vis of img "monkey5" to false
end preOpenCard
```

9. Add the following code to the Panda card:

```
on preOpenCard
    set the vis of img "panda1" to true
    set the vis of img "panda2" to false
    set the vis of img "panda3" to false
    set the vis of img "panda4" to false
    set the vis of img "panda5" to false
    set the vis of img "panda6" to false
    set the vis of img "panda7" to false
    set the vis of img "panda8" to false
end preOpenCard
```

We are now ready to program our individual animation sequences. As you will see in the next three steps, we will implement a brief pause before staring the animation sequence. This will help ensure that the animation does not start until the card is fully loaded and the user is ready.

10. Add the following code to the Dog card:

```
on openCard
    wait 1 sec
    --
    repeat for 3 times
        set the vis of img "dog2" to true
        set the vis of img "dog1" to false
        wait 150 millisecs
        set the vis of img "dog3" to true
        set the vis of img "dog2" to false
        wait 150 millisecs
        set the vis of img "dog4" to true
        set the vis of img "dog3" to false
        wait 150 millisecs
        set the vis of img "dog5" to true
        set the vis of img "dog4" to false
        wait 150 millisecs
        set the vis of img "dog6" to true
        set the vis of img "dog5" to false
        wait 150 millisecs
        set the vis of img "dog7" to true
        set the vis of img "dog6" to false
        wait 150 millisecs
        set the vis of img "dog8" to true
        set the vis of img "dog7" to false
        wait 150 millisecs
        set the vis of img "dog9" to true
```

```
        set the vis of img "dog8" to false
        wait 150 millisecs
        set the vis of img "dog10" to true
        set the vis of img "dog9" to false
        wait 150 millisecs
        set the vis of img "dog1" to true
        set the vis of img "dog10" to false
        wait 150 millisecs
    end repeat
end openCard
```

The first part of this code contains the statement `wait 1 sec`. This is really to compensate for slower mobile devices. The rest of the code is encapsulated in a `repeat` loop. We simply display the next image in the sequence, make the previous image invisible, wait 150 milliseconds, and then move forward in the sequence. If we did not wait, at least briefly, between each sequence, the mobile device would flash the individual images too quickly for the user to see.

11. Add the following code to the Monkey card:

```
on openCard
    wait 1 sec
    --
    repeat for 3 times
        set the vis of img "monkey2" to true
        set the vis of img "monkey1" to false
        wait 150 millisecs
        set the vis of img "monkey3" to true
        set the vis of img "monkey2" to false
        wait 150 millisecs
        set the vis of img "monkey4" to true
        set the vis of img "monkey3" to false
        wait 150 millisecs
        set the vis of img "monkey5" to true
        set the vis of img "monkey4" to false
        wait 150 millisecs
        set the vis of img "monkey1" to true
        set the vis of img "monkey5" to false
        wait 150 millisecs
    end repeat
end openCard
```

This code contains the 1-second preanimation pause just like we implemented on the Dog card. The repeat loop is similar to what we coded on the Dog card, but with only five images.

12. Add the following code to the Panda card:

```
on openCard
   wait 1 sec
   --
   repeat for 3 times
      set the vis of img "panda2" to true
      set the vis of img "panda1" to false
      wait 150 millisecs
      set the vis of img "panda3" to true
      set the vis of img "panda2" to false
      wait 150 millisecs
      set the vis of img "panda4" to true
      set the vis of img "panda3" to false
      wait 150 millisecs
      set the vis of img "panda5" to true
      set the vis of img "panda4" to false
      wait 150 millisecs
      set the vis of img "panda6" to true
      set the vis of img "panda5" to false
      wait 150 millisecs
      set the vis of img "panda7" to true
      set the vis of img "panda6" to false
      wait 150 millisecs
      set the vis of img "panda8" to true
      set the vis of img "panda7" to false
      wait 150 millisecs
      set the vis of img "panda1" to true
      set the vis of img "panda8" to false
      wait 150 millisecs
   end repeat
end openCard
```

This code replicates the code we used for the Dog and Monkey cards. There were eight panda images, so we merely sequence the display of those images with an interval of 150 milliseconds.

Objective Complete - Mini Debriefing

We have completely programmed our **Jungle Dance Party** mobile application. We added navigational control to the application by programming the buttons on the main interface as well as the **Enough** buttons on the Dog, Monkey, and Panda cards. Our coding included adding the preOpenCard and openCard scripts for each of the three animal cards.

Classified Intel

As much of our code on the three animal cards is identical, we can save a lot of time by copying and pasting code between cards. It is important to ensure all the pasted code is reviewed so that there are no references to objects on another card.

Adding optional sound

Let's make this app a bit more interesting. We will upload three sound files, one for each animal. We will use the sound button on the main interface to allow the user to enable/disable sound.

Engage Thrusters

1. Add the following script at the stack level:

```
global theSound

on openStack
    put "on" into theSound
    set the icon of btn "sound" on card "Main" to 394
end openStack
```

We instantiated a global variable (theSound) to keep track of the user's desire to hear or suppress sound effects. In the openStack script, we set the initial condition to "on" so that, by default, the app will play sound effects.

2. Edit the script of the sound button on the Main card so that it matches the following code:

```
on mouseUp
    global theSound

    if theSound is "on" then
        put "off" into theSound
        set the icon of me to 390
    else
        put "on" into theSound
        set the icon of me to 394
    end if
end mouseUp
```

This code handles switching between "on" and "off" conditions of the global variable theSound.

3. Import the `dog.wav`, `monkey.wav`, and `panda.wav` audio files.

4. Add the following first line to the on `openCard` script of the Dog card:

   ```
   global theSound
   ```

   We need to declare our global variable so that we can reference it later in the code.

5. Add the following three lines of code immediately following the `repeat for 3 times` line of code on the Dog card:

   ```
   if theSound is "on" then
       play audioclip "dog.wav"
   end if
   ```

   Here, we simply check to see if `theSound` is "`on`" or "`off`" and either play or do not play the appropriate audio clip. In the next four steps, we will repeat these code changes for the Monkey and Panda cards.

6. Add the following first line to the on `openCard` script of the Monkey card:

   ```
   global theSound
   ```

   We need to declare our global variable so that we can reference it later in the code.

7. Add the following three lines of code immediately following the `repeat for 3 times` line of code on the Monkey card:

   ```
   if theSound is "on" then
       play audioclip "monkey.wav"
   end if
   ```

8. Add the following first line to the on `openCard` script of the Panda card:

   ```
   global theSound
   ```

   We need to declare our global variable so that we can reference it later in the code.

9. Add the following three lines of code immediately following the `repeat for 3 times` line of code on the Panda card:

   ```
   if theSound is "on" then
       play audioclip "panda.wav"
   end if
   ```

Objective Complete - Mini Debriefing

That's it. You uploaded three audio clips into your LiveCode application and add the necessary code to play them based on user preference.

Mission Accomplished

In this project, we developed a **Jungle Dance Party** mobile application using a single stack and four cards. We used a series of images to create an animation effect on three of the four cards. The fourth card was used for navigation. We included audio files and gave control of their use to our user.

The following screenshot shows the completed game's main interface:

A Hotshot Challenge

Your Hotshot challenge for this project is to give users control of how fast or how slow the animals are animated. In this project, we used 150 milliseconds to control the animation speed. Give your users the ability to adjust that for each animal. Once you accomplish this, you'll have a real Jungle Dance Party!

Project 8

Creating the My Database Mobile App

In this project, we will create the **My Database** app. We will develop our app so that users can create and manage their personal home inventory. Their inventory will be searchable and sortable. We will permit information such as item name, category, room where the item is located, purchase price, and date purchased. Our mobile app will have a simple design so that we can focus on interacting with the database.

Creating mobile applications that make use of databases can be quite complex. This project is merely an introduction to using databases for your mobile apps. In order to create robust mobile applications that make full use of databases, you'll need to go beyond the basics presented in this project.

Mission Briefing

Our mobile app will consist of one stack and four cards. The first card will present the user with a simple interface that provides six options:

- ▶ **Create**: This will allow the user to create a new database
- ▶ **Open**: This option will open a previously created database
- ▶ **Add**: Using this feature, users will be able to add information to the database
- ▶ **View**: We will provide users with the ability to view data they previously entered into the database
- ▶ **Query**: This will be the search function
- ▶ **Close**: Users should close the database when they are finished using it

The second, third, and fourth cards will be for the Add, View, and Query functions respectively.

The following diagram is a mockup of our app's main interface:

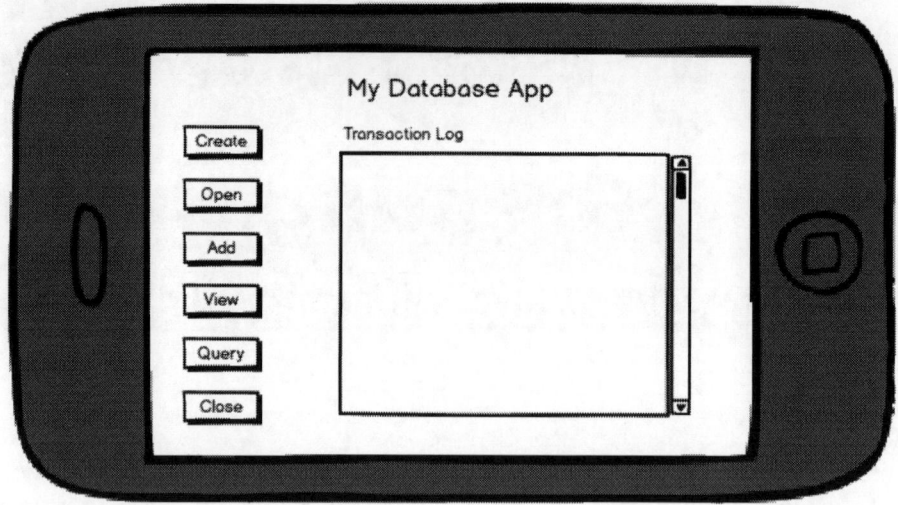

Why Is It Awesome?

A lot of mobile applications collect or manage data. This data can be a simple as a user's profile settings or as complex as stock exchange information. With LiveCode, we have several methods of storing data to include labels, tables, data charts, and external files. Of course, we can also use databases that are embedded in our app or connect to external databases. When we have more than a small amount of data to deal with, using databases can make our apps more efficient.

Your Hotshot Objectives

Use the following brief bullet points outlining the eight major tasks required to complete the project:

- ▶ Creating the main stack
- ▶ Creating the user interface
- ▶ Programming the Create database function
- ▶ Programming the Open and Close database functions
- ▶ Creating the Add Record card and functionality
- ▶ Creating the View card and functionality
- ▶ Creating the Query card and functionality

Mission Checklist

Before getting started, it is important that you have a firm understanding of database vocabulary. The following table is of database terms and their meaning:

Term	Description
Database	A collection of related data stored systematically.
Field	Fields hold one piece of data such as last name, dates, color, etc.
Record	A group of related fields.
Table	A data structure similar to a spreadsheet or matrix used for storing data. Columns indicate the field and rows indicate specific records.

Creating the main stack

Our first task is to create the main stack for our My Database mobile app. For this application, we will only have one stack and four cards. First, we will create the main stack.

Engage Thrusters

1. Let's begin by creating a new main stack named `MyDatabase`. Using the properties inspector, make the following customizations to the main stack:

    1. Change the size of the stack to `480` x `320` pixels. This will give us a landscape orientation.

    2. Set the name of the stack to `MyDatabase`.

    3. Set the title of the stack to `My Database`.

    4. Set the background color to white.

2. Rename the default card to `Main`.

Objective Complete - Mini Debriefing

When we created the main stack, LiveCode created a default card for us. In our next task, we will configure the default card to house our main user interface.

Creating the user interface

In this task, we will create the user interface. The app's interface will consist of a title label, six rectangular buttons, an additional label field, and a list box.

As you work through the steps in this task, refer back to the interface mockup so you have a clear picture of what we are doing.

Engage Thrusters

1. Drag a Label field onto the card `Main` and make the following customizations using the properties inspector:

    1. Set the width to `470` and the height to `36`.

    2. Set the location to `239, 26`.

    3. Set the name of the field to `Title`.

    4. Set the text size to **24**.

    5. Center-align the text.

    6. Change the contents to `My Database App`.

    7. Set the text (foreground color) to black.

2. Drag a Label field onto the card `Main` and make the following customizations using the properties inspector:

    1. Set the width to `128` and the height to `28`.

    2. Set the location to `211, 74`.

    3. Set the name of the field to `LogTitle`.

    4. Set the text size to **14**.

    5. Left-align the text.

    6. Change the contents to `Transaction Log`.

    7. Set the foreground color to black.

3. Drag a Rectangle Button onto the card and make the following customizations using the properties inspector:

    1. Set the width to `82` and the height to `23`.

    2. Set the location to `59, 77`.

    3. Set the name of the button to `Create`.

4. Drag a Rectangle Button onto the card and make the following customizations using the properties inspector:

   1. Set the width to `82` and the height to `23`.

   2. Set the location to `59, 120`.

   3. Set the name of the button to `Open`.

5. Drag a Rectangle Button onto the card and make the following customizations using the properties inspector:

   1. Set the width to `82` and the height to `23`.

   2. Set the location to `59, 163`.

   3. Set the name of the button to `Add`.

6. Drag a Rectangle Button onto the card and make the following customizations using the properties inspector:

   1. Set the width to `82` and the height to `23`.

   2. Set the location to `59, 207`.

   3. Set the name of the button to `View`.

7. Drag a Rectangle Button onto the card and make the following customizations using the properties inspector:

   1. Set the width to `82` and the height to `23`.

   2. Set the location to `59, 250`.

   3. Set the name of the button to `Query`.

8. Drag a Rectangle Button onto the card and make the following customizations using the properties inspector:

   1. Set the width to `82` and the height to `23`.

   2. Set the location to `59, 293`.

   3. Set the name of the button to `Close`.

9. Drag a Scrolling Field onto the card `Main` and make the following customizations using the properties inspector:

   1. Set the width to `300` and the height to `214`.

   2. Set the location to `298, 197`.

   3. Set the name of the field to `log`.

   4. Set the text size to **14**.

   5. Left-align the text.

   6. Set the text (foreground color) to black.

Objective Complete - Mini Debriefing

After completing the nine steps in this section, your interface should look similar to the following screenshot. We were able to create this interface by using only three types of objects: labels, buttons, and a scrolling list field. Our interface consists of a title, six buttons, a transaction log, and a transaction log label.

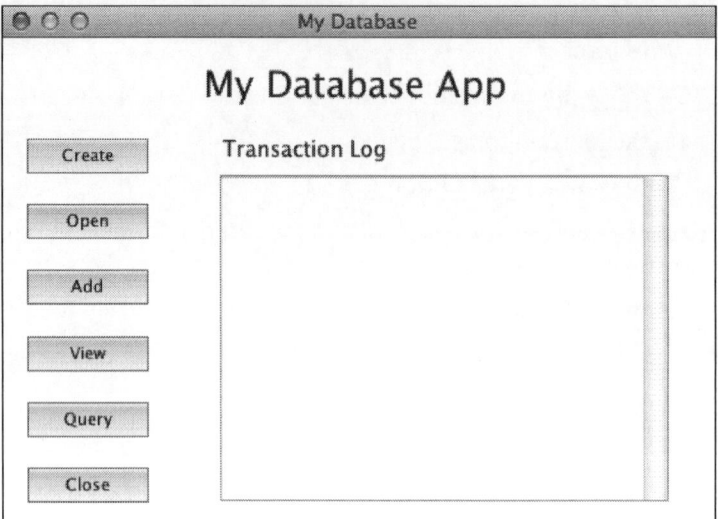

Programming the Create database function

When you work with databases in LiveCode, the first thing you must do is to establish a connection to the database. In this task, we will code the Create button to create a new database. In the subsequent task, we will code the open and close functions.

Engage Thrusters

1. Add the following code to the **Create** button:

```
on mouseUp
    dbConnect
end mouseUp
```

This code calls the dbConnect command, which we will program in the next step.

2. Add the following code to the **Main** card's script:

```
command dbConnect
    global dbPath, dbID
    local tLog

    # SECTION ONE
    put specialFolderPath("documents") & "/packt.sqlite" into
dbPath

    # SECTION TWO
    put revOpenDatabase("sqlite", dbPath, , , , ) into dbID

    # SECTION THREE
    put fld "log"into tLog
    put "Database Created: ID " & dbID & return before tLog
    put tLog into fld "log"
end dbConnect
```

As you can see, we start the `dbConnect` command by declaring two global variables and one local variable. The `dbPath` variable contains the path for the database. LiveCode requires that the path point to an area that the user has write access to. The `dbID` variable will store the newest database connection ID. The `tLog` local variable will be used in section three of our code.

Section one of our code creates the path for the database and stores it in the global `dbPath` variable.

Section two creates a new database and stores the ID in the global `dbID` variable.

In section three, our code puts a new message at the top of the transaction log. To do this, we capture the log's current text and store it in the local `tLog` variable. We then construct our next transaction report and add it to the `tLog` contents using the `before` keyword. Last, we dump the contents of the `tLog` variable into the `log` field. This might seem a laborious approach, but it is necessary and very quick.

3. Since we started putting data in the transaction log field (`log`), we will want to ensure that field is cleared each time the app is opened. To accomplish this, enter the following code at the stack level:

```
on openStack
    put empty into fld "log" on card "Main"
end openStack
```

Objective Complete - Mini Debriefing

In three easy steps, we created the ability for users to create databases using our mobile app. When we use the **Create** button, we will see output results in the transaction log as illustrated in the following screenshot:

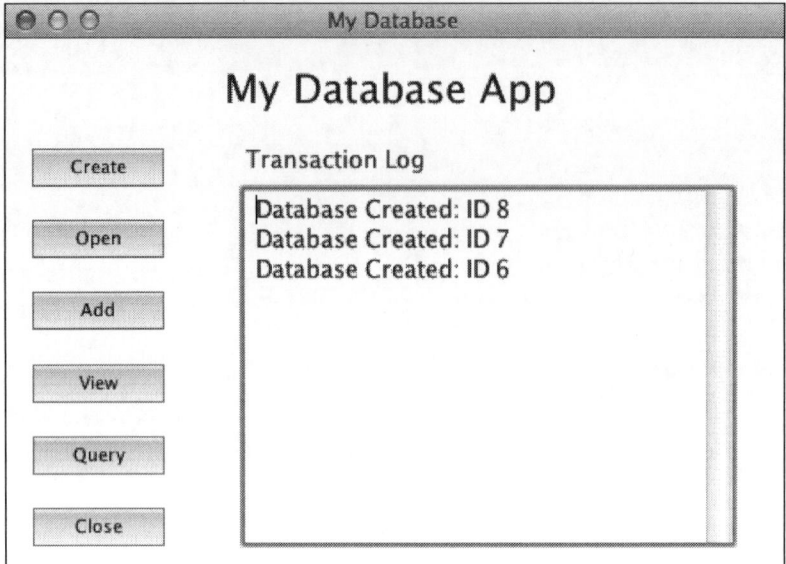

Classified Intel

When you create a database using the steps outlined in this task, an `sqlite` file is created on your mobile device's storage medium. In our example, the file would be named `packt.sqlite`. Where this file is located depends on which mobile device you are using.

Programming the Open and Close database functions

In the previous task, we created a database from scratch. In this task, we will code the Open and Close buttons so that we can open a previously created database and close the open database connection.

Engage Thrusters

1. Add the following code to the **Open** button:

```
on mouseUp
  dbConnect2
end mouseUp
```

This code calls the `dbConnect2` command, which we will program in the next step.

2. Add the following code to the **Main** card's script:

```
command dbConnect2
  global dbPath, dbID
  local tLog

  # SECTION ONE
  answer files "Select a database file to open:" with type
"sqlite"
  put it into dbPath

  # SECTION TWO
  put revOpenDatabase("sqlite", dbPath, , , , ) into dbID

  # SECTION THREE
  put fld "log"into tLog
  put "Database " & dbPath & " Opened: ID " & dbID &
    return before tLog
  put tLog into fld "log"
end dbConnect2
```

Our `dbConnect2` command is very similar to the `dbConnect` command we coded in our previous task. The differences are in sections two and three.

Section two now asks for a file from the user. The `ask` files with type command opens a standard dialog box so that the user can select a specific file. The results are put into the global `dbPath` variable.

In section three, we modified our transaction log output to show that we opened, instead of created, a database.

3. All that is left for us to accomplish in this task is to close the database. To do that, add the following code to the **Close** button's script:

```
on mouseUp
  global dbID
  local tLog

  # SECTION ONE
```

```
          revCloseDatabase dbID

          # SECTION TWO
          put fld "log"into tLog
          put "Database Closed: ID " & dbID & return before tLog
          put tLog into fld "log"
     end mouseUp
```

In section one of this code, we make a call to the `revCloseDatabase` command and pass the current database connection ID (`dbID`). Next, in section two, we output an appropriate entry in the transaction log.

Objective Complete - Mini Debriefing

In three easy steps, we created the ability for users to create databases using our mobile app. When we use the **Create** button, we will see output results in the transaction log as illustrated in the following screenshot:

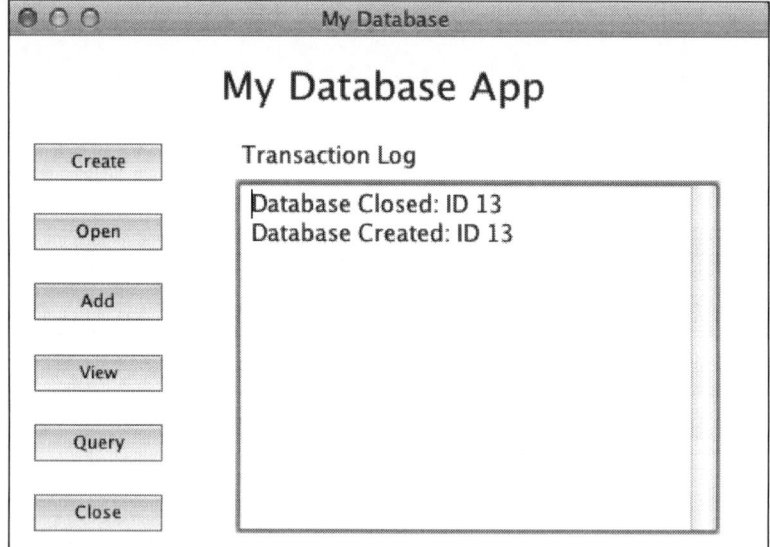

Classified Intel

When apps are programmed with LiveCode, databases are automatically closed when the user quits the app. It is considered good programming practice to close the databases as soon as your app no longer requires an active connection.

Creating the Add Record card and functionality

In this task, we will create an Add card so that users can add data to their database.

Engage Thrusters

1. Add the following code to the **Add** button's script.

    ```
    on mouseUp
        go to card "Add"
    end mouseUp
    ```

2. Create a new card and name it **Add**.

3. Drag a Label field onto the card **Add** and make the following customizations using the properties inspector:

    1. Set the width to `470` and the height to `36`.

    2. Set the location to `239, 26`.

    3. Set the name of the field to `Title`.

    4. Set the text size to **24**.

    5. Center-align the text.

    6. Change the contents to `Add Data to My Database`.

    7. Set the foreground color to black.

4. Drag a Rectangle Button onto the card and make the following customizations using the properties inspector:

    1. Set the width to `82` and the height to `23`.

    2. Set the location to `61, 73`.

    3. Set the name of the button to `Table`.

    4. Set the label of the button to `Add Table`.

5. Drag a Rectangle Button onto the card and make the following customizations using the properties inspector:

    1. Set the width to `82` and the height to `23`.

    2. Set the location to `53, 299`

    3. Set the name of the button to `Back`.

6. Add the following code to the **Back** Button:

```
on mouseUp
    go to card "Main"
end mouseUp
```

The **Back** button is now programmed to allow the user to navigate back to the main screen.

7. Add the following code to the **Table** Button:

```
on mouseUp
  global dbID
  local tSQL, tLog, tResults

  # SECTION ONE
  put "CREATE TABLE inventory (item char(10), " & \
    "category char(12), room char(10), price " & \
    "integer, pDate date)" into tSQL

  # SECTION TWO
  revExecuteSQL dbID, tSQL
  put it into tResults
  if tResults is not a number then
    put "no" into tResults
  end if

  # SECTION THREE
  put fld "log" on card "Main" into tLog
  put "Table " & quote & " Created: " & tResults & \
    " records impacted" & return before tLog
  put tLog into fld "log" on card "Main"
end mouseUp
```

Section one of this code compiles an SQL statement and puts it into the local variable tSQL.

In section two, we execute the SQL statement by using the revExecuteSQL statement. We merely pass the connection ID (dbID) and SQL statement (tSQL); LiveCode does the rest for us. We also evaluate the return value of the revExecuteSQL statement. The statement will return the number of rows impacted by the statement.

We put an appropriate entry into the transaction log on the **Main** card in section three of the code.

Next we will create the ability for users to add records to the new table.

8. Drag a Label field onto the card **Add** and make the following customizations using the properties inspector:

    1. Set the width to `100` and the height to `21`.

    2. Set the location to `150, 112`.

    3. Set the name of the field to `Item Label`.

    4. Change the contents to `Item Name`.

9. Drag a Label field onto the card **Add** and make the following customizations using the properties inspector:

    1. Set the width to `100` and the height to `21`.

    2. Set the location to `150, 142`.

    3. Set the name of the field to `Category Label`.

    4. Change the contents to `Category`.

10. Drag a Label field onto the card **Add** and make the following customizations using the properties inspector:

    1. Set the width to `100` and the height to `21`.

    2. Set the location to `150, 172`.

    3. Set the name of the field to `Room Label`.

    4. Change the contents to `Room`.

11. Drag a Label field onto the card **Add** and make the following customizations using the properties inspector:

    1. Set the width to `100` and the height to `21`.

    2. Set the location to `150, 202`.

    3. Set the name of the field to `Price Label`.

    4. Change the contents to `Price`.

12. Drag a Label field onto the card **Add** and make the following customizations using the properties inspector:

    1. Set the width to `100` and the height to `21`.

    2. Set the location to `150, 232`.

    3. Set the name of the field to `Date Label`.

    4. Change the contents to `Purchase Date`.

13. Drag a Text Entry Field onto the card **Add** and make the following customizations using the properties inspector:

    1. Set the width to 100 and the height to 21.
    2. Set the location to 266, 112.
    3. Set the name of the field to item.

14. Drag a Text Entry Field onto the card **Add** and make the following customizations using the properties inspector:

    1. Set the width to 100 and the height to 21.
    2. Set the location to 266, 142.
    3. Set the name of the field to category.

15. Drag a Text Entry Field onto the card **Add** and make the following customizations using the properties inspector:

    1. Set the width to 100 and the height to 21.
    2. Set the location to 266, 172.
    3. Set the name of the field to room.

16. Drag a Text Entry Field onto the card **Add** and make the following customizations using the properties inspector:

    1. Set the width to 100 and the height to 21.
    2. Set the location to 266, 202.
    3. Set the name of the field to price.

17. Drag a Text Entry Field onto the card **Add** and make the following customizations using the properties inspector:

    1. Set the width to 100 and the height to 21.
    2. Set the location to 266, 232.
    3. Set the name of the field to pDate.

18. Drag a Rectangle Button onto the card and make the following customizations using the properties inspector:

    1. Set the width to 82 and the height to 23.
    2. Set the location to 265, 271.
    3. Set the name of the button to Record.
    4. Set the label of the button to Add Record.

19. Add the following code to the **Record** button:

```
on mouseUp
  global dbID
  local tSQL, tLog, tResults
  local tData1, tData2, tData3, tData4, tData5

  # SECTION ONE
  put the text of fld "item" into tData1
  put the text of fld "category" into tData2
  put the text of fld "room" into tData3
  put the text of fld "price" into tData4
  put the text of fld "pDate" into tData5
  --
  put "INSERT into inventory VALUES (" & \
    tData1 & comma & tData2 & comma & \
    tData3 & comma & tData4 & comma & \
    tData4 & ");" into tSQL

  # SECTION TWO
  revExecuteSQL dbID, tSQL
  put it into tResults
  if tResults is not a number then
    put "no" into tResults
  end if

  # SECTION THREE
  put fld "log" on card "Main" into tLog
  put "Record Added" & return before tLog
  put tLog into fld "log" on card "Main"

  # SECTION FOUR
  clearValues
end mouseUp
```

Section one of this code compiles an SQL statement and puts it into the local variable tSQL. As you can see, values are taken from the text input fields on the **Add** card.

In section two, we execute the SQL statement by using the revExecuteSQL statement.

Section three is where we log our output to the transaction log on the **Main** card.

In the final section, section four, we make a call to the `clearValues` command. We will program that command in the next steps.

20. Add the following `openCard` code at the card level of the **Add** card:

```
on openCard
   clearValues
end openCard
```

21. Add the following code at the card level of the **Add** card:

```
command clearValues
   put empty into fld "item"
   put empty into fld "category"
   put empty into fld "room"
   put empty into fld "price"
   put empty into fld "pDate"
end clearValues
```

We will use the `clearValues` command to ensure no data is left in the input text fields after each record is added and each time the card is opened.

Objective Complete - Mini Debriefing

After completing the 21 steps in this task, you will have an interface that facilitates the creation of an inventory table in the database. Also, the user can create records to add to the table. Data elements are `item`, `category`, `room`, `price`, and `purchase date`. Your interface and results should be similar to the following screenshots:

Creating the View card and functionality

Now that our mobile app can create a database and add a table, and now that we can add records to the database, we need a way to view the database information. We'll accomplish that in this task.

Engage Thrusters

1. Add the following code to the View button's script on the Main card.

    ```
    on mouseUp
      go to card "View"
    end mouseUp
    ```

2. Create a new card and name it `View`.

3. Drag a Label Field onto the card **View** and make the following customizations using the properties inspector:

    1. Set the width to `470` and the height to `36`.

    2. Set the location to `239, 26`.

    3. Set the name of the field to `Title`.

    4. Set the text size to **24**.

    5. Center-align the text.

6. Change the contents to `View My Database`.

7. Set the foreground color to black.

4. Drag a Rectangle Button onto the card and make the following customizations using the properties inspector:

 1. Set the width to `82` and the height to `23`.

 2. Set the location to `53,299`

 3. Set the name of the button to `Back`.

5. Add the following code to the **Back** button:

```
on mouseUp
   go to card "Main"
end mouseUp
```

6. Drag a Scrolling List Field onto the card and make the following customizations using the properties inspector:

 1. Set the width to `416` and the height to `198`.

 2. Set the location to `240,161`.

 3. Set the name of the field to `viewPort`.

7. At the card level of the **View** card, enter the following code:

```
on openCard
  global dbID
  local tSQL, tResults

  # SECTION ONE
  put empty into fld "viewPort"

  # SECTION TWO
  put "SELECT * from inventory;" into tSQL
  put revDataFromQuery(tab,return,dbID,tSQL) into
    tResults
   put tResults into fld "viewPort"
end openCard
```

Objective Complete - Mini Debriefing

Now that you completed the steps in this task, you have a method of retrieving and displaying the contents of the database's inventory table. Your interface for the **View** card should be similar to the following screenshot:

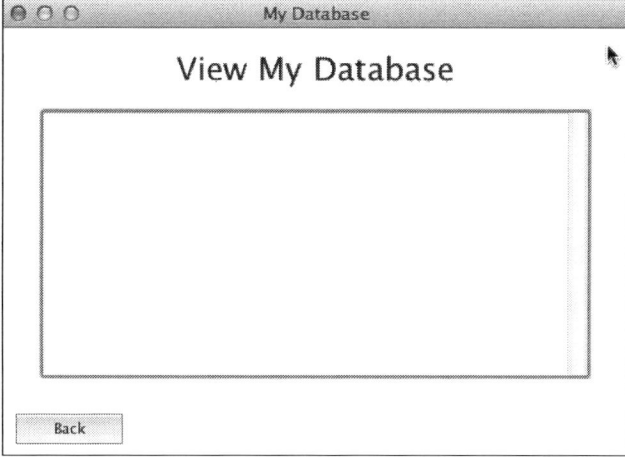

Classified Intel

When you save your mobile application as a standalone application, you will need to include the appropriate database support. This setting is available in the **Standalone Application Settings** window. The following screenshot provides the details:

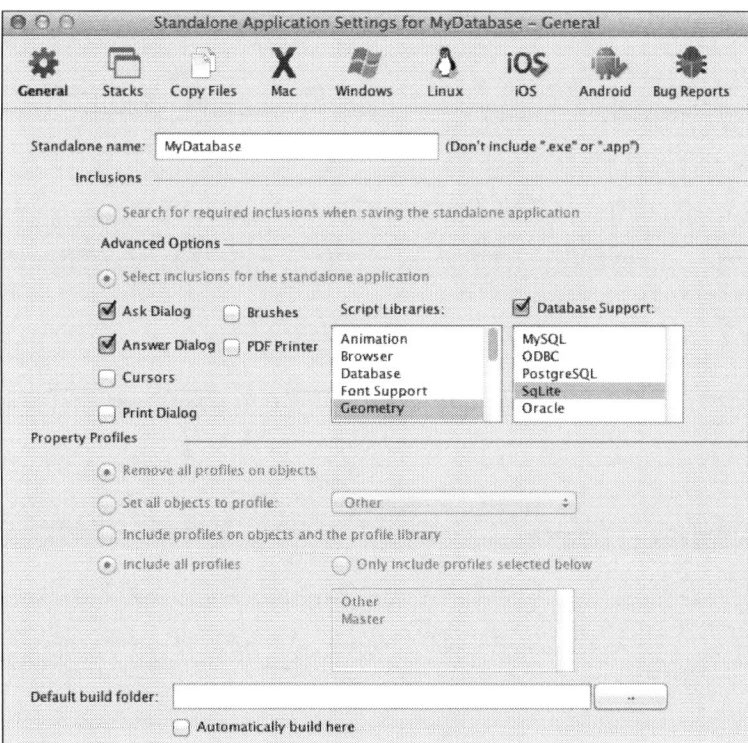

Creating the Query card and functionality

The last thing for us to accomplish is to provide users with the ability to request specific data from their database. This is accomplished through the use of SQL commands.

Engage Thrusters

1. Add the following code to the **Query** button's script on the **Main** card:

```
on mouseUp
   go to card "query"
end mouseUp
```

2. Create a new card and name it Query.

3. Drag a Label field onto the card **Query** and make the following customizations using the properties inspector:

   1. Set the width to 470 and the height to 36.

   2. Set the location to 239, 26.

   3. Set the name of the field to Title.

   4. Set the text size to **24**.

   5. Center-align the text.

   6. Change the contents to Query My Database.

   7. Set the foreground color to black.

4. Drag a Rectangle Button onto the card and make the following customizations using the properties inspector:

   1. Set the width to 82 and the height to 23.

   2. Set the location to 53, 299

   3. Set the name of the button to Back.

5. Add the following code to the **Back** button.

```
on mouseUp
   go to card "Main"
end mouseUp
```

6. At the card level of the "Query" card, enter the following code:

```
/*
Functionality for this card is
part of the Hotshot Challenge
at the end of the chapter.
*/
```

Objective Complete - Mini Debriefing

In this task, we created the shell and navigation controls for the **Query** card. Functionality requires moderate to advanced SQL statements, which is beyond the scope of this book. It is not all that difficult and so it is being left for you to handle in the Hotshot Challenge.

Your interface should be similar to the following screenshot:

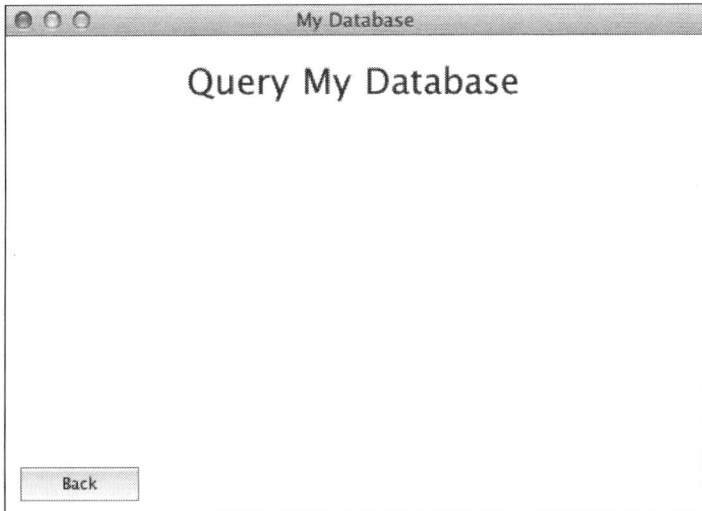

Mission Accomplished

You did it! Database work is not the easiest and it might not be as much fun as programming games. As you have seen, LiveCode does some of the heavy lifting when it comes to database work.

We created a simple My Database mobile application that supports the creation, opening, closing, and viewing of database data. We even included functionality to create an inventory table and upload data in to that table of the database.

Your completed user interface should be similar to the following screenshot:

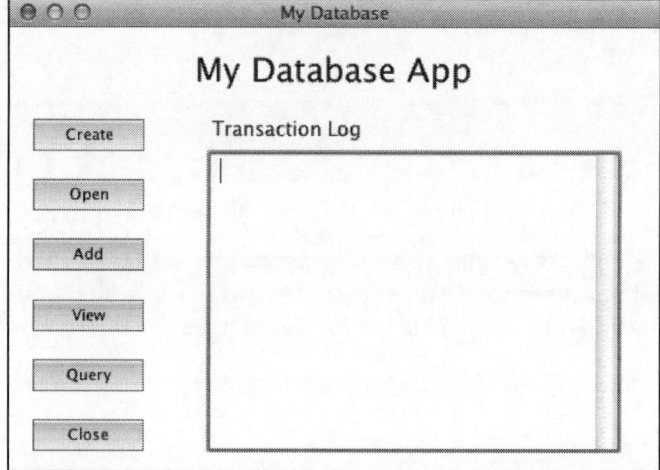

A Hotshot Challenge

For this Hotshot Challenge, you will make modifications to the My Database App. Accomplish the following to complete your challenge:

- Make the appropriate changes to the **Create** button's functionality so that when a new database is created, there is a check to see if that database already exists. This will prevent the user from accidentally overwriting their database.

- Add error checking to the **Close** button so that an error is displayed in the transaction log when a user attempts to close a database that is not open.

- Complete the functionality on the **Query** card.

Good luck!

Project 9

Advanced Fun with the Advanced Fun Mobile App

In this project, we will create the **Advanced Fun** mobile app. We will use six of LiveCode's more advanced features and put them all in one app. Our app will contain a main menu with buttons leading to six cards, each featuring a different advanced feature.

As you start developing more advanced mobile applications with LiveCode, you'll likely need to use one or more of the features covered in this project. Keep your project ideas in mind while you work through this project.

Mission Briefing

Our mobile app will consist of one stack and seven cards. The first card will present the user with a simple interface that provides the following six options:

- ▶ **All About Me**: We will demonstrate what information LiveCode can determine about the user's device
- ▶ **Traveler**: This option will demonstrate both drag-and-drop functionality along with contextually aware objects
- ▶ **Script Grabber**: We will have objects give other objects scripts
- ▶ **Custom Properties**: Here we will have LiveCode supporting custom properties of objects

▶ **Textual Fun**: Here we will demonstrate how to evaluate and manipulate text

▶ **Arrays**: Our final option will focus on arrays as variables

Each of the six options listed will be featured on separate cards within the same main stack.

Here is a mockup of our app's main interface:

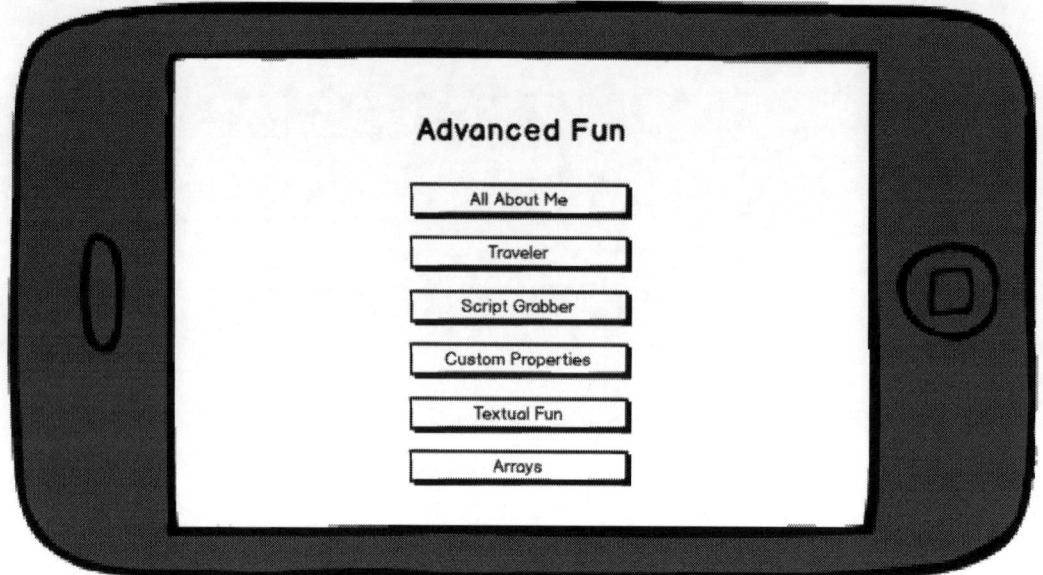

Why Is It Awesome?

LiveCode is a full-featured and very capable programming language. Our **Advanced Fun** mobile app project will feature some of LiveCode's more advanced features. It is important to have a good understanding of all your programming language's capabilities while you are developing mobile apps. When you know what LiveCode's capabilities are, you are more apt to use them to your advantage. When appropriate, you can use the advanced features to make your app more efficient, interesting, and fun.

Your Hotshot Objectives

We have eight primary tasks to complete in order to realize our vision of the Advanced Fun mobile app. They are as follows:

▶ Creating the main stack

▶ Creating the user interface

▶ Programming the All About Me option

- ▶ Programming the Traveler option
- ▶ Programming the Script Grabber option
- ▶ Programming the Custom Properties option
- ▶ Programming the Textual Fun option
- ▶ Programming the Arrays option

Creating the main stack

Our first task is to create the main stack for our Advanced Fun mobile app. For this application, we will only have one stack and seven cards.

Engage Thrusters

1. Let's begin by creating a new main stack named `Advanced Fun`. Using the properties inspector, make the following customizations to the main stack:

    1. Change the size of the stack to `480` x `320` pixels. This will give us a landscape orientation.
    2. Set the name of the stack to `AdvancedFun`.
    3. Set the title of the stack to `Advanced Fun`.
    4. Set the background color to white.

2. Rename the default card to `Main`.
3. Save the stack.

Objective Complete - Mini Debriefing

When we created the main stack, LiveCode created a default card for us. In our next task, we will configure the default card to house our main user interface.

Creating the user interface

In this task, we will create the user interface. The app's interface will consist of a title label and six rectangular buttons.

As you work through the steps in this task, refer back to the interface mockup so you have a clear picture of what we are doing.

Engage Thrusters

1. Drag a Label field onto the card Main and make the following customizations using the properties inspector:

    1. Set the width to 470 and the height to 36.
    2. Set the location to 239, 26.
    3. Set the name of the field to Title.
    4. Set the text size to **24**.
    5. Embolden and center the text.
    6. Change the contents to Advanced Fun.
    7. Set the text (foreground color) to black.

2. Drag a Rectangle Button onto the card and make the following customizations using the properties inspector:

    1. Set the width to 160 and the height to 23.
    2. Set the location to 239, 85.
    3. Set the name of the button to AboutMe.
    4. Set the label of the button to All About Me.
    5. Set the fill (background color) to blue.
    6. Set the text (foreground color) to white.
    7. Set the text size to **14**.
    8. Embolden the text.
    9. Add the following script to this button:

        ```
        on mouseUp
            go to card (short name of me)
        end mouseUp
        ```

3. Drag a Rectangle Button onto the card and make the following customizations using the properties inspector:

    1. Set the width to 160 and the height to 23.
    2. Set the location to 239, 124.
    3. Set the name of the button to Traveler.
    4. Set the label of the button to Traveler.
    5. Set the background color to blue.
    6. Set the foreground color to white.

7. Set the text size to **14**.

8. Bold the text.

9. Add the following script to this button:

```
on mouseUp
    go to card (short name of me)
end mouseUp
```

4. Drag a Rectangle Button onto the card and make the following customizations using the properties inspector:

    1. Set the width to `160` and the height to `23`.

    2. Set the location to `239, 163`.

    3. Set the name of the button to `ScriptGrabber`.

    4. Set the label of the button to `Script Grabber`.

    5. Set the background color to blue.

    6. Set the foreground color to white.

    7. Set the text size to **14**.

    8. Embolden the text.

    9. Add the following script to this button:

    ```
    on mouseUp
        go to card (short name of me)
    end mouseUp
    ```

5. Drag a Rectangle Button onto the card and make the following customizations using the properties inspector:

    1. Set the width to `160` and the height to `23`.

    2. Set the location to `239, 201`.

    3. Set the name of the button to `CustomP`.

    4. Set the label of the button to `Custom Properties`.

    5. Set the background color to blue.

    6. Set the foreground color to white.

    7. Set the text size to **14**.

    8. Embolden the text.

    9. Add the following script to this button:

    ```
    on mouseUp
        go to card (short name of me)
    end mouseUp
    ```

6. Drag a Rectangle Button onto the card and make the following customizations using the properties inspector:

    1. Set the width to 160 and the height to 23.

    2. Set the location to 239, 240.

    3. Set the name of the button to Text Fun.

    4. Set the label of the button to Textual Fun.

    5. Set the background color to blue.

    6. Set the foreground color to white.

    7. Set the text size to **14**.

    8. Embolden the text.

    9. Add the following script to this button:

    ```
    on mouseUp
        go to card (short name of me)
    end mouseUp
    ```

7. Drag a Rectangle Button onto the card and make the following customizations using the properties inspector:

    1. Set the width to 160 and the height to 23.

    2. Set the location to 239, 279.

    3. Set the name of the button to Arrays.

    4. Set the label of the button to Arrays.

    5. Set the background color to blue.

    6. Set the foreground color to white.

    7. Set the text size to **14**.

    8. Embolden the text.

    9. Add the following script to this button:

    ```
    on mouseUp
        go to card (short name of me)
    end mouseUp
    ```

Objective Complete - Mini Debriefing

After completing the seven steps in this section, your interface should look similar to the following screenshot. Our interface is simple with just one text label and six rectangular buttons.

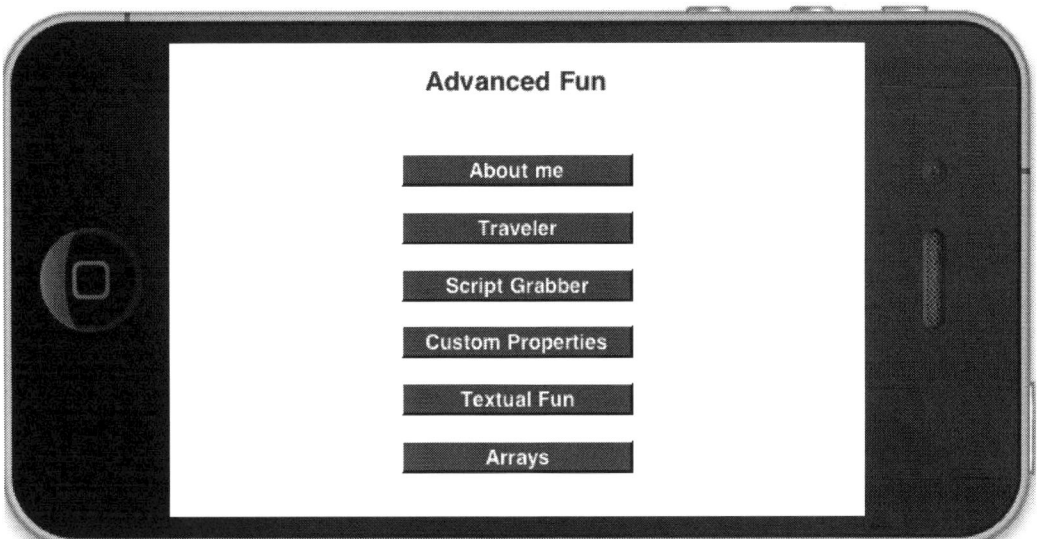

Classified Intel

For each button, we added the script `go to card (short name of me)`. In the next six tasks, we will create additional six cards. By giving the cards the same name as the buttons, we can refer to them more easily. This is another advanced feature.

Programming the All About Me option

For this task we will create a new card with one button and one text field. Next, we will add a script to the button that displays information about the user's device in the text field.

Engage Thrusters

1. Create a new card and name it `AboutMe`.

2. Drag a Rectangle Button onto the card and make the following customizations using the properties inspector:

    1. Set the width to `82` and the height to `23`.

    2. Set the location to `49, 17`.

    3. Set the name of the button to `Back`.

    4. Set the label of the button to `Back`.

    5. Set the background color to blue.

    6. Set the foreground color to white.

7. Set the text size to **12**.

8. Add the following script to the **Back** button.

```
on mouseUp
    go to card "Main"
end mouseUp
```

3. Drag a Default Button onto the card and make the following customizations using the properties inspector:

1. Set the width to `200` and the height to `23`.

2. Set the location to `240, 56`.

3. Set the name of the button to `Action`.

4. Set the label of the button to `What do I know?`.

5. Set the background color to blue.

6. Set the foreground color to white.

7. Set the text size to **14**.

8. Embolden the text.

4. Drag a Scrolling Field onto the card and make the following customizations using the properties inspector:

1. Set the width to `384` and the height to `148`.

2. Set the location to `240, 180`.

3. Set the name of the button to `Output`.

5. Add the following code to the card **AboutMe**:

```
on openCard
    put empty into fld "Output"
end openCard
```

This code will ensure each time the user selects the **All About Me** option that the **Output** field will be empty.

6. Add the following script to the **Action** button:

```
on mouseUp
    local sect1, sect2, sect3, sect4
    local tOS, tMemory

    # SECTION ONE
    put empty into fld "output"
```

```
# SECTION TWO
put "Today is : " & the date & return & \
    "The time is: " & the time into sect1


# SECTION THREE
put "Your host name is: " & the hostname & return & \
    "Your IP Address is: " & the hostNameToAddress of the
hostName into sect2


# SECTION FOUR
put "Your system is: " & the systemVersion into sect3


# SECTION FIVE
put hasMemory(3*1024*1024) into tMemory
if tMemory then
   put "You have at least 3 MB of RAM available" into sect4
else
   put "You have less than 3 MB of RAM available" into sect4
end if


# SECTION SIX
put sect1 & return & sect2 & return & sect3 & return & sect4
into fld "output"
end mouseUp
```

We start this button's code by declaring several local variables. The rest of our code is organized into four sections. Each of these sections uses the corresponding local variable (`sect1`, `sect2`, `sect3`, or `sect4`) to store the results for later output.

The `tOS` variable stores the user's operating system, and the `tMemory` variable is used in the fifth section.

The first section of the script simply clears the **Output** field by putting `empty` into it. The second section gets the date and time from the user's system and puts the formatted results into the variable `sect1`. The third section of our script obtains the hostname and IP address of the user's device. This information is placed in the `sect2` local variable. The fourth section gets and displays the system version of the user's device. If the user's device is a Mac, the `systemVersion` function returns three integers such as `10.7.5`. If the user is using Windows, the function will return a string beginning with the word `Windows`. In the case of mobile devices, the `systemVersion` function will return the actual version of the OS such as 5.1 or 6.0.1. The output for this section is put in the `sect3` local variable.

The code in the fifth section determines if the user's device has at least 3 MB of memory available using the `hasMemory()` function. This function returns `true` if the specified amount of memory is available to the user; otherwise `false` is returned. Our code formats the output and places it in the `sect4` local variable.

In our final section of code, the sixth section, we simply display the contents of the `sect1`, `sect2`, `sect3`, and `sect4` local variables, separated by a `return`, in the **Output** field.

Objective Complete - Mini Debriefing

As you can see in the following sample output screenshot, we have completed this task and have the ability to see information about our system. Some of the output was blacked out for security purposes.

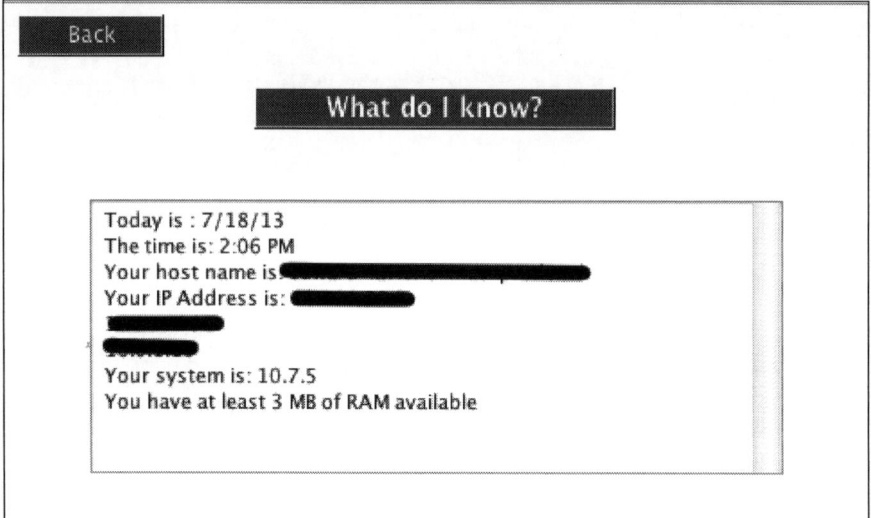

Programming the Traveler option

For this task, we will create an interface that permits the user to drag-and-drop an object over one of three geographic areas. We will add code so that the system can tell us where the user dropped the object.

Engage Thrusters

1. Create a new card and name it `Traveler`.

2. Drag a Rectangle Button onto the card and make the following customizations using the properties inspector:

   1. Set the width to `82` and the height to `23`.

   2. Set the location to `49, 17`.

   3. Set the name of the button to `Back`.

   4. Set the label of the button to `Back`.

   5. Set the background color to blue.

   6. Set the foreground color to white.

   7. Set the text size to **12**.

   8. Add the following script to the **Back** button:

      ```
      on mouseUp
          go to card "Main"
      end mouseUp
      ```

3. Drag a Label field onto the card Traveler and make the following customizations using the properties inspector:

   1. Set the width to `378` and the height to `21`.

   2. Set the location to `283, 18`.

   3. Set the name of the field to `Instructions`.

   4. Set the text size to **14**.

   5. Embolden and center the text.

   6. Change the contents to `Drag the car to a country`.

   7. Set the foreground color to black.

4. Import the `US_140x93.png` image file to the Traveler card and make the following customizations using the properties inspector:

   1. Set the location to `92, 202`.

   2. Change the name of the image to `US`.

5. Import the `UK_93x145.png` image file to the Traveler card and make the following customizations using the properties inspector:

   1. Set the location to `240, 176`.

   2. Change the name of the image to `UK`.

6. Import the `IT_115x145.png` image file to the Traveler card and make the following customizations using the properties inspector:

   1. Set the location to `395, 174`.

   2. Change the name of the image to `IT`.

7. Import the `car.png` image file to the Traveler card and make the following customizations using the properties inspector:

   1. Set the location to `92, 78`.

8. Drag a Label field onto the Traveler card and make the following customizations using the properties inspector:

   1. Set the width to `438` and the height to `27`.

   2. Set the location to `239, 295`.

   3. Set the name of the field to `Results`.

   4. Set the text size to **12**.

   5. Embolden and center the text.

   6. Set the foreground color to black.

9. Add the following script at the card level on the Traveler card:

```
on preOpenCard
    set the loc of img "car.png" to 92,78
    put empty into fld "Results"
end preOpenCard
```

This code will reset the location of the car image and ensure that no text is displayed in the Results field.

10. Add the following code to the `car.png` image:

```
on mouseDown
    grab me
end mouseDown

on mouseUp
    if the loc of me is within the rect of img "US" then
        put "You are in the United States" into fld "Results"
    else if the loc of me is within the rect of img "UK" then
        put "You are in the United Kingdom" into fld "Results"
    else if the loc of me is within the rect of img "IT" then
```

```
      put "You are in Italy" into fld "Results"
  else
      put "You are no where special" into fld "Results"
  end if
end mouseUp
```

There are two parts to the code we just entered. First is the `mouseDown` handler. When the user clicks or taps the car, they will have essentially grabbed or selected the object to be moved. Now the user can freely move the car around the screen. When the player releases the car object, the `mouseUp` handler will be executed.

The `mouseUp` handler simply checks to see if the car is located inside one of the country rectangles. An appropriate message is displayed in the Results field.

Objective Complete - Mini Debriefing

Having followed the 10 steps in this task, your user interface should be similar to the following screenshot:

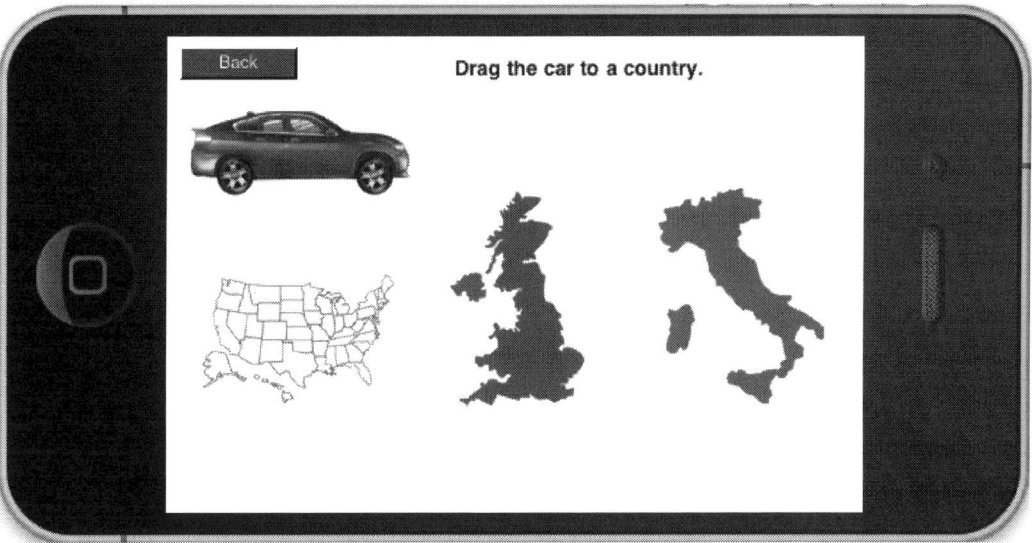

As you can see in the following screenshot, the car has been moved to Italy and the results are displayed at the bottom of the screen:

Programming the Script Grabber option

For this task, we will create a new **ScriptGrabber** card and add functionality so that a **Try Me** button's script can be changed during program execution.

Engage Thrusters

1. Create a new card and name it `ScriptGrabber`.

2. Drag a Rectangle Button onto the card and make the following customizations using the properties inspector:

    1. Set the width to `82` and the height to `23`.

    2. Set the location to `49`, `17`.

    3. Set the name of the button to `Back`.

    4. Set the label of the button to `Back`.

    5. Set the background color to blue.

    6. Set the foreground color to white.

    7. Set the text size to **12**.

8. Add the following script to the **Back** button.

```
on mouseUp
   go to card "Main"
end mouseUp
```

3. Drag a Label field onto the ScriptGrabber card and make the following customizations using the properties inspector:

   1. Set the width to 378 and the height to 21.
   2. Set the location to 283, 18.
   3. Set the name of the field to Instructions.
   4. Set the text size to **14**.
   5. Embolden and center the text.
   6. Change the contents to Pick a Script to Grab.
   7. Set the foreground color to black.

4. Drag a Rectangle Button onto the card and make the following customizations using the properties inspector:

   1. Set the width to 82 and the height to 23.
   2. Set the location to 217, 61.
   3. Set the name of the button to Normal.
   4. Set the label of the button to Normal.

5. Drag a Rectangle Button onto the card and make the following customizations using the properties inspector:

   1. Set the width to 82 and the height to 23.
   2. Set the location to 365, 61.
   3. Set the name of the button to Opposite.
   4. Set the label of the button to Opposite.

6. Drag a Push Button onto the card and make the following customizations using the properties inspector:

   1. Set the width to 82 and the height to 23.
   2. Set the location to 291, 99.
   3. Set the name of the button to Try Me.
   4. Set the label of the button to Try Me.

7. Drag a Scrolling Field onto the card and make the following customizations using the properties inspector:

    1. Set the width to 384 and the height to 148.

    2. Set the location to 248, 206.

    3. Set the name of the button to Output.

8. Add the following code to the ScriptGrabber card:

```
on preOpenCard
    set the script of btn "Try Me" to empty
    --
    put empty into fld "Output"
end preOpenCard
```

This code accomplishes two things just prior to the ScriptGrabber card being opened. First, it removes any scripts assigned to the **Try Me** button. Second, it clears out the **Output** text field.

9. Drag a Rectangle Button onto the card and make the following customizations using the properties inspector:

    1. Set the width to 82 and the height to 23.

    2. Set the location to 103, 297.

    3. Set the name of the button to btnNormal.

    4. Add the following code to this button:

```
on mouseUp
    put "Normal: Up means Up" into fld "Output"
end mouseUp

on mouseDown
    put "Normal: Down means Down" into fld "Output"
end mouseDown
```

    5. Set **Visible** of the button to false.

The code for this button will send text messages to the **Output** field to indicate that the normal button code is being used.

10. Drag a Rectangle Button onto the card and make the following customizations using the properties inspector:

    1. Set the width to `82` and the height to `23`.

    2. Set the location to `205, 297`.

    3. Set the name of the button to `btnOpposite`.

    4. Add the following code to this button:

    ```
    on mouseUp
        put "Opposite: Up means Down" into fld "Output"
    end mouseUp

    on mouseDown
        put "Opposite: Down means Up" into fld "Output"
    end mouseDown
    ```

    5. Set **Visible** of the button to false.

       The code for this button will send text messages to the **Output** field to indicate that the normal button code is being used.

11. Add the following code to the **Normal** button:

    ```
    on mouseUp
        set the script of btn "Try Me" to script of btn "btnNormal"
    end mouseUp
    ```

    This code will copy the script from the `btnNormal` button to the **Try Me** button.

12. Add the following code to the **Opposite** button:

    ```
    on mouseUp
        set the script of btn "Try Me" to script of btn "btnOpposite"
    end mouseUp
    ```

    This code will copy the script from the btnOpposite button to the **Try Me** button.

Objective Complete - Mini Debriefing

After you complete the 12 steps outlined in this task, you will have an interface on your **ScriptGrabber** card similar to the following screenshot:

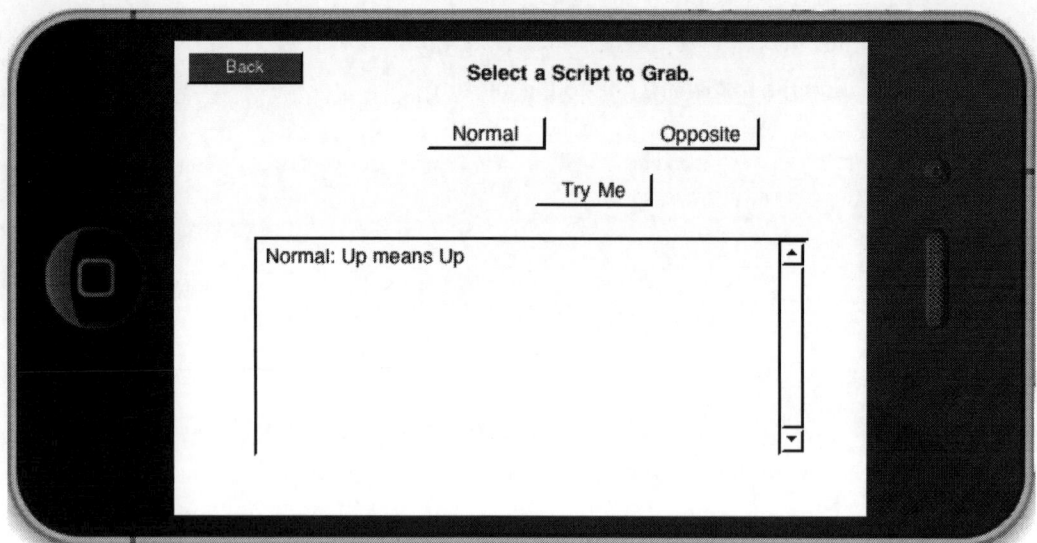

As you can see, the **Try Me** button can emulate the code from either hidden button (**Normal** and **Opposite**).

Classified Intel

Assigning scripts to objects is an advanced technique afforded to us by LiveCode. There are, of course, limitations to how many lines of a script you can assign to objects once the program is running. By default, you can use up to 10 statements.

Programming the Custom Properties option

Custom properties provide us with tremendous flexibility to manage objects in our mobile apps. Objects in LiveCode have properties such as location, rect, size, various colors, and countless other properties. What if you want to create an object such as an avatar for a mobile game? You might want to give it properties such as health, stamina, coins, dexterity, age, hair color, and more. LiveCode affords us that type of programming flexibility.

In this task, we will create a car with custom properties.

Engage Thrusters

1. Create a new card and name it `CustomP`.

2. Drag a Rectangle Button onto the card and make the following customizations using the properties inspector:

    1. Set the width to `82` and the height to `23`.

    2. Set the location to `49, 17`.

    3. Set the name of the button to `Back`.

    4. Set the label of the button to `Back`.

    5. Set the background color to blue.

    6. Set the foreground color to white.

    7. Set the text size to **12**.

    8. Add the following script to the Back button.
       ```
       on mouseUp
           go to card "Main"
       end mouseUp
       ```

3. Drag a Label field onto the card CustomP and make the following customizations using the properties inspector:

    1. Set the width to `378` and the height to `21`.

    2. Set the location to `283, 18`.

    3. Set the name of the field to `Instructions`.

    4. Set the text size to **14**.

    5. Embolden and center the text.

    6. Change the contents to `Click Buttons to learn about me.`

    7. Set the foreground color to black.

4. Import the `car.png` image file to the CustomP card and make the following customizations using the properties inspector:

    1. Set the location to `240, 160`.

    2. Change the name to `car`.

5. Select the `car` image and select **Custom Properties** in the properties inspector. Refer to the following screenshot:

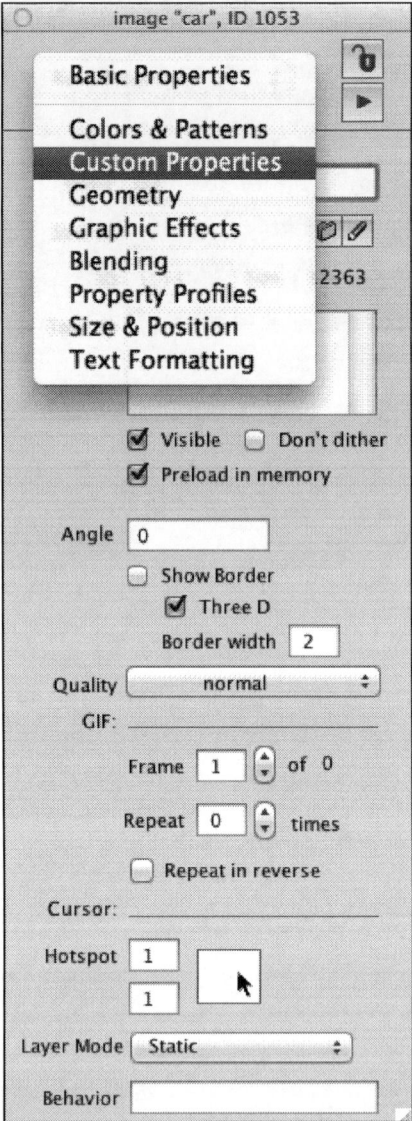

To add custom properties, you will click on the plus sign in the **Custom Properties** area of the **Custom Properties** dialog window. When you do this, a pop-up input box appears. Enter the name of your custom property there.

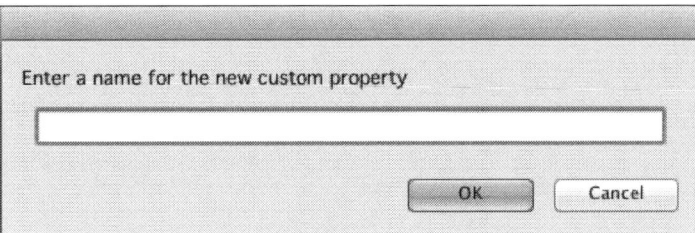

In this dialog box, enter `color` and click on the **OK** button or tap the *return* (Mac)/ *Enter* (Windows) key.

6. Now that you have created the first custom property of your car, you need to assign it a value. With the new custom property name selected, type `black` in the **Property Contents** input box. Refer to the following screenshot for details:

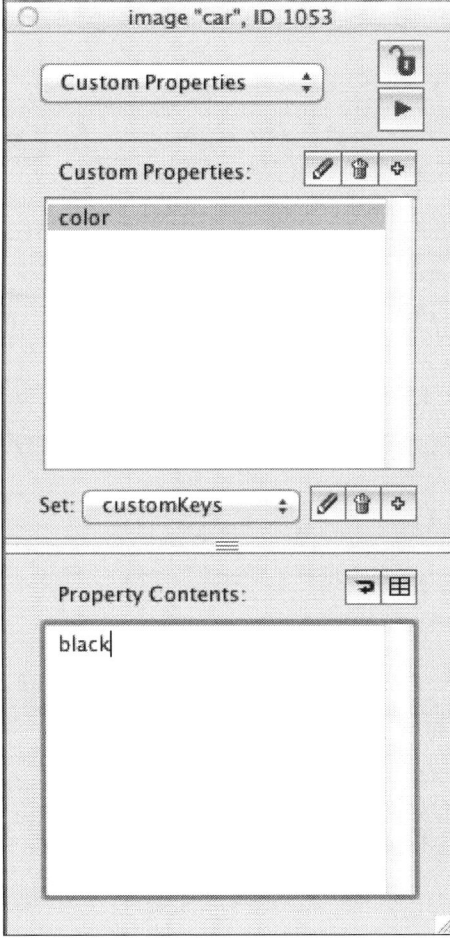

7. Add the following additional custom properties for the `car` image:

Custom property	Property content
year	2013
wheels	4
doors	2
body	sport
miles	10,319
speed	139

8. Drag a Label field onto the CustomP card and make the following customizations using the properties inspector:

    1. Set the width to `148` and the height to `34`.

    2. Set the location to `238, 207`.

    3. Set the name of the field to `Property`.

    4. Set the text size to **14**.

    5. Embolden and center the text.

    6. Set the foreground color to black.

9. At the card level, add the following code to the CustomP card:

```
on preOpenCard
    put empty into fld "Property"
end preOpenCard
```

    This code will ensure that the **Property** label is blank when the card is first opened.

10. Drag a Rectangle Button onto the CustomP card and make the following modifications using the properties inspector:

    1. Set the width to `82` and the height to `23`.

    2. Set the location to `77, 97`.

    3. Set the name of the button to color.

    4. Add the following script to the button:

```
on mouseUp
    local tProp

    put the short name of me into tProp
    put the tProp of img "car" into fld "Property"
end mouseUp
```

This code will display the property contents for the color custom property. The output will be displayed in the Property field that we placed just under the car.

11. Drag a Rectangle Button onto the CustomP card and make the following modifications using the properties inspector:

    1. Set the width to 82 and the height to 23.

    2. Set the location to 77, 152.

    3. Set the name of the button to body.

    4. Add the following script to the button:

```
on mouseUp
   local tProp

   put the short name of me into tProp
   put the tProp of img "car" into fld "Property"
end mouseUp
```

This code will display the property contents for the body custom property. The output will be displayed in the **Property** field that we placed just under the car.

12. Drag a Rectangle Button onto the CustomP card and make the following modifications using the properties inspector:

    1. Set the width to 82 and the height to 23.

    2. Set the location to 77, 207.

    3. Set the name of the button to doors.

    4. Add the following script to the button:

```
on mouseUp
   local tProp

   put the short name of me into tProp
   put the tProp of img "car" into fld "Property"
end mouseUp
```

This code will display the property contents for the doors custom property. The output will be displayed in the **Property** field that we placed just under the car.

13. Drag a Rectangle Button onto the CustomP card and make the following modifications using the properties inspector:

    1. Set the width to 82 and the height to 23.

    2. Set the location to 240, 97.

    3. Set the name of the button to speed.

    4. Add the following script to the button:

    ```
    on mouseUp
       local tProp

       put the short name of me into tProp
       put the tProp of img "car" into fld "Property"
    end mouseUp
    ```

    This code will display the property contents for the speed custom property. The output will be displayed in the **Property** field that we placed just under the car.

14. Drag a Rectangle Button onto the CustomP card and make the following modifications using the properties inspector:

    1. Set the width to 82 and the height to 23.

    2. Set the location to 405, 97.

    3. Set the name of the button to year.

    4. Add the following script to the button:

    ```
    on mouseUp
       local tProp

       put the short name of me into tProp
       put the tProp of img "car" into fld "Property"
    end mouseUp
    ```

    This code will display the property contents for the year custom property. The output will be displayed in the **Property** field that we placed just under the car.

15. Drag a Rectangle Button onto the CustomP card and make the following modifications using the properties inspector:

    1. Set the width to `82` and the height to `23`.

    2. Set the location to `405, 152`.

    3. Set the name of the button to `miles`.

    4. Add the following script to the button:

    ```
    on mouseUp
       local tProp

       put the short name of me into tProp
       put the tProp of img "car" into fld "Property"
    end mouseUp
    ```

    This code will display the property contents for the miles custom property. The output will be displayed in the **Property** field that we placed just under the car.

16. Drag a Rectangle Button onto the CustomP card and make the following modifications using the properties inspector:

    1. Set the width to `82` and the height to `23`.

    2. Set the location to `405, 207`.

    3. Set the name of the button to `wheels`.

    4. Add the following script to the button:

    ```
    on mouseUp
       local tProp

       put the short name of me into tProp
       put the tProp of img "car" into fld "Property"
    end mouseUp
    ```

    This code will display the property contents for the wheels custom property. The output will be displayed in the **Property** field that we placed just under the car.

Objective Complete - Mini Debriefing

With the 16 steps in this task completed, we will have a fully functional example of using custom properties. The user interface should be similar to the following screenshot:

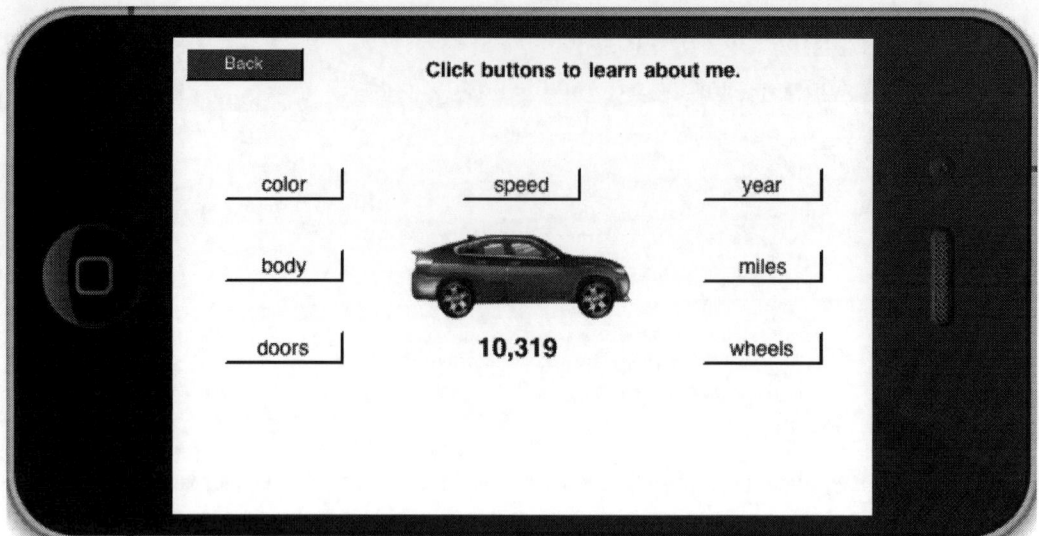

Classified Intel

You cannot create custom properties whose name is already in use by LiveCode such as **style**. If your new custom property name clashes with a built-in reserved word, LiveCode will let you know with a friendly error message.

Programming the Textual Fun option

LiveCode provides us with powerful control over text. We can evaluate entire strings, lines, chunks, words, or individual characters. In this task, we will have a little bit of fun with input provided to us by the user. We will create a new card titled **TextFun** that will simply ask the user for input and present a **Process** button. Once that button is clicked/tapped, our code will do the rest.

Engage Thrusters

1. Create a new card and name it `TextFun`.

2. Drag a Rectangle Button onto the card and make the following customizations using the properties inspector:

    1. Set the width to `82` and the height to `23`.

    2. Set the location to `49, 17`.

    3. Set the name of the button to `Back`.

    4. Set the label of the button to `Back`.

    5. Set the background color to blue.

    6. Set the foreground color to white.

    7. Set the text size to **12**.

    8. Add the following script to the **Back** button.

    ```
    on mouseUp
        go to card "Main"
    end mouseUp
    ```

3. Drag a Label field onto the card TextFun and make the following customizations using the properties inspector:

    1. Set the width to `168` and the height to `28`.

    2. Set the location to `98, 61`.

    3. Set the name of the field to `Instructions`.

    4. Set the text size to **12**.

    5. Embolden and left-align the text.

    6. Set the foreground color to black.

4. Drag a Text Entry Field onto the TextFun card and make the following customizations using the properties inspector:

    1. Set the width to `272` and the height to `21`.

    2. Set the location to `318, 61`.

    3. Set the name of the field to `userInput`.

5. Drag a Rectangle Button onto the card and make the following customizations using the properties inspector:

    1. Set the width to 82 and the height to 21.

    2. Set the location to 413, 92.

    3. Set the name of the button to Process.

    4. Set the label of the button to Process.

6. Drag a Scrolling Field onto the card and make the following customizations using the properties inspector:

    1. Set the width to 384 and the height to 148.

    2. Set the location to 248, 206.

    3. Set the name of the button to Output.

7. Add the following code to the card level of the TextFun card:

```
on preOpenCard
    put empty into fld "userInput"
    put empty into fld "Output"
end preOpenCard
```

This code empties the user input text field and the **Output** scrolling text field each time the card is opened.

8. Add the following code to the **Process** button:

```
on mouseUp
    local theInput, sect1, sect2, sect3, sect4, sect5
    local tVowel, tConsonant, tOther, tBackwards, tReverse

    # SECTION ONE
    put empty into fld "Output"
    put the text of fld "userInput" into theInput
    put 0 into tVowel
    put 0 into tConsonant
    put 0 into tOther

    # SECTION TWO
    put "Words: " & the number of words of theInput & \
            return & "First Word: " & word 1 of theInput  & \
            return & "Last Word: " & last word of theInput into sect1

    # SECTION THREE
    put "Characters: " & the number of chars of theInput into sect2
```

```
    # SECTION FOUR
    repeat with x = 1 to (the len of theInput)
        if char x of theInput is among the chars of "aeiou" then
            add 1 to tVowel
        else if char x of theInput is among the chars of
"bcdfghjklmnpqrstvwxyz" then
            add 1 to tConsonant
        else
            add 1 to tOther
        end if
    end repeat
    put "Vowels: " & tVowel & return & \
        "Consonants: " & tConsonant & return & \
        "Special Characters: " & tOther into sect3

    # SECTION FIVE
    repeat with x = the len of theInput down to 1
        put char x of theInput after tBackwards
    end repeat
    put "Backwards: " & tBackwards into sect4

    # SECTION SIX
    repeat with x = the number of words of theInput down to 1
        put word x of theInput after tReverse
        put space after tReverse
    end repeat
    put "Reverse Words: " & tReverse into sect5

    # SECTION SEVEN
    put sect1 & return & sect2 & return & sect3 & return & \
        sect4 & return & sect5 into fld "Output"
end mouseUp
```

Our code starts by declaring 11 local variables. Here, each of these variables will be discussed in the related section of code.

The code in the first section accomplishes a few things. First, it puts `empty` into the `Output` field. We do this to avoid confusion. Next, we take the user input and put it into the `theInput` variable. This makes referencing the user's text more efficient in later code. The third thing this section of code does is to put zero (`0`) into three local variables: `tVowel`, `tConsonant`, and `tOther`. If we do not put a numeric value in these variables, we run the risk of future errors. If we never use one of those variables and did not initialize it, any attempt to use that variable would result in unwanted results.

The second section of the code calculates the number of words, the first word, and the last word of the user input. We can simply use `the number of words`, `word 1`, and `last word` to obtain those results.

In the third section, we determine the number of characters by using `the number of characters of theInput` statement. Note that even spaces count as characters.

The fourth section is a bit more complicated. Here we count how many of the characters are vowels, how many are consonants, and how many are neither a vowel or consonant. The easiest way to accomplish this is to use a `repeat` loop using a local variable that starts at one (1) and goes to the last character, which we can determine by using `the len` or `the length`. As you can see with the provided code, for each character we evaluate it using the `is among` function.

In the fifth section, we have another `repeat` loop that starts with the last letter and works backwards to the first letter. Each character is put into a local variable, one after the other.

The sixth section is similar to the code in the fifth section. The difference is that in the fifth section, we used the `repeat` loop to go through the user input one character at a time. With the sixth section's code, we loop through the input one word at a time. Words are delineated by spaces.

Finally, the seventh section is where we combine the previous sectional inputs and post the results in the **Output** field.

Objective Complete - Mini Debriefing

With the 8 steps in this task completed, we will have a fully functional example of using custom properties. The user interface should be similar to the following screenshot:

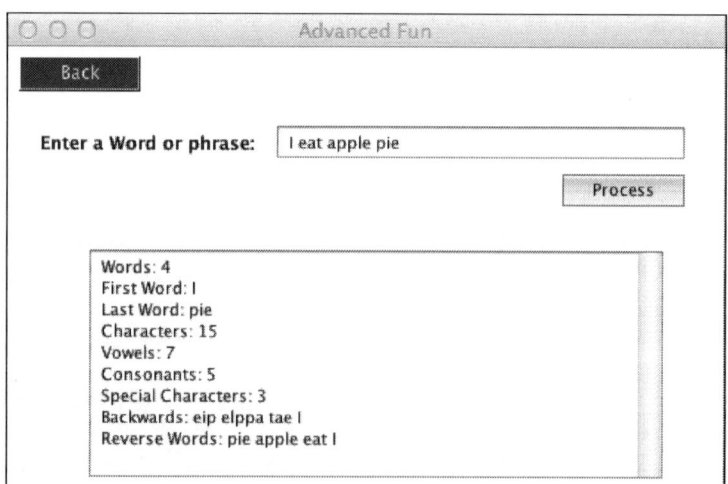

Programming the Arrays option

Arrays are a way to organize data in memory. You can think of arrays as being as simple as a list or as complicated as a spreadsheet. We use arrays in programming to help make our code efficient and to logically store data.

In this task we will create an array, populate it, sort it, and search it.

Engage Thrusters

1. Create a new card and name it `Arrays`.

2. Drag a Rectangle Button onto the card and make the following customizations using the properties inspector:

    1. Set the width to `82` and the height to `23`.

    2. Set the location to `49, 17`.

    3. Set the name of the button to `Back`.

    4. Set the label of the button to `Back`.

    5. Set the background color to blue.

    6. Set the foreground color to white.

    7. Set the text size to **12**.

    8. Add the following script to the **Back** button:

       ```
       on mouseUp
           go to card "Main"
       end mouseUp
       ```

3. Drag a Scrolling Field onto the card and make the following customizations using the properties inspector:

    1. Set the width to `384` and the height to `164`.

    2. Set the location to `248, 214`.

    3. Set the name of the button to `Output`.

    4. Set **Three D** to false.

4. Drag a Rectangle Button onto the card and make the following customizations using the properties inspector:

    1. Set the width to 82 and the height to 23.

    2. Set the location to 73, 79.

    3. Set the name of the button to Create.

    4. Set **Three D** to false.

    5. Add the following script to the Create button:

```
on mouseUp
    global gArrayFun

    put empty into gArrayFun
    put "gArrayFun Array initialized" into fld "Output"
end mouseUp
```

    This code initializes the global array gArrayFun and puts an appropriate message in our output box. Refer to the following screenshot for details:

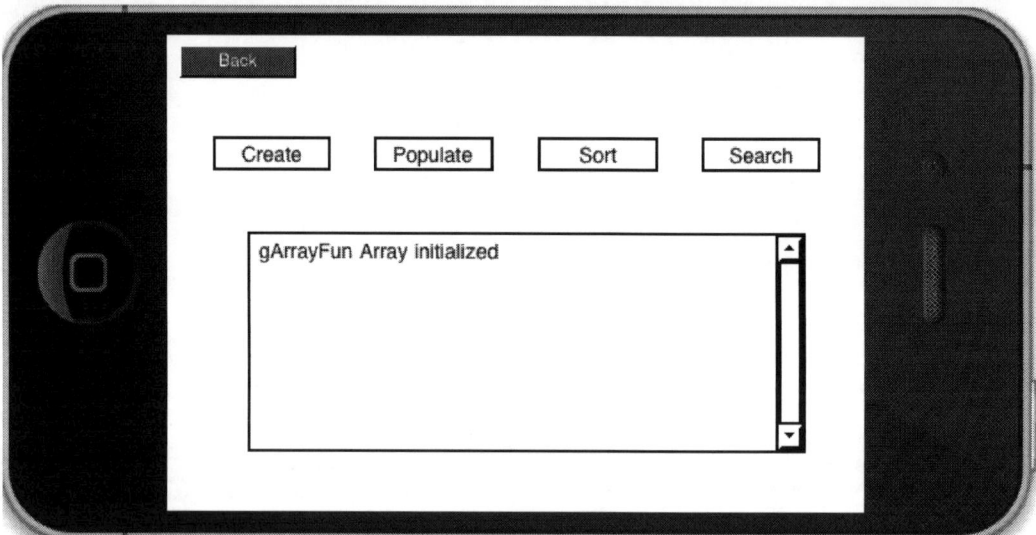

5. Drag a Rectangle Button onto the card and make the following customizations using the properties inspector:

   1. Set the width to `82` and the height to `23`.

   2. Set the location to `185`, `79`.

   3. Set the name of the button to `Populate`.

   4. Set **Three D** to false.

   5. Add the following script to the **Populate** button.

```
on mouseUp
    global gArrayFun
    local tOutput

    # SECTION ONE
    put "American Buffalo" into gArrayFun[1]
    put "Wild Pig" into gArrayFun[2]
    put "Komodo Dragon" into gArrayFun[3]
    put "Prairie Dog" into gArrayFun[4]
    put "Giant Panda" into gArrayFun[5]
    put "Water Buffalo" into gArrayFun[6]
    put "Elephant Seal" into gArrayFun[7]
    put "Irish Setter" into gArrayFun[8]
    put "Sea Urchin" into gArrayFun[9]
    put "Guinea Pig" into gArrayFun[10]

    # SECTION TWO
    repeat with x = 1 to 10
        put gArrayFun[x] & return after tOutput
    end repeat

    put tOutput into fld "Output"
end mouseUp
```

The first section of this code populates 10 animal names into the array. Each array location is referenced in brackets after the array name. In the second section, the code steps through the array, populating the local variable tOuptut, one line at a time with the values held in the array. As you can see from the following screenshot, the array values are displayed as they were entered, not in any other order:

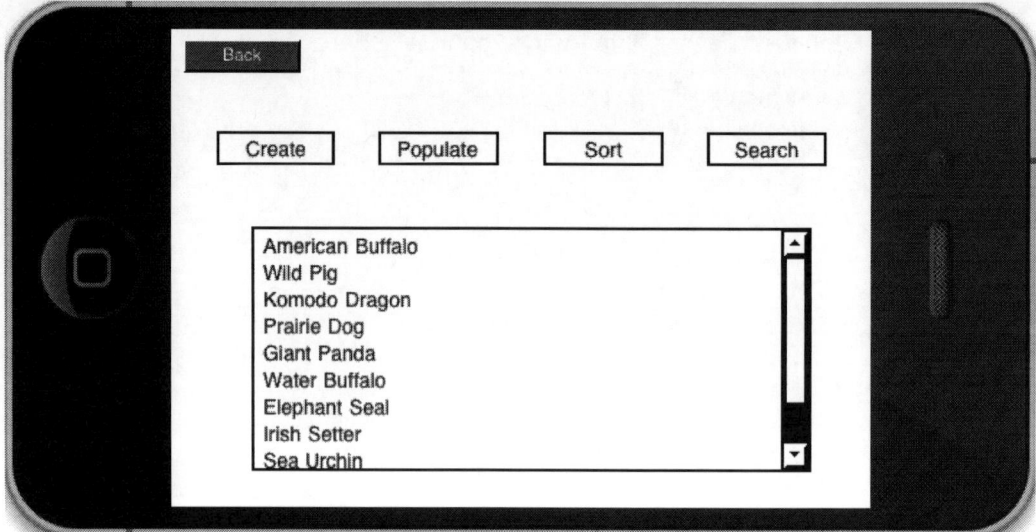

6. Drag a Rectangle Button onto the card and make the following customizations using the properties inspector:

    1. Set the width to 82 and the height to 23.

    2. Set the location to 297, 79.

    3. Set the name of the button to Sort.

    4. Set **Three D** to false.

    5. Add the following script to the **Sort** button:

```
on mouseUp
    global gArrayFun
    local tData

    # SECTION ONE
    combine gArrayFun using return
    sort lines of gArrayFun
    put gArrayFun into fld "Output"
```

```
      # SECTION TWO
  put gArrayFun into tData
  repeat with x = 1 to 10
    put line x of tData into gArrayFun[x]
  end repeat
end mouseUp
```

This code does two things. First, in the first section, it uses the `combine` function to convert our `gArrayFun[]` array into a regular variable. This allows us to sort the new variable's lines. At the end of this section's code, we output the sorted results in our **Output** field.

In the second section, we need to put the sorted data back into an array. We do this by stepping through a `repeat` loop, one variable at a time until all values are back in the array. This time, they are in the sorted order. Here is a screenshot of our results:

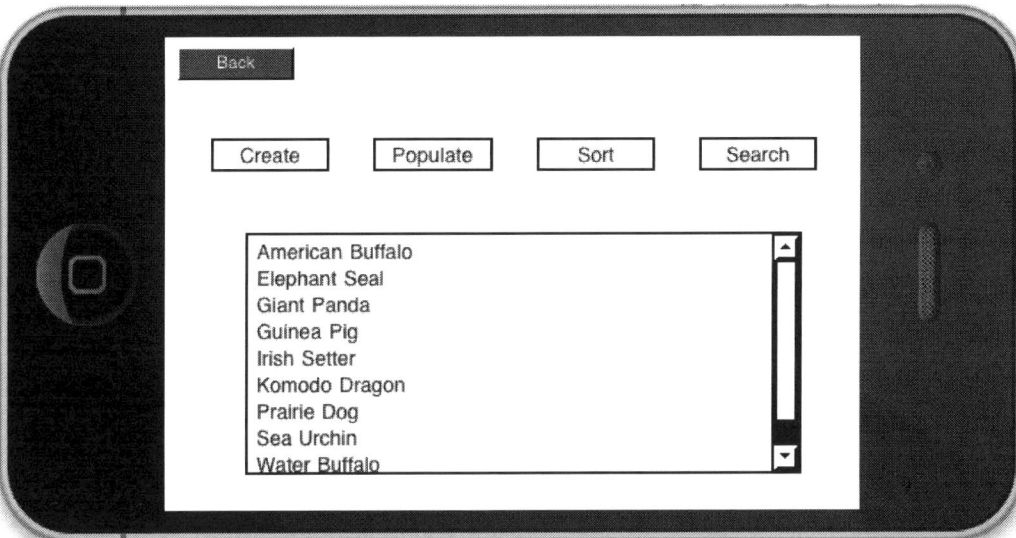

7. Drag a Rectangle Button onto the card and make the following customizations using the properties inspector:

    1. Set the width to 82 and the height to 23.

    2. Set the location to 409, 79.

    3. Set the name of the button to Search.

    4. Set **Three D** to false.

5. Add the following script to the **Search** button:

```
on mouseUp
   global gArrayFun
   local userInput, tResults

   # SECTION ONE
   ask "What do you want to search for?" titled
   "Enter Search Criteria"
   put it into  userInput

   # SECTION TWO
   repeat with x = 1 to 10
      if userInput is among the words of gArrayFun[x] then
         put gArrayFun[x] & return after tResults
         end if
      end repeat

      # SECTION THREE
      put "Your Search Results:" & return & tResults into
      fld "Output"
end mouseUp
```

In the first section of this code, we prompt the user for input and place that input into the `userInput` local variable. For testing, you can use the word `Pig`, as there are multiple occurrences of it in our array. Refer to the following screenshot for details:

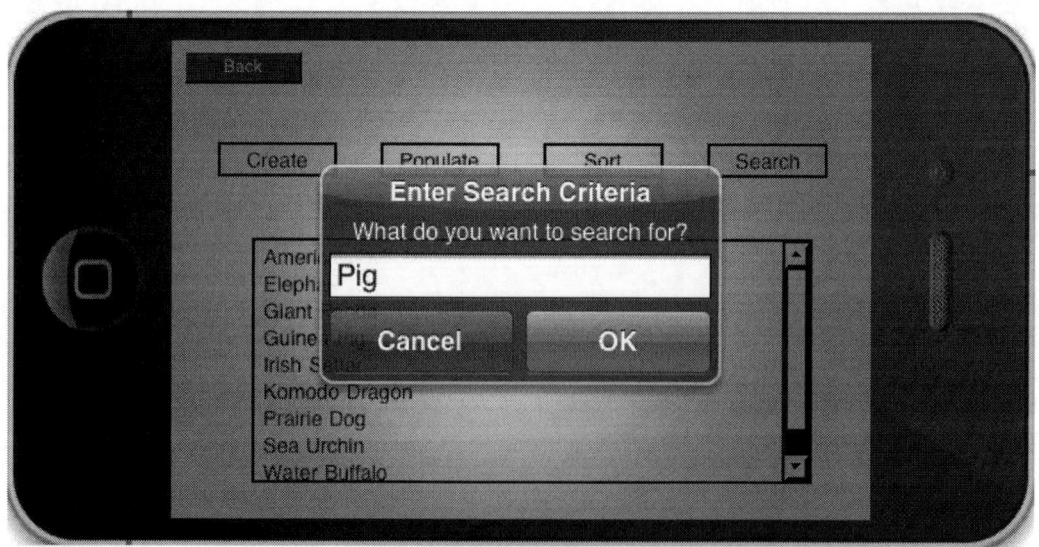

In the second section, we use a `repeat` loop to check each value in our array. We are checking to see if the search criterion we entered (`Pig`) is contained (`is among`) the array values. If we find a match, we add the full array value and a return in the `tResults` local variable.

In the third section, we output the results to the **Output** field. Refer to the following screenshot for results:

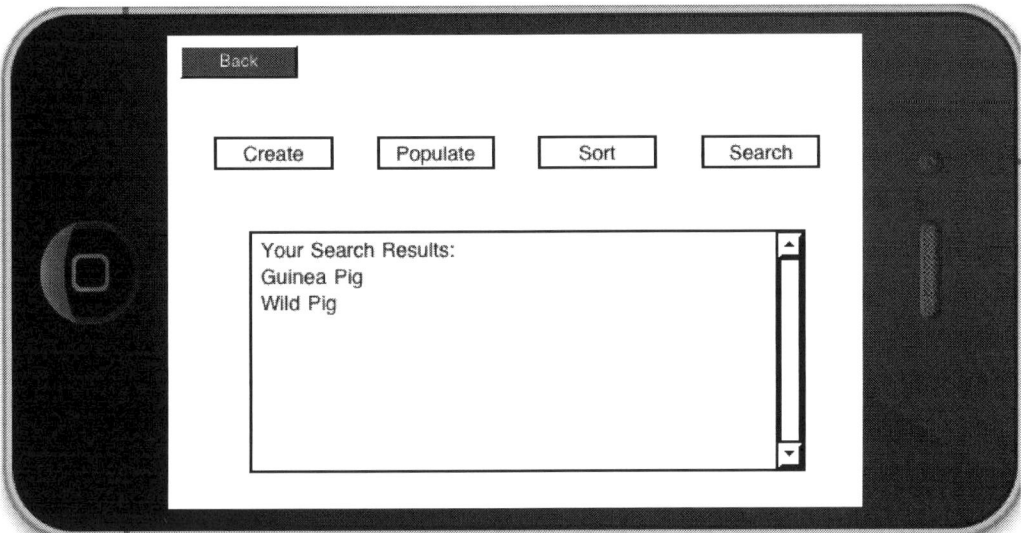

8. At the card level, add the follow script to the Arrays card:

```
on preOpenCard
    put empty into fld "Output"
end preOpenCard
```

This script simply clears the output scrolling list field each time the card is opened.

Objective Complete - Mini Debriefing

We completed this task in only eight steps. Our **ArrayFun** card has functionality to create, populate, sort, and search our array. Our final UI, before any of the buttons are selected, is depicted in the following screenshot:

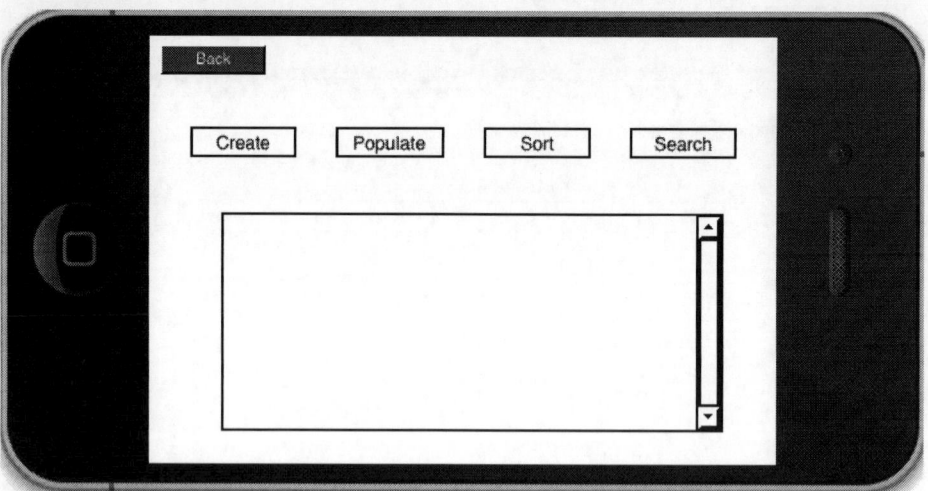

Mission Accomplished

Our project consisted of creating a single mobile application that demonstrates six sets of advanced features of LiveCode. Our main interface is shown in the following screenshot:

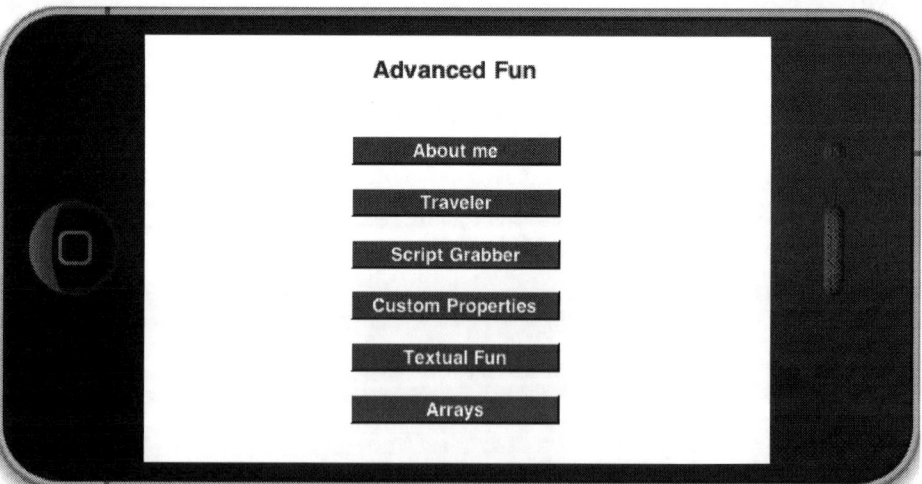

The advanced features we demonstrated included detecting system information, contextually aware objects, assigning scripts to objects programmatically, assigning and using custom properties, evaluating and manipulating text, and arrays.

A Hotshot Challenge

Your Hotshot challenge for this project has the following two parts:

> **Part 1**: Revisit the **All About Me** functionality we created in the first task. Modify the code so that you can precisely (within 1 MB) display how much RAM is available to a user .

> **Part 2**: Update the **ArraysFun** card functionality so that the appropriate error handling is in place. For example, you cannot search or sort an array that has not been created or populated.

Good luck!

Project 10

In-app Purchases and Advertising for iOS and Android

There are three primary ways to make money from mobile applications. The most traditional method is to sell your app via the app store / marketplace associated with your distribution platform (that is, iOS or Android). Two additional methods of earning revenue are to allow users to purchase digital goods from within your app and to support third-party advertising. In this project, we will explore how to implement in-app purchases and advertising using LiveCode.

Mission Briefing

For this final project, we will build an application that incorporates in-app purchasing and in-app advertising. There will be some specific differences in how we implement these schemas depending upon our targeted development platform. We will highlight those differences so there is no confusion.

Our application will consist of a single stack and single card housing a simple user interface. We will have a title, five buttons, and an on-screen persistent ad.

We will call our app **IAPAA** for **in-app purchases and advertising**.

The following diagram is a mockup of our app's main interface:

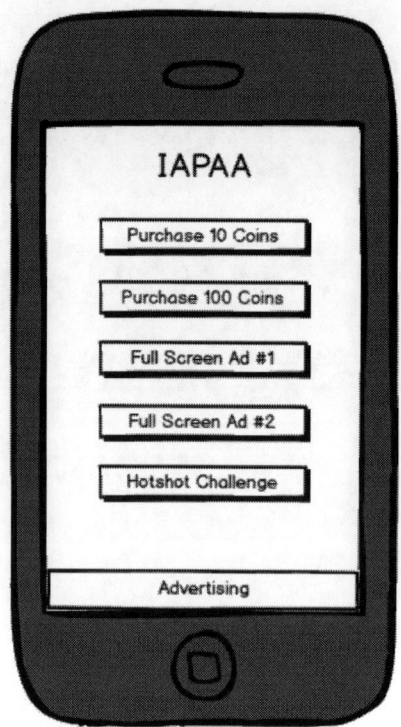

Why Is It Awesome?

This project will help you learn how to implement in-app purchasing and advertising using LiveCode. This is an important skillset to have. The good news is that it is not terribly difficult. Once you complete this project, you will be able to incorporate in-app advertising and purchasing in your own mobile apps.

You will learn how to implement these two important features for both iOS and Android devices.

Your Hotshot Objectives

In order to complete this project, you will progress through the following tasks:

- ▶ Creating the main stack
- ▶ Creating the user interface
- ▶ Integrating on-load advertising
- ▶ Integrating banner advertising

> ▸ Integrating Full Screen Ad #1
>
> ▸ Integrating Full Screen Ad #2
>
> ▸ Integrating in-app purchases

Creating the main stack

Let's start by creating the main stack for our IAPAA mobile app. For this application, we will only have one stack and one card. First, we will create the main stack.

Engage Thrusters

1. Let's begin by creating a new main stack named `IAPAA`. Using the properties inspector, make the following customizations to the main stack:

    1. Change the size of the stack to `480 x 320` pixels. This will give us a portrait orientation.

    2. Set the name of the stack to `IAPAA`.

    3. Set the title of the stack to `IAPAA`.

    4. Set the background color to white.

2. Rename the default card to `Main`.

Objective Complete - Mini Debriefing

When we created the main stack, LiveCode created a default card for us. In our next task, we will configure the **Main** card to house our user interface.

Creating the user interface

You are now ready to create the user interface for your IAPAA mobile application. Our interface will only consist of a single title and five buttons.

Engage Thrusters

1. Drag a Label field onto the card **Main** and make the following customizations using the properties inspector:

    1. Set the width to `316` and the height to `36`.

    2. Set the location to `160, 38`.

    3. Set the name of the field to `Title`.

4. Set the text size to **24**.

5. Bold and center-align the text.

6. Change the contents to `IAPAA`.

7. Set the foreground color to black.

2. Drag a Rectangle Button onto the card and make the following customizations using the properties inspector:

    1. Set the width to `275` and the height to `36`.

    2. Set the location to `160, 102`.

    3. Set the name of the button to `coins_10`.

    4. Set the label of the button to `Purchase 10 Coins`.

    5. Set the background color to blue.

    6. Set the foreground color to white.

    7. Set the text size to **18**.

    8. Bold the text.

3. Drag a Rectangle Button onto the card and make the following customizations using the properties inspector:

    1. Set the width to `275` and the height to `36`.

    2. Set the location to `160, 163`.

    3. Set the name of the button to `coins_100`.

    4. Set the label of the button to `Purchase 100 Coins`.

    5. Set the background color to blue.

    6. Set the foreground color to white.

    7. Set the text size to **18**.

    8. Bold the text.

4. Drag a Rectangle Button onto the card and make the following customizations using the properties inspector:

    1. Set the width to `275` and the height to `36`.

    2. Set the location to `160, 223`.

    3. Set the name of the button to `full_ad1`.

    4. Set the label of the button to `Full Screen Ad #1`.

5. Set the background color to blue.

6. Set the foreground color to white.

7. Set the text size to **18**.

8. Bold the text.

5. Drag a Rectangle Button onto the card and make the following customizations using the properties inspector:

    1. Set the width to `275` and the height to `36`.

    2. Set the location to `160, 284`.

    3. Set the name of the button to `full_ad2`.

    4. Set the label of the button to `Full Screen Ad #2`.

    5. Set the background color to blue.

    6. Set the foreground color to white.

    7. Set the text size to **18**.

    8. Bold the text.

6. Drag a Rectangle Button onto the card and make the following customizations using the properties inspector:

    1. Set the width to `275` and the height to `36`.

    2. Set the location to `160, 344`.

    3. Set the name of the button to `hotshot`.

    4. Set the label of the button to `Hotshot Challenge`.

    5. Set the background color to blue.

    6. Set the foreground color to white.

    7. Set the text size to **18**.

    8. Bold the text.

Objective Complete - Mini Debriefing

The user interface was pretty quick to create. We only added one text label and five buttons to our main stack's default card. So far, we have not added any scripts to implement in-app purchases or advertising. We will accomplish that in subsequent tasks.

Your interface should look similar to the following screenshot:

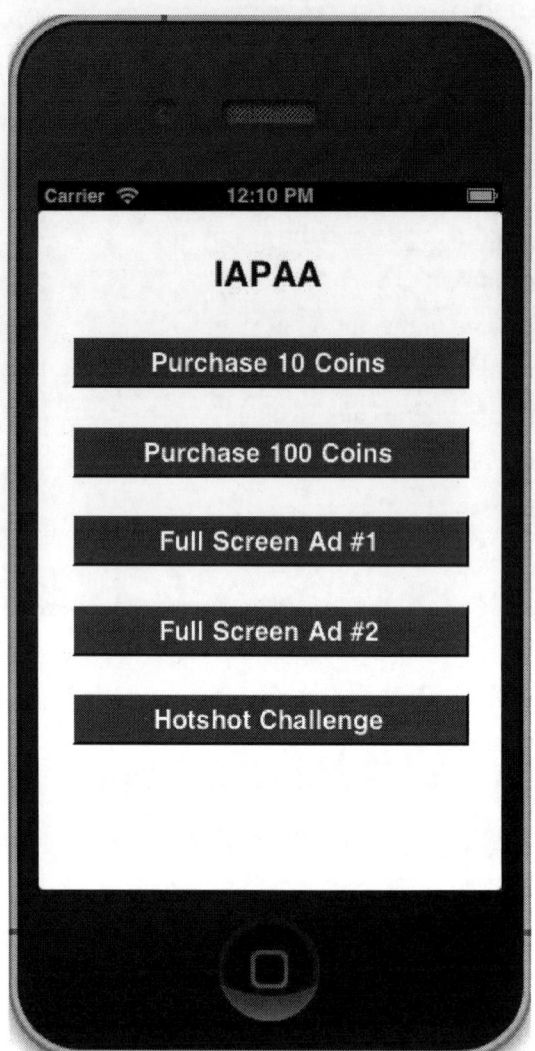

Classified Intel

You'll note that we left empty space at the bottom of our interface. That is where we will place our banner ad in a later task.

Integrating on-load advertising

There are a host of advertising agencies that support in-app mobile advertising. The one we will use for this task is inner-active, an app monetization service. It supports several types of advertising, all free to the developer. More importantly, **RunRev**, the owners of LiveCode, have a partnership with inner-active. This makes integrating in-app advertising relatively easy.

For this task, we will add an advertisement when the app is initially loaded. No changes to our UI will be required.

Prepare for Lift Off

You will need to create a free account at inner-active. Their site is `www.inner-active.com`. You will also need a LiveCode account (also free). You should have created your LiveCode account when you obtained your copy of LiveCode.

Once you have these accounts, you will be ready to proceed with this task.

Engage Thrusters

1. Log in to your LiveCode account and select the **Store** link at the top of the page. At the LiveCode store, select the **Advertising** link in the left-hand side navigation pane. Refer to the following image for details:

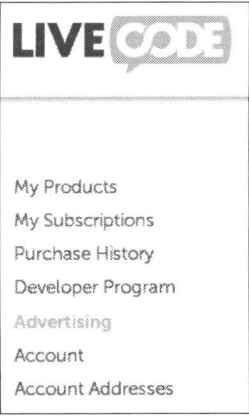

2. Login to your inner-active account via the LiveCode site.

 If you are new to inner-active, you should take the time to explore the **Settings** tab where you can configure your profile information to include payment details.

3. Select the **Add App** tab and enter the information as shown in the following screenshot:

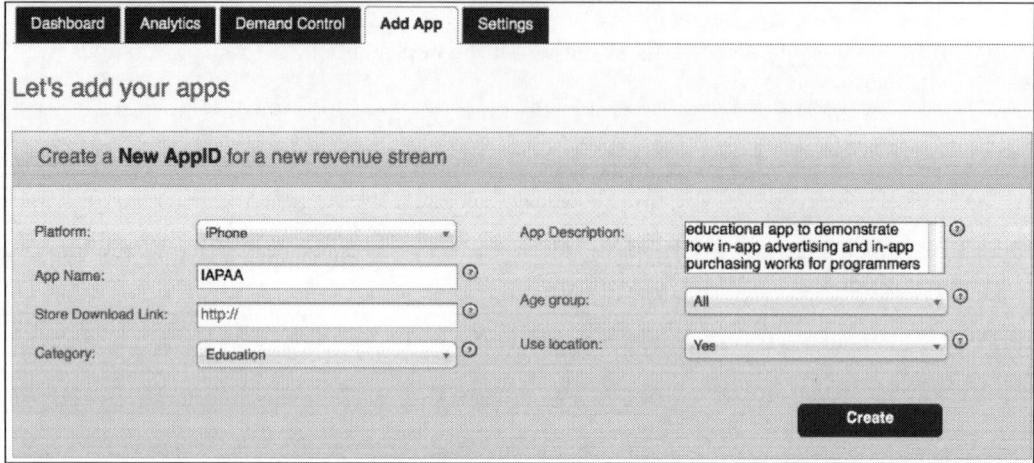

1. Select **iPhone** for the **Platform**.

2. Enter IAPAA for the **App Name**.

3. Leave the **Store Download Link** section blank.

4. Select **Education** for the **Category**.

5. Enter the following **App Description:** educational app to demonstrate how in-app advertising and in-app purchasing works for programmers.

6. Leave the **Age Group** set to **All**.

7. Select **Yes** for **Use Location**.

4. Click the **Create** button to create a new App ID. In just a few moments, you will have an App ID created for you. Take note of the App ID; you will use it in your mobile application in the next step. This App ID will be used by inner-active to track the amount of advertising your app receives.

 Your App ID will be unique. The **three19_IAPAA_iPhone** App ID is used in this project for illustrative purposes. You should be sure to use your own App ID so that any ad revenue and statistics are correctly attributed to you.

5. Next, we will add LiveCode script to our application so that a full screen ad will be displayed each time the app is launched. Enter the following lines of code in the **Main** card.

```
on preOpenCard
  mobileAdRegister "three19_IAPAA_iPhone"
  mobileAdCreate "Ad001", "full screen", (0,0)
end preOpenCard
```

LiveCode gives us the ability to add mobile advertising with as few as two lines of code. Our first line of code makes a call to the `mobileAdRegister` command. We pass this command the App ID created by inner-active. This command allows us to use the App ID along with other LiveCode functions.

Our second line of code uses the `mobileAdCreate` command to instantiate the ad. We passed three parameters to the command. First, we pass `Ad001` as the name of the ad. This can be anything we want it to be. We can reference the ad by the name we assign just as if it were a global variable. The second parameter is `full screen` as the type. LiveCode allows us the option to have a banner, text, or full screen ad. If no type is passed, a banner ad will be created. Finally, we pass the top left pixel location of our ad `(0,0)`.

When you test the app in a simulator, or on your actual device, you should have a full screen ad displayed as illustrated in the following screenshot:

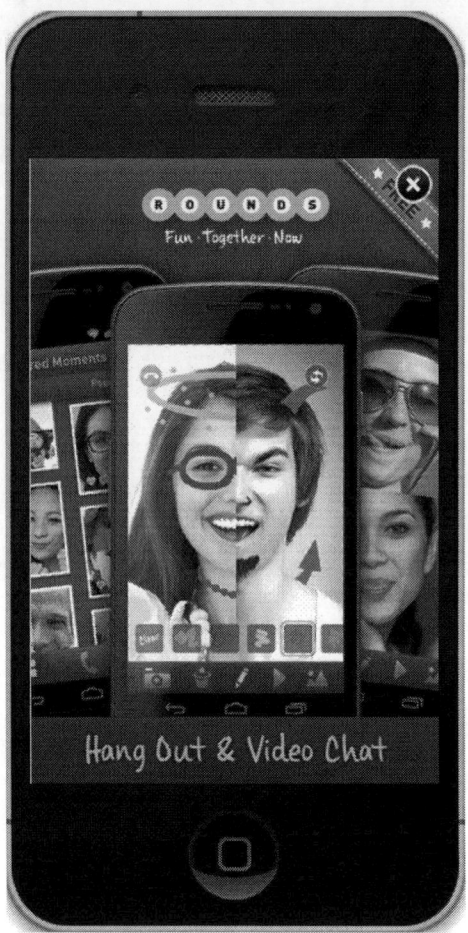

Objective Complete - Mini Debriefing

In this task, we created an inner-active mobile app monetization account. Using that account and two lines of code, we created a full screen ad that will be displayed each time the app is loaded.

Integrating banner advertising

In this task, we will add a banner advertisement to our main screen using the `mobileAdCreate` command.

Engage Thrusters

Add the following code to the **Main** card script:

```
on openCard
  local adData

  put "30" into adData["refresh"]
  put "24" into adData["age"]
  put "Female" into adData["gender"]

  mobileAdCreate "Ad002", "banner", (0,410), adData
end openCard
```

This is the only code we need to add a banner advertisement on the main card. As you can see, we created a local array called `adData`. We use this array to hold values for `refresh`, `age`, and `gender`. There are additional attributes available including distribution id, phone number, keywords, coordinates, and location.

For our example, we only use the `refresh`, `age`, and `gender` attributes. Refresh refers to how often you want the ad to refresh. The default is two minutes, but you can enter a value between 30 and 300 seconds. The age refers to the age of the target user. The gender value can be `male`, `female`, `m`, or `f`.

The call to the `mobileAdCreate` command now includes the ad name (`Ad002`), type (`banner`), location (`0,410`), and metadata (`adData`).

Objective Complete - Mini Debriefing

For this task we entered code in the openCard command to facilitate adding a banner on the bottom of the application's main screen. We set the ad to refresh every 30 seconds and targeted 24 year-old females. The following screenshot shows our work in action:

Integrating Full Screen Ad #1

Our next task is to program the button labelled **Full Screen Ad #1**. We will do this by adding code to the **full_ad1** button.

Engage Thrusters

Add the following code to the button **full_ad1**:

```
on mouseUp

    # SECTION ONE
    set the vis of btn "coins_10" to false
    set the vis of btn "coins_100" to false
    set the vis of btn "full_ad1" to false
    set the vis of btn "full_ad2" to false
    set the vis of btn "movie_ad" to false

    # SECTION TWO
    mobileAdSetVisible "Ad002", false

    # SECTION THREE
    mobileAdCreate "Ad003", "text", (0,240)

    # SECTION FOUR
    wait 15 seconds
    mobileAdSetVisible "Ad003", false
    mobileAdSetVisible "Ad002", true
    --
    set the vis of btn "coins_10" to true
    set the vis of btn "coins_100" to true
    set the vis of btn "full_ad1" to true
    set the vis of btn "full_ad2" to true
    set the vis of btn "movie_ad" to true


end mouseUp
```

There are four sections to this code. The first two sections hide the on screen objects so that our new ad can be clearly displayed. In the first section, we are setting the visibility of our five buttons to false. In the second section, we make a call to the `mobileAdSetVisible` command and pass `Ad002` (our banner ad) and `false` to it. This tells LiveCode to hide that specific ad.

In section three, we instantiate a new ad and give it the name `Ad003`. The second parameter we pass is `text`, which is one of the three types (banner, text, and full screen) that we can use. Our final parameter is the starting location for the ad on screen.

Our final section, section four, waits 15 seconds, hides the new full screen text ad (`Ad003`), redisplays the banner ad (`Ad002`), and sets the interface buttons to `true`.

Objective Complete - Mini Debriefing

This task was made easy by LiveCode's mobile ad support library. We introduced the `mobileAdSetVisible` command so that we can selectively display and hide ads we create with the `mobileAdCreate` command.

The following screenshot shows our new full screen ad:

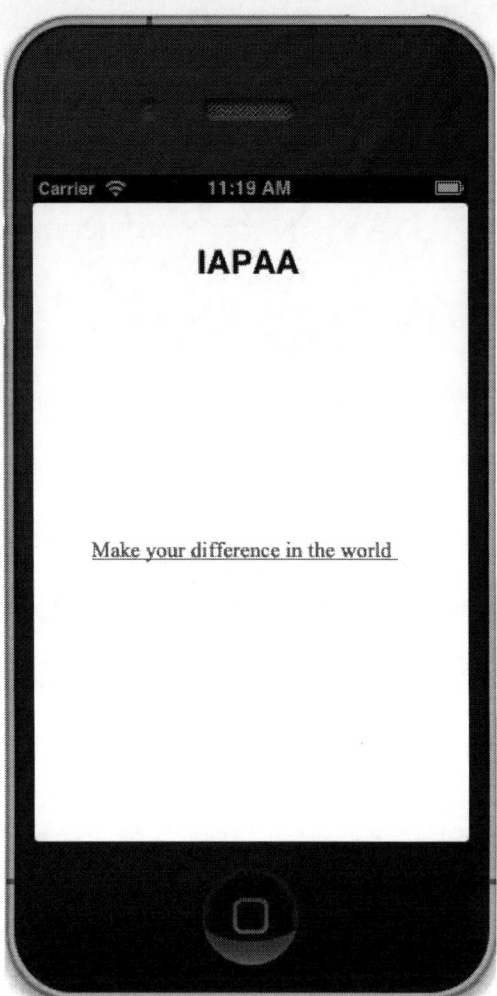

Integrating Full Screen Ad #2

Some mobile application developers place ads that are displayed when the user navigates between cards. We can handle this task with another call to the `mobileAdCreate` command. After you finish this task, you will be able to click on the button labelled **Full Screen Ad #2** to see a new full screen ad. The ad will remain in place until the user closes out of it by clicking the **x** in the upper right-hand corner.

Engage Thrusters

Add the following lines of code to the script of button **full_ad2**:

```
on mouseUp
  local adData

  put "45" into adData["age"]
  put "male" into adData["gender"]

  mobileAdCreate "Ad004", "full screen", (0,0), adData
end mouseUp
```

We created a new full screen ad titled `Ad004` and targeted 45 year-old males.

When instantiated, the full screen ad will remain on screen until the user closes it. Tapping the **x** in the upper right-hand corner will close the ad. This technique is used when you want your users to see the ad and force them to close it.

Objective Complete - Mini Debriefing

We created an additional full screen add by making a call to the `mobileAdCreate` command.

Integrating in-app purchases

Integrating in-app purchases is a complex task; and it is different for iOS and Android mobile apps. In this task, we will cover the key commands and processes used for integrating in-app purchases on iOS devices.

Prepare for Lift Off

In order to complete this task, you will need to have **Apple Developer** and **iTunes Connect** accounts.

Engage Thrusters

1. Log in to your **iTunes Connect** account and ensure you have accepted the most recent **iOS Paid Applications Agreement** from Apple. The agreement can be found in the **Contracts, Tax, and Banking** section of the **iTunes Connect** site. The following screenshot shows the message that will be displayed to you when you have not accepted the most current agreement:

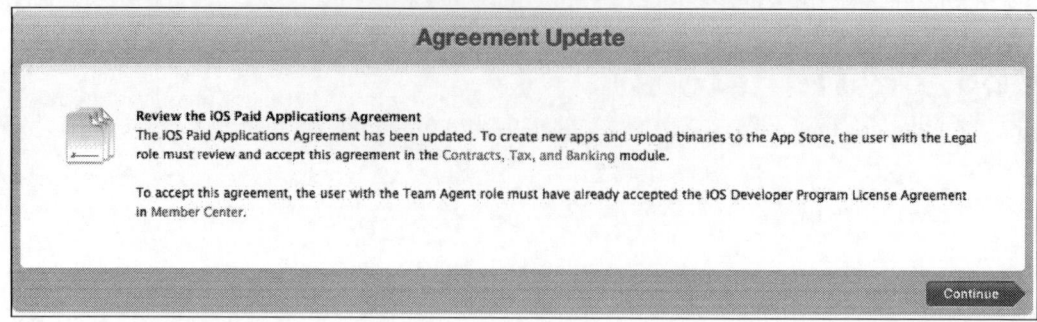

2. Add your app to **iTunes Connect**. Once you have the required information entered, select the **Manage In-App Purchases** button. You are now ready to select the **Create New** button. Refer to the following screenshot for details:

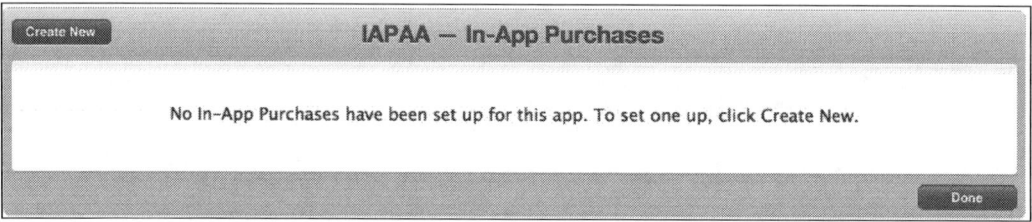

3. Next, you will be prompted to select a purchase type. For the purpose of this task, select **Consumable**. Refer to the following screenshot for a detailed description of that purchase type:

Consumable

A consumable In-App Purchase must be purchased every time the user downloads it. One-time services, such as fish food in a fishing app, are usually implemented as consumables.

Select

4. You will be presented with a web form that has several mandatory fields:

    ❑ **Reference Name**: This is used for your reference. A typical reference name would be **10 Coin Pack**.

    ❑ **Product ID**: This is a unique product identifier. A typical product ID would be **IAPAA10CoinPack**.

    ❑ **Price Tier**: This is used to select the purchase price associated with the reference name.

    You will need to add at least one language and a screenshot. Once you have all this information entered, you can select **Save**. The result will be in the form of a unique Apple ID that you will use in LiveCode.

    The example in the following screenshot shows four purchases for non-consumable items. This means that once the user makes the purchase, they will always have the purchased item.

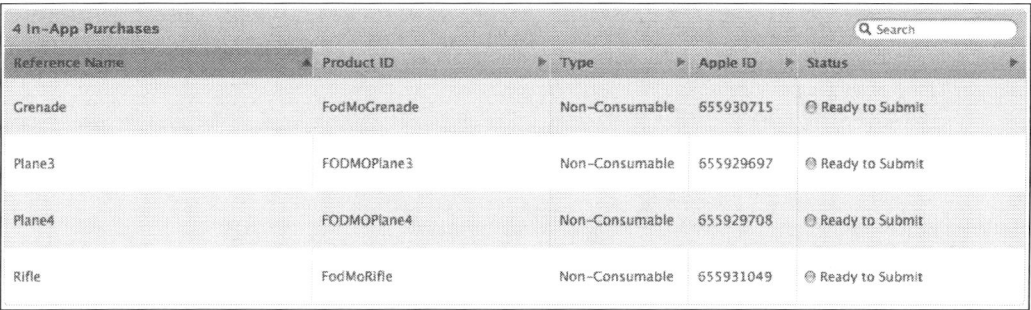

5. Now you are ready to write the necessary code in LiveCode to support the in-app advertising. There are several LiveCode commands and functions that you should become familiar with. A brief summary of these commands and functions is provided in the following table. You should consult the LiveCode

Command / Function	Description
mobileCanMakePurchase()	This function returns "true" or "false."
mobilePurchaseCreate productID	This command creates a new purchase.
mobilePurchases()	This function returns a list of all active purchases.
mobilePurchaseConfirmDelivery purchaseID	This command is used to communicate with the App Store to confirm purchase fulfillment.

Objective Complete - Mini Debriefing

That is it; you completed this task. It is clear that LiveCode is only one part of the solution regarding iOS in-app purchases. You must also have an Apple Developer and iTunes Connect account.

Mission Accomplished

You completed this project and now have sufficient experience to implement in-app advertising in your own mobile applications. You also have an idea of what it takes to support in-app purchases.

Your final app interface should look similar to the following screenshot:

A Hotshot Challenge

Your final Hotshot challenge is to program the **Hotshot Challenge** button in this project. Create a unique mobile ad experience based on the work you competed in this project.

Have fun and good luck!

Mobile App Development Primer

Developing apps for mobile devices requires knowledge of the platform-specific submission process. LiveCode allows you to publish apps in iOS and Android formats, and there are unique considerations for both. This appendix covers preparing your LiveCode apps for submission to the appropriate app store.

iOS apps

There are several settings to pay attention to prior to submitting your app to Apple's App Store. Fortunately, LiveCode gives us control of all of these settings in a single **Standalone Application Settings** dialog screen.

The Standalone Application Settings window

As you can see in the following screenshot, the **Standalone Application Settings** dialog window has a large number of options that must be reviewed prior to publishing an iOS binary file:

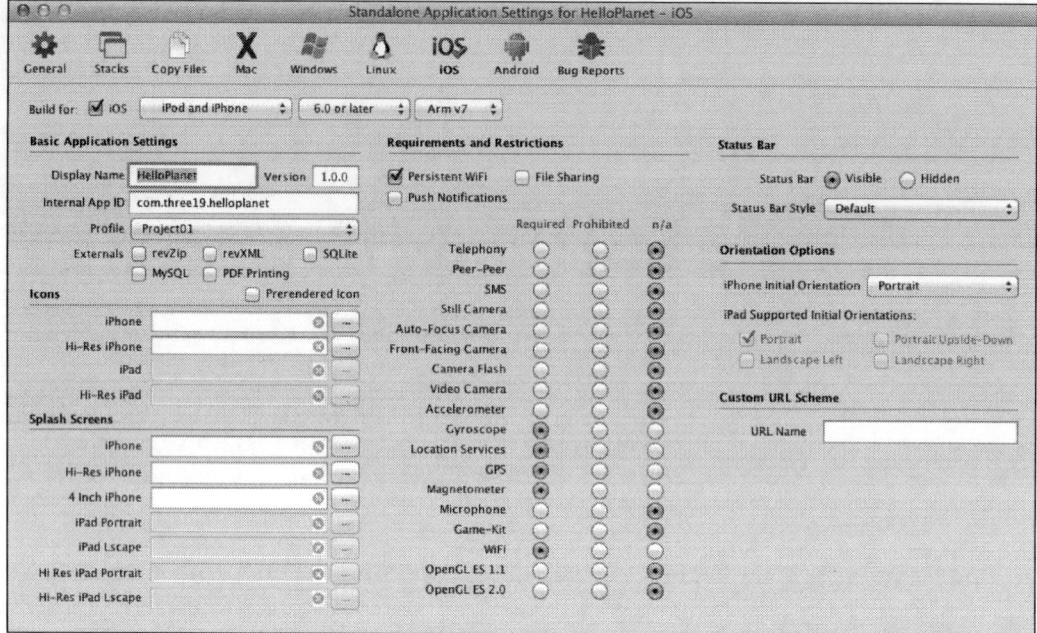

This dialog window's options are divided into four sections as indicated in the following screenshot:

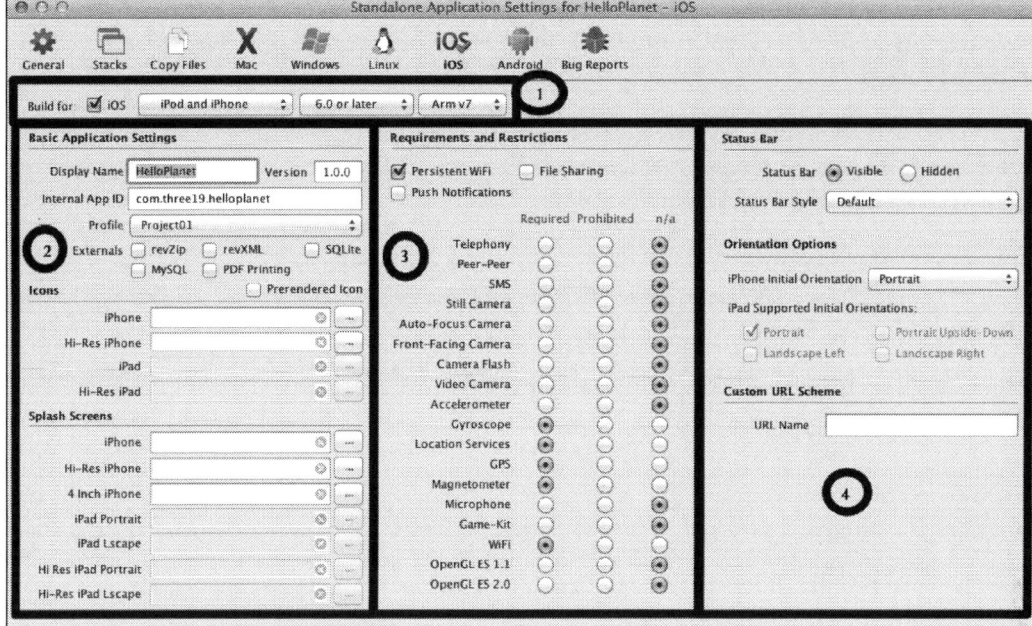

The first section is the **Build for:** area of the window.

If you want LiveCode to publish a binary for iOS, the **iOS** checkbox must be selected.

You will use the first pull-down menu to select which iOS device or devices you want your app to support. The options are: **iPod, iPhone and iPad**, **iPod and iPhone**, and **iPad**.

The second pull-down menu dictates what the minimum iOS version that your app will support. The available options include: **3.1.3 or later**, **4.0 or later**, **5.0 or later**, and **6.1 or later**.

The third pull-down menu allows you to select which instruction set to build for. There are three options available as follows:

- ► **Universal**: This generates a build for ARMv6 and ARMv7 devices. Selecting this option will result in a larger binary file.
- ► **Arm v6**: This build will run on ARMv6 and ARMv7 devices.
- ► **Arm v7**: This binary will only work on ARMv7 devices.

The second section is comprised of **Basic Application Settings**, **Icons**, and **Splash Screens**.

There are five settings in the **Basic Application Settings** area of the dialog. The descriptions for each of these settings are as follows:

- ► **Display Name**: This is the label that will be displayed on the SpringBoard or Home screen of the iOS device
- ► **Version**: The version number entered must match the data you enter in the App Store
- ► **Internal App ID**: This is the bundle identifier that matches your iOS provisioning profile
- ► **Profile**: Here you will select the provisioning profile associated with your app
- ► **Externals**: If your app uses any of the listed externals, they must be selected here prior to generating a binary file

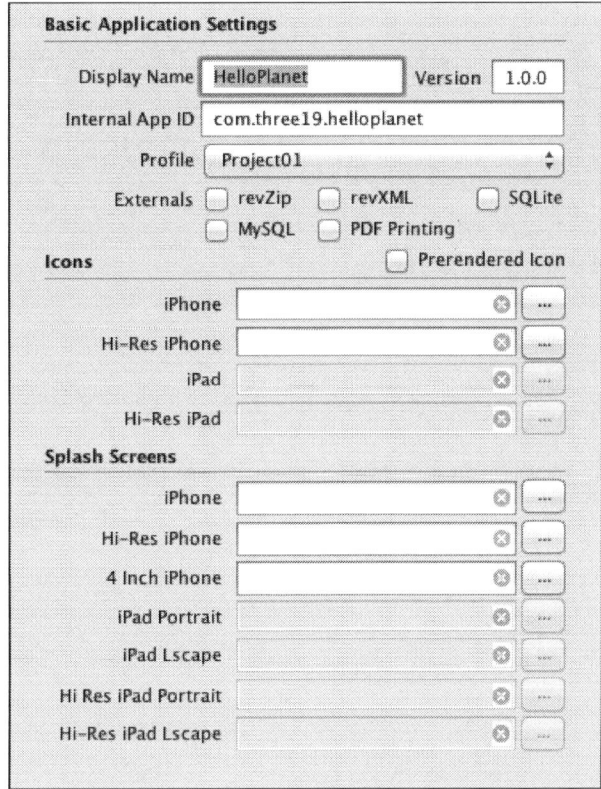

 Apple's requirements for app icons are very specific. It is a good idea to review those requirements prior to submitting each app. This will help ensure that you are apprised of any changes from Apple.

Based on your target devices, you will need to provide two or four icons. Each icon's size requirement is listed as follows:

► **iPhone** – 57 x 57 pixels

► **Hi-Res iPhone** – 114 x 114 pixels

► **iPad** – 72 x 72 pixels

► **Hi-Res iPad** – 144 x 144 pixels

There is also a **Prerendered Icon** checkbox. Selecting this box indicates that your icons already have a tint and glossy effect applied to them. Again, check the current Apple submission requirements.

The next area of this section is **Splash Screens**. There are up to seven splash screens that you will need to provide, depending upon your device and orientation selections. Dimensions of each splash screen are listed as follows:

- ▸ **iPhone** – 320 x 480 pixels

- ▸ **Hi-Res iPhone** – 640 x 960 pixels

- ▸ **4 Inch iPhone** – 640 x 1,136 pixels

- ▸ **iPad Portrait** – 768 x 1,024 pixels

- ▸ **iPad Lscape** – 1,024 x 768 pixels

- ▸ **Hi-Res iPad Portrait** – 1,536 x 2,048 pixels

- ▸ **Hi-Res iPad Lscape** – 2,048 x 1,496 pixels

The third section is **Requirements and Restrictions**. There are three checkboxes and 18 radio box selections to be made in the **Requirements and Restrictions** area of the dialog box.

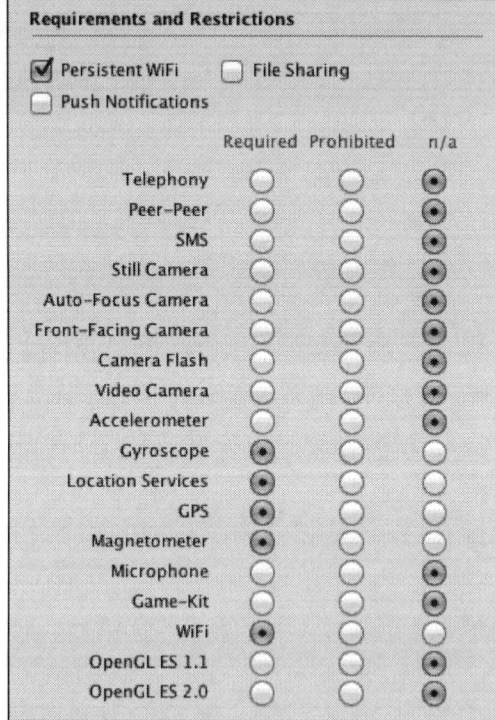

- ▸ **Persistent WiFi**: Select this option if your mobile app requires a persistent Wi-Fi connection to operate.

- ▶ **File Sharing**: This feature refers to the **File Sharing** option in iTunes. Select this option if your app requires iTunes file sharing to be enabled.

- ▶ **Push Notifications**: Select this option if your app will be programmed to receive push notifications.

- ▶ Use the 18 radio buttons to designate which services your app needs or should be prohibited from using.

The fourth and last section is comprised of **Status Bar**, **Orientation Options**, and **Custom URL Scheme**.

This final area of the **Standalone Application Settings** dialog window is as follows:

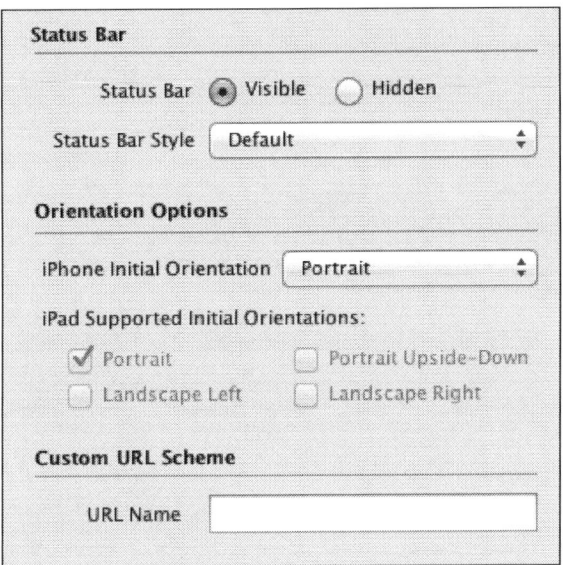

- ▶ **Status Bar**: Here, you can select if you want the iOS device's status bar to be visible or hidden while your application is on screen. If you select **Visible**, you will also want to select a **Status Bar Style** option. The style options are **Default**, **Black Opaque**, and **Black Translucent**.

- ▶ **Orientation Options**: Set the **iPhone Initial Orientation** field to **Portrait**, **Portrait Upside-Down**, **Landscape Left**, or **Landscape Right**. If your app will be deployed on iPads, you will select one or more of the **iPad Supported Initial Orientations** options.

 Initial orientations are important because they determine which splash screen to display while your app is loading.

> ▶ **Custom URL Scheme**: This feature allows you to design a custom URL that can be used to launch your app from within another app.

Android apps

When we develop apps for Android devices, we have several specific settings to set in the **Standalone Application Settings** dialog screen.

As you can see in the following screenshot, the **Standalone Application Settings** dialog window has a large number of options that must be reviewed prior to publishing an Android binary file:

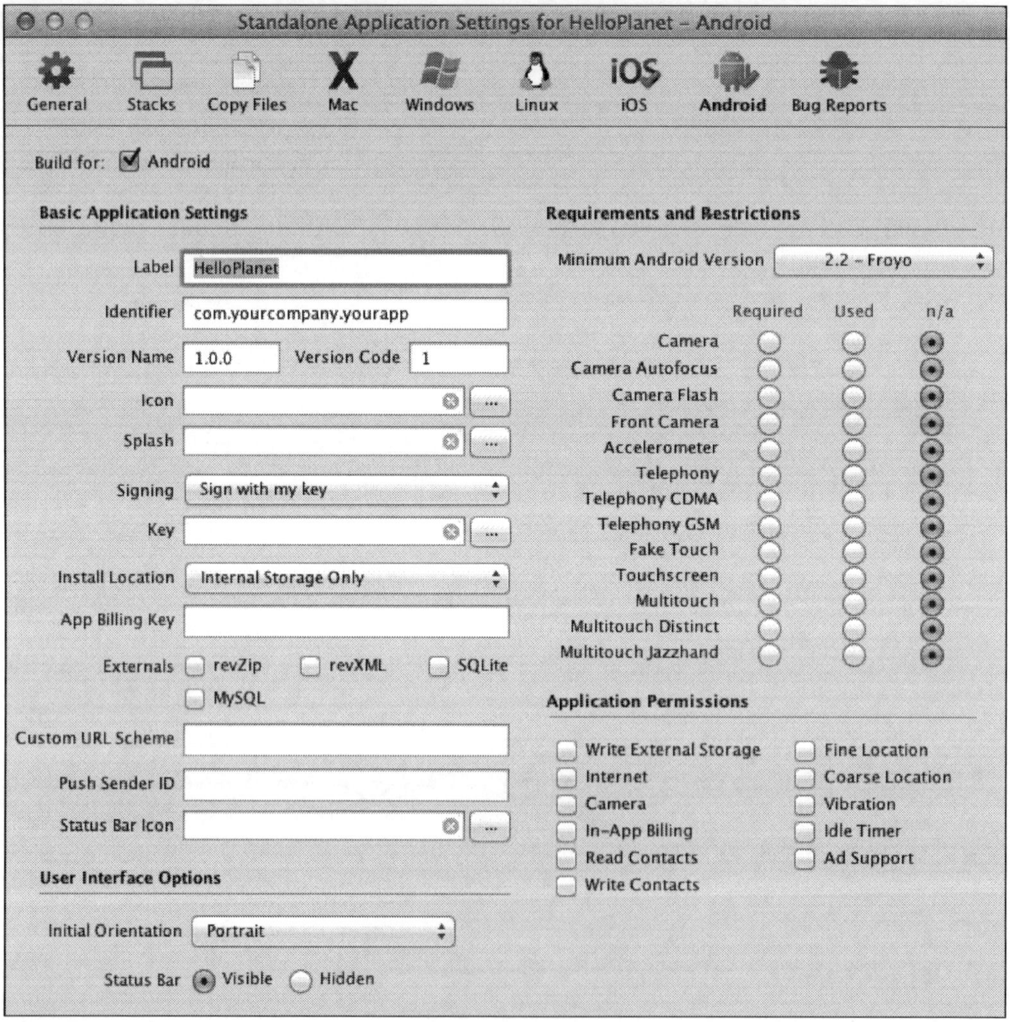

This dialog window's options are divided into five sections as indicated in the following screenshot:

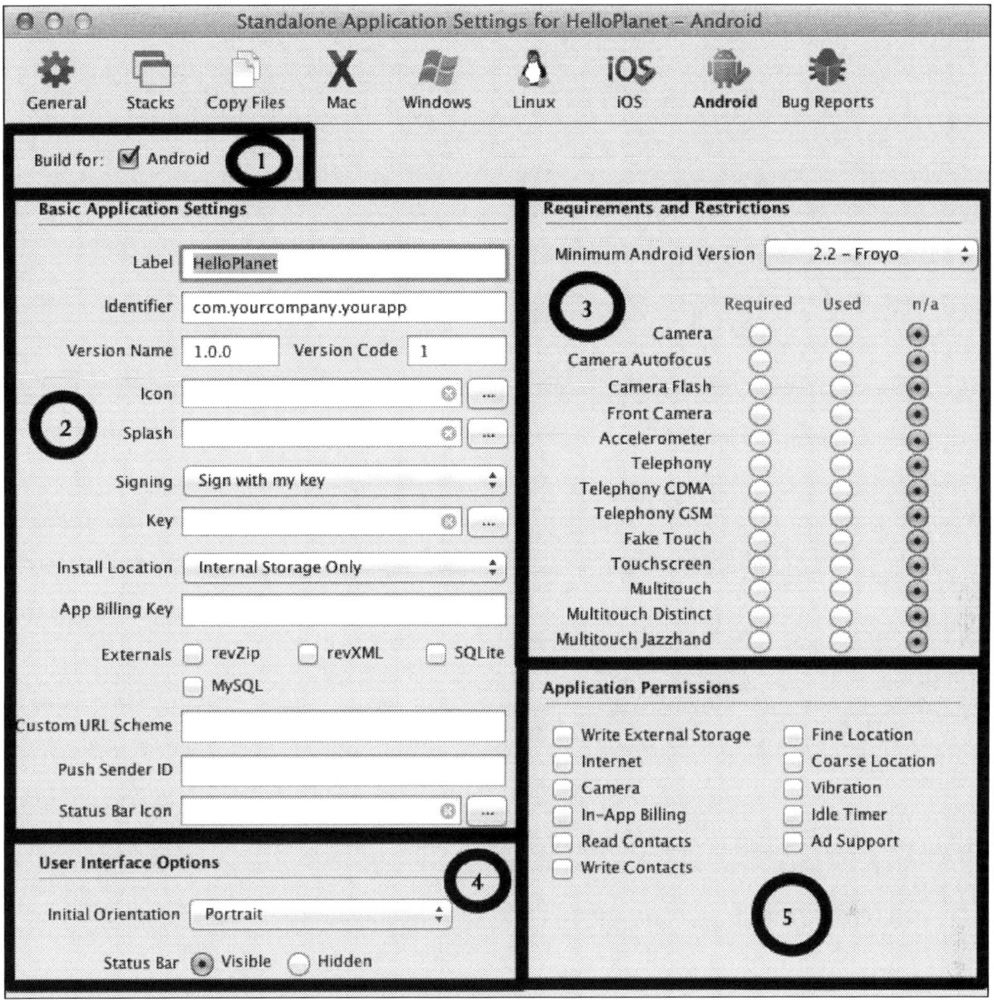

The first section is the **Build for:** area of the window.

The **Build for:** option provides us with the ability to select and deselect the option to publish a binary file formatted for Android devices.

The second section is **Basic Application Settings**.

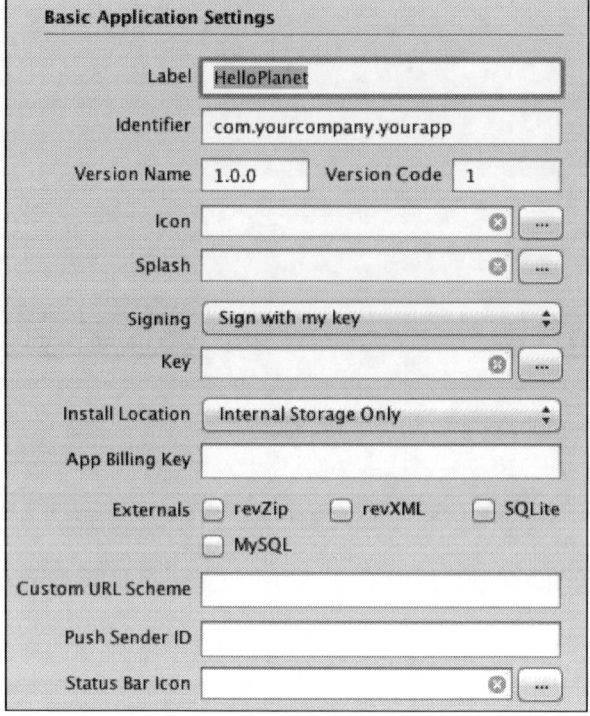

There are several settings in the **Basic Application Settings** area of the dialog window. The description for each of these settings is as follows:

▸ **Label**: This is the label that will be displayed on the launch screen of the Android device.

▸ **Identifier**: This is a unique identifier specific to your app.

▸ **Version Name**: This is the version of your app in a human-readable format.

▸ **Version Code**: This is the version number used by the Android OS.

▸ **Icon**: This is where you will upload your app's launch icon.

▸ **Splash**: If you have a personal or educational LiveCode license, you will upload a splash screen image here. If you have a commercial license, this does not apply to you.

▸ **Signing**: You are presented with three options: **Sign with my key**, **Sign for development only**, and **Do not sign**.

▸ **Key**: This setting links to a key-store file that is used when the **Sign with my key** option within **Signing** is selected.

- ▸ **Install Location**: This is where you set your app's preference for storing data. The options are **Internal Storage Only, Allow External Storage**, and **Prefer External Storage**.

- ▸ **App Billing Key**: This is where you will enter your billing key from your Android Play Store account. This key is used for in-app purchases.

- ▸ **Externals**: If your app uses any of the listed externals, they must be selected here prior to generating a binary file.

- ▸ **Custom URL Scheme**: This feature allows you to design a custom URL that can be used to launch your app from within another app.

- ▸ **Push Sender ID**: This is a unique project number associated with your app. This ID is used while you are using push notifications.

- ▸ **Status Bar Icon**: Here you will upload your status bar icon.

The third section is **Requirements and Restrictions**.

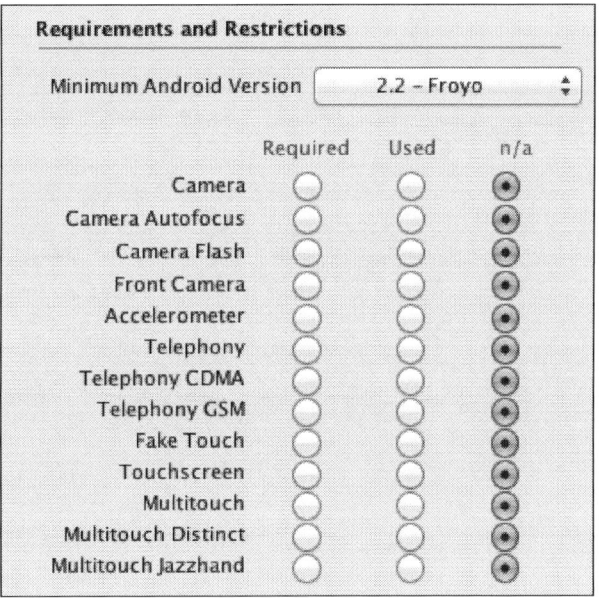

The first section of the **Requirements and Restrictions** area allows you to indicate the minimum Android version that must be installed on a user's device for your app to run. The options include **2.2 - Froyo, 2.3 - Gingerbread, 2.3.3, 3.0 - Honeycomb**, and **3.1**.

The section contains 13 sets of radio buttons. These buttons allow you to select which services are required, used, or not applicable.

The fourth section is **User Interface Options**.

In this section of the dialog window, you select your app's initial orientation (**Portrait** or **Landscape**) and whether or not to display the status bar.

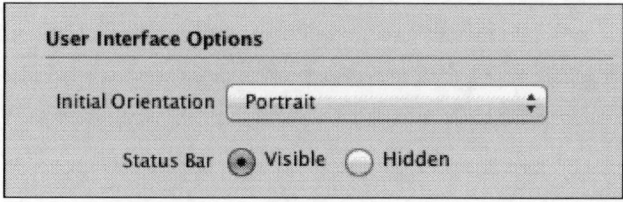

The fifth and final section is **Application Permissions**.

This final section of the **Standalone Application Settings** dialog window is where you will select which services and accesses your app will use.

Index

P

panda button 181
Panda card, Jungle Dance Party app project
  creating 179, 180
Picker card 105
picker menu interface
  creating 103, 104
picture question card
  creating 137-140
Pop card 100
pop-up dialogs
  using 8-10
pop-up menu interface
  creating 99, 100
portrait orientation 32
preOpenCard commands 181
Prerendered Icon checkbox 273
programming 7
project brief
  about 7
  advantages 7
  checklist 8
  objectives 8
project shell
  creating 83, 84
pull-down menu interface
  creating 88-92

Q

Query card
  creating 208

R

random() function 74
random numbers
  using 73, 74
R button 73
record 191
resetCoconuts command 162
RunRev 257

S

score
  adding 143-148

scoring schema
  adding 166, 167
ScriptGrabber card 224
Script Grabber option
  programming 224-228
sequencing question card
  creating 127-133
shell game 151
short answer question card
  creating 134-136
Standalone Application Settings window 207
Store link 257
Submit button 134, 147
Swipe card 85
swiping menu interface
  creating 85-88

T

Tab card 102
table 191
Table Button 200
tab menu interface
  creating 101, 102
Textual Fun option
  programming 236-240
theInput variable 239
Thimblerig 151
time of the day
  detecting 10
timeup command 13
Traveler option
  programming 221-224
true/false question card
  creating 117-121
Try Me button 224

U

user input
  accepting 57
  calculation function, programming 62
  clear command, programming 63, 64
  equals button, programming 64, 65
  evaluating 11-15
  global variables, creating 57, 58
  global variables, initializing 57, 58

Thank you for buying
LiveCode Mobile Development Hotshot

About Packt Publishing

Packt, pronounced 'packed', published its first book "*Mastering phpMyAdmin for Effective MySQL Management*" in April 2004 and subsequently continued to specialize in publishing highly focused books on specific technologies and solutions.

Our books and publications share the experiences of your fellow IT professionals in adapting and customizing today's systems, applications, and frameworks. Our solution based books give you the knowledge and power to customize the software and technologies you're using to get the job done. Packt books are more specific and less general than the IT books you have seen in the past. Our unique business model allows us to bring you more focused information, giving you more of what you need to know, and less of what you don't.

Packt is a modern, yet unique publishing company, which focuses on producing quality, cutting-edge books for communities of developers, administrators, and newbies alike. For more information, please visit our website: www.packtpub.com.

Writing for Packt

We welcome all inquiries from people who are interested in authoring. Book proposals should be sent to author@packtpub.com. If your book idea is still at an early stage and you would like to discuss it first before writing a formal book proposal, contact us; one of our commissioning editors will get in touch with you.

We're not just looking for published authors; if you have strong technical skills but no writing experience, our experienced editors can help you develop a writing career, or simply get some additional reward for your expertise.

Corona SDK Mobile Game Development: Beginner's Guide

ISBN: 978-1-84969-188-8   Paperback: 408 pages

Create monetized games for iOS and Android with minimum cost and code

1. Build once and deploy your games to both iOS and Android

2. Create commercially successful games by applying several monetization techniques and tools

3. Create three fun games and integrate them with social networks such as Twitter and Facebook

HTML5 Mobile Development Cookbook

ISBN: 978-1-84969-196-3   Paperback: 254 pages

Over 60 recipes for building fast, responsive HTML5 mobile websites for iPhone 5, Android, Windows Phone, and Blackberry

1. Solve your cross-platform development issues by implementing device and content adaptation recipes

2. Maximum action, minimum theory allowing you to dive straight into HTML5 mobile web development

3. Incorporate HTML5-rich media and geo-location into your mobile websites

Please check **www.PacktPub.com** for information on our titles

Flash iOS Apps Cookbook

ISBN: 978-1-84969-138-3   Paperback: 420 pages

100 practical recipes for developing iOS apps with Flash Professional and Adobe AIR

1. Build your own apps, port existing projects, and learn the best practices for targeting iOS devices using Flash

2. How to compile a native iOS app directly from Flash and deploy it to the iPhone, iPad or iPod touch

3. Full of practical recipes and step-by-step instructions for developing iOS apps with Flash Professional

Unity iOS Essentials

ISBN: 978-1-84969-182-6   Paperback: 358 pages

Develop high performance, fun iOS games using Unity 3D

1. Learn key strategies and follow practical guidelines for creating Unity 3D games for iOS devices

2. Learn how to plan your game levels to optimize performance on iOS devices using advanced game concepts

3. Full of tips, scripts, shaders, and complete Unity 3D projects to guide you through game creation on iOS from start to finish

Please check **www.PacktPub.com** for information on our titles

Printed in Great Britain
by Amazon.co.uk, Ltd.,
Marston Gate.